JOHN HENRY CARDINAL NEWMAN

The Oriel portrait by George Richmond:
Newman in his last year in the Church of England

PETER M. CHISNALL

John Henry Cardinal Newman

A man of courage, conflict and conviction

ST PAULS

ST PAULS Publishing
187 Battersea Bridge Road, London SW11 3AS, UK

ISBN 085439 613 6

Set by TuKan DTP, Fareham, Hampshire,UK
Printed by Interprint Ltd, Marsa, Malta

ST PAULS is an activity of the priests and brothers
of the Society of St Paul who proclaim the Gospel
through the media of social communication

Contents

*List of Illustrations, which are used by kind permission
of Birmigham Oratory.*

The Oriel Portrait by George Richmond: Newman in
      his last year in the Church of England
Newman and Ambrose in Rome 1846
Birmingham Oratory: Italian Renaissance style. The domed
      Oratory was added as a memorial to Cardinal Newman
Pope Leo XIII: 'I always had a cult for Newman'
Bust of Newman by Sir Richard Westmacott, a school
      fellow and lifetime friend
The House at Littlemore: Newman's rural retreat

Preface

It has ever been a hobby of mine (unless it be a truism, not a hobby) that a man's life lies in his letters.
LD XX.443, Mrs John Mozley (Jemima), 18 May 1863.

John Henry Newman was a man of many parts: a dedicated scholar, a highly talented writer, a religious poet of unusual merit, an ecclesiastical activist, a visionary and also a powerful protagonist and controversialist. Fearlessly, he challenged contemporary attitudes and belief both in the Church of England and later, in the Roman Catholic Church which he entered when almost half way through his long life. As an Anglican, he had played a leading role in the Oxford Movement – he wrote most of the *Tracts for the Times.* He relished argument; the challenge of controversy fired his intellect and emotions, and stimulated his influential writings. Essentially, Newman was versatile: an eminent scholar and an ambitious activist. He readily crossed swords with leading politicians like Gladstone and Peel as well as prominent clerics such as Archbishop Cullen of Dublin and the novelist-clergyman Charles Kingsley. He was the founder-president of the Catholic University of Ireland (forerunner of University College Dublin – UCD). From this involvement, Newman produced *The Idea of a University,* which stressed that religion should have a recognised place in higher education. But he also emphasised that a university was not a seminary or a convent; its role was to prepare young people to take their place in the world. *The*

Idea of a University remains today a source of inspiration for educationalists around the world. As a religious activist, Newman founded, with papal authority, the first English Oratory. In Birmingham, he and a small group of his Oxford contemporaries developed this community of secular priests living under a modified Rule of St Philip Neri, the 16th century founder of Oratorianism. Later, Newman established the Oratory School, a public school for the sons of Catholic gentry and the rising middle classes. Throughout his life, he vigorously promoted the role of the Catholic laity; he wanted them to become better educated, to come out of the ghetto, and contribute to political and social life at all levels. He demanded that the clergy should willingly recognise the important role of the laity in the Church. Newman disliked exaggerated Ultramontanism; he felt uneasy about excessive dependence on emotional appeals and satisfactions in religion. His own religious convictions were deeply held, but his personal piety was not ostentatious. Throughout his life, Newman kept up a vast correspondence with politicians, prelates, intimate friends and the many others who sought his pastoral care. In this book, excerpts from correspondence give illuminating insights into his character and manifold interests and activities. Many misunderstood him, some even reviled him, while others regarded him as an apparent failure. But his influence is clearly evident today both in the Catholic Church and in religious discussion and development elsewhere. Like many luminaries of history, he was perhaps before his time, but with the passing of time Newman is increasingly recognised 'for what he was, an incomparable communicator of the new horizons on which the eyes of Christians should be firmly focused.

ACKNOWLEDGEMENTS

This short book has had a long maturation; it has developed from dedicated reading of Newman's *Letters and Diaries,* and other historical sources. It does not aspire to be a complete biography – others have already done this well – instead it focuses on specific aspects of Newman's long and eventful life, and considers them in relation to the regeneration of English Catholicism. Essentially, it is a book for those who would like to know more about one of the most renowned churchmen of the Victorian era.

I am deeply indebted to those who have given generously of their time and expertise during my researches, and I thank them heartily for their encouragement and help:

Dr Peter Nockles, John Rylands Library, University of Manchester;
David C.Sheehy, Archivist, Archdiocese of Dublin;
Fr Liam Rigney, Archdiocese of Dublin;
Gerard Tracey, Archivist, The Oratory, Birmingham

I also thank the editorial and publishing staff of ST PAULS Publishing, whose skills have greatly contributed to this text.

1

Prelude

JOHN Henry Newman made a most distinguished and distinctive contribution to English Roman Catholicism in the 19th century – of which his life spanned virtually the whole epoch – so our understanding of the influence of specific aspects of his life and work is enriched if it is viewed against the background of the historical development of the Roman Catholic Church in England since the Reformation. In this introductory chapter, important events and issues in political and ecclesiastical spheres which profoundly affected English Roman Catholics as they gradually progressed from penal subjection to emancipation and legal recognition are identified and discussed. This approach, founded on an examination of leading historical sources concerned with religious life in England over almost three centuries, aims to give insights into the nature of the beliefs, practices and organisation of Roman Catholicism in England, without which a consideration of Newman's manifold influence might well be less effective or, indeed, less rewarding.

The Reformation in England was largely precipitated by Henry VIII's concern about the Tudor dynasty. Unlike Lutheranism and Calvinism, the Church of England was founded on statute law, and between 1531-34 a series of statutes abolished the traditional ties between Rome and

England, and set up the king as the spiritual as well as the temporal ruler. Because this fundamental religious change was enshrined in statute law, it was deeply rooted in constitutional matters and involved the monarch and Parliament itself. Henry, it is said, was compelled to follow a course of action which, at first, he scarcely desired.[1]

During the short reign of Edward VI (1547-53), widespread doctrinal and liturgical reforms took place. England seemed to be joining the mainstream of the Reformation in Europe. But this period was also punctuated by a series of rebellions motivated by a potent mixture of political and religious causes. The Western Rising (1549) was the largest of these insurrections.[2]

Any hope of a smooth restoration of power to Roman Catholics when Mary (daughter of Catherine of Aragon) acceded in 1553 was soon dashed by Parliament's refusal to restore sequestrated church lands and its restricting of the power of Papal Bulls in England. Although all the Reformation statutes were repealed, Mary failed to a large extent to secure the re-conversion of the people, and the persecutions also alienated many. Her marriage to Philip II of Spain added to public concern and distaste. Over a comparatively short period, conflicting religious doctrines were enforced by law, and it was not until the reign of Elizabeth I (1558-1603) that an established Church of England finally emerged. During this time, the majority of the clergy 'appear to have acquiesced as readily in the Elizabethan settlement of 1559 – in the Acts of Supremacy and Uniformity – as they had in the Marian restoration'.[3] However, the religious situation was far from settled, and the new Oath of Supremacy was rejected by all except one of the bishops, as well as by the heads of Oxford and Cambridge colleges; all were deprived of their offices. On the continent, meanwhile, the Council of Trent (1545-63) reaffirmed what was held to be the apostolic traditions and teaching authority of the Roman Catholic Church as related to the Scriptures, the intrinsic nature and power of the sacraments, papal authority, and the distinctive role of women in marriage and the family; and strict clerical disciplines were laid down. The dictates of conscience were declared to be above the power of princes and the magistracy.

Calvinist views certainly influenced the development of Protestant thought in England; this was singularly evident when more extreme Protestants – who had spent the Marian years in exile – were given influential positions in the cathedrals, churches and universities. Like Calvin, they recognised the importance of 'godly magistrates', and of the nobility and gentry in spreading Protestantism.[4] With Calvin's approval, the Geneva Bible (1560) became the most popular vernacular Bible of the Elizabethan era. Liturgical preferences matched those of the reformers on the continent; cultural developments in church services, ornamentation and architecture were discouraged. Apart from financial pressures, Elizabeth had little interest in architecture and, like her father, no ambition of vying with the lavish magnificence of the French kings, notably Francis I.

The deliberate despoliation of cathedrals and churches, the dissolution of the monasteries, and the dispersion or destruction of great libraries, significantly reduced ecclesiastical patronage, and the general hostile attitudes towards Rome affected cultural and social life in England.[5]

The fundamental religious upheavals which followed from the break with Rome, and the sufferings and deprivations imposed on those who stuck doggedly to their old beliefs resulted in what one historian has described as a 'continuity in some sense', linking these men and women with their deep-rooted cultural beliefs and practices.[6]

In 1570, Pope Pius V excommunicated Elizabeth with the Bull *Regnans in Excelsis*, which absolved Roman Catholic subjects from their allegiance. Inevitably, this led to intense resentment and to political and religious suspicions and intrigues, which were frequently placed at the door of Catholics.[7] Those who 'openly refused to conform to the laws of the unitary Protestant establishment',[8] were styled 'recusants' and were subjected to the harsh penalties of the penal laws. These directly denied political, civil and personal freedoms to dissidents – who included Protestant nonconformists.[9] Fines, sequestration of property, imprisonment, torture and even execution were among the penalties exacted from the few who, under the leadership of some prominent Roman Catholic families, dared publicly to disregard the law. Most, however, observed the law requiring their attendance at Sunday services at the local parish church. These so-called 'church papists' tended to retain, secretly, their Roman Catholic beliefs; some had been priests. Between the recusants and the Church papists there was no clear line.[10]

During the late 1570s, newly ordained priests arrived secretly in England from Douai, where a seminary had been founded by William Allen, an Oxford don and member of a minor gentry family from Lancashire, who later became a Roman Catholic priest. He was created a cardinal in 1587, and is 'regarded by most Catholic scholars as the saviour of English Roman Catholicism'.[11] But it has been argued by Bossy that while he has more claims than anyone else to be remembered as the founder of the English Roman Catholic community, he had originally distinctly modest objectives for the Douai establishment. Its development into a missionary foundation may well be said to be due more to its distinguished scholars, such as Edmund Campion, than to Allen himself. But as the missionary impetus grew, Allen 'visibly shed his earlier inhibitions' and emerged as a prophet of the active missionary ideal'.[12]

These 'seminary priests', regarded as traitors under English law, were to suffer severe hardship, punishment and, in the case of one hundred and twenty three of them in Elizabeth's reign, execution for ministering to the Roman Catholics in England.[13] At the time of Elizabeth's death in 1603, it has been estimated that there were about 300 missionary priests in England;[14] this number peaked at 750 by 1640, but a long-term decline after 1700 reduced numbers to fewer than 400.[15]

All through these times a regular flow of anti-Catholic literature inflamed public opinion; the most influential of these publications was probably Foxe's *Acts and Monuments of these Latter Days*, known popularly as 'The Book of Martyrs', which first appeared in 1563. This sensationally written book passed through many editions, traducing Roman Catholicism, representing it as associated with treason, doctrinal and liturgical perversions, and intellectual degradation. Norman notes 'the ideology of anti-Catholicism which, enshrined in Foxe's book, was to dog English Roman Catholicism for centuries'.[16]

James I (1603-25) 'seemed anxious to avoid further action against Roman Catholics',[17] but further legal harassment of Roman Catholics followed a 'whole series of plots and projected coups d'état' popularly associated with Roman Catholics.[18] 'If Roman Catholics were bad, Jesuits were worse... they were the papacy's elite shock troops, the Waffen SS of 17th century Roman Catholicism'.[19] The penal laws, which tended to be erratically enforced on the whole,[20] were applied with vigour when popular feelings about Roman Catholicism were aroused.

Charles I's reign (1625-49) was beset by constitutional problems culminating in the English Civil War, and his eventual defeat and execution. During his reign a surprising degree of toleration towards Roman Catholic worship was apparent in Court circles, largely due to the influence of Charles's French wife, Henrietta Maria. Court Roman Catholicism contrasted distinctly with the habitual discretion of the country gentry, who remained loyal to the old faith. Informal diplomatic contacts with Rome were resumed. But Charles was under suspicion of harbouring papist sympathies, and he was virtually forced to agree to re-activation of the penal laws and to a rigorous hunting-down of Roman Catholic priests, of whom twenty were executed during 1641-46.[21]

The Commonwealth period of government (1649-60) which followed Charles I's execution, was marked by further penal legislation at first, but this was relaxed, later, to some degree. Mathew comments that it is not surprising that the period of Cromwell's rule in England was marked by severity, in view of the fact that English Roman Catholicism was closely identified with the royal cause. Most of the Puritan leaders were strongly Protestant in their connections and 'generally without even a vague Catholic friendship'.[22]

The restoration of the Stuart monarchy in 1680 seemed to hold out great hopes for Roman Catholics, but these were not to be fulfilled. Charles II attempted to balance toleration towards Roman Catholics with equal liberties for Protestant Dissenters, but he had to bear in mind his forbears' constitutional problems and his own precarious position.

In 1661 the Corporation Act restricted membership of corporations to professing members of the established Church, and since members of Parliament were largely chosen from these corporate bodies, the disability on Catholics was doubled. A new Act of Uniformity in 1662 was imposed on the clergy and also on schoolmasters; those who refused to conform were deprived of their posts. Other restrictive legislation followed, to the dismay of Roman Catholics who had petitioned the king for repeal of the penal laws. This, however, was the prerogative of Parliament. Further, the royal finances badly needed bolstering, and recusancy fines seemed to offer the king some prospect of clearing his burdensome debts. Nevertheless, despite repeated efforts by the Treasury, 'the total collected was ridiculously small', and in 1680 the Privy Council reported that Roman Catholics had developed secret methods of protecting their estates from any sizeable demands made on them.[23] In 1662 Charles issued a Declaration of Indulgence suspending the penal laws but public outcry forced him to withdraw it. The following year a Bill of Indulgence was introduced into Parliament but thrown out.[24]

The penal laws were, therefore, largely unproductive financially because of poor or reluctant administration and also because of large-scale exemptions granted to prominent local Roman Catholic families. According to the Recusancy returns of 1671, only half the counties had enforced the laws at all.[25] They were, however, largely effective in excluding Roman Catholics from public life and social influence. This isolation was amplified by the first Test Act of 1673 which was deliberately designed to frustrate any attempts to suspend anti-Roman Catholic legislation, and was a setback to incipient religious toleration. The Act imposed a sacramental test, a declaration against Transubstantiation, and demanded new oaths of allegiance and supremacy from all who held public office. A second Test Act in 1678 excluded Roman Catholic peers from the House of Lords. This increased the political penalties endured by Roman Catholics, who had been excluded from the Commons since 1563.[26]

In this environment, when Papists were accused of responsibility for both the Great Plague of 1665 and the Great Fire of London in the following year, Titus Oates's fantastic allegations, known as the 'Popish Plot', found willing listeners. His accusations against Roman Catholics were listened to by the Privy Council 'with amazement', and his answers to 'questions on points of simple fact... clearly showed him to be a liar'. But the fear of popery was so widespread that it caused the government to ignore Oates's downright deception, to play down the evidence of his nefarious character, and to institute a new onslaught against Roman Catholics.[27] 'Parliament reinforced the penal laws and the worst persecution of Roman Catholics since the reign of Elizabeth began'.[28] The Archbishop of Armagh, Oliver Plunket, was brought over from Ireland, and a 'flock of witnesses from Dublin, whose brogue could scarcely be comprehended by Englishmen' gave testimony. The king 'agreed quite happily that Plunket was innocent, but said that his enemies were still waiting for him to make a false step'.[29] He was condemned to death by Judge Jeffreys, and was the last of the Roman Catholic clergy to be executed in England for their faith. As Leys puts it, 'the Popish Plot was the last organised persecution of Englishmen for religious causes'.[30]

In the end, Oates was convicted of perjury after a lengthy trial in 1685, and 'was unofficially released from prison in December 1688. On 11 March 1689, with King James deposed and King William on the throne, he petitioned Parliament for redress'.[31] To extricate themselves from a political problem, the new Whig judges requested the king to grant Oates a free pardon, which he did without delay. As noted already, Charles's policies and behaviour were much affected by affairs of State. He would seem to have been a rather reluctant participant in the anti-Roman Catholic behaviour which scarred his reign. On his deathbed he was, in fact, reconciled to the Roman Catholic faith.[32]

Towards the close (1623) of James I's reign, Rome had introduced a new method of ecclesiastical government for the Roman Catholic Church in England; it lasted only nine months due to the death of the newly-appointed vicar-apostolic. The system was re-introduced in 1685, when Rome appointed a vicar-apostolic to take charge of the growing Roman Catholic body in England: in 1600, this community numbered about 40,000, increased to 60,000 by 1650, and levelled off until about 1720.[33] In 1688 three additional vicars-apostolic were 'consecrated with considerable pomp in three royal palaces'.[34] These four dignitaries acted independently in their own districts but were under the jurisdiction of the Prefect of Propaganda in Rome, the Vatican office responsible for the Roman Catholic Church's activities in 'mission' countries. The four districts were: the northern, covering from Scotland to a line drawn roughly from the Dee to the Humber; the western, which covered all of Wales and south-western England to the Dorset coast; the London district, which included all the home counties and Bedfordshire and Berkshire; and the rest of England lay in the midlands district. The boundaries of these districts did not coincide with any of the ancient sees or provinces in order to avoid likely misunderstandings about the missionary efforts now being made. Despite this, John Leyburn, a former president of Douai and vicar-apostolic for the London district, was arrested and imprisoned in the Tower for two years.[35] The office of vicar-apostolic was to continue through to the middle of the 19th century until, in 1850, the restoration of the Roman Catholic hierarchy took place, as is discussed later.

James II (1685-88) had been converted to Roman

Catholicism in 1672, when he was Duke of York. His accession greatly cheered his co-religionists, who started to open up old chapels and to build new ones. He unwisely promulgated, as Charles II had in 1662, a general Declaration of Indulgence and was unsuccessful in this attempted appeasement. It appeared that people might be willing to extend toleration in practice but wished that the penal laws should remain. He then had preliminary investigations made into the feasibility of repealing the penal laws; again his ambitions were frustrated

Instead, he re-issued his Declaration of Indulgence but this proposed general remission was firmly rejected once more. The birth of a son and heir to the throne, who would be baptised a Roman Catholic on account of his mother's religion, so startled some influential Englishmen that they invited William of Orange, husband of James's daughter Mary and a Protestant, to come over and restore what they perceived to be their ancient liberties. James's weak health and ineffectual response to this direct challenge led to his deposition and flight into exile. Some Protestants 'as well as Papists joined the king in exile, for many of the Church of England disapproved of revolution'.[36] This brief, inglorious reign was the last Roman Catholic monarchy of England. James's well meaning but ill-advised political interventions probably hardened residual anti-Roman Catholic feelings. The Roman Catholics themselves anxiously speculated about whether a new wave of religious persecution would arise.

They had not long to wait. The 'Revolution Parliament' of 1689, after passing the Bill of Rights limiting the royal prerogative, then prescribed new oaths of allegiance and supremacy with penalties of fines and imprisonment for dissidents. Further, the Habeas Corpus Act 'was suspended by William III... and he was thus able to imprison any suspect without trial'.[37] Existing penal legislation remained on the statute book. Although the properties of many Roman Catholics were burnt, and some priests and people sought refuge abroad, widespread persecution did not flare up.

Fears of a second Stuart Restoration were increased by the death of Queen Mary in 1694. Suspicions of Jacobite plotting led to the Trial of Treasons Act of 1696; this was of great significance to Roman Catholics because it conferred rights to prepare their cases before being brought to trial. Nevertheless, it remained a treasonable act for a Catholic priest to say Mass or for people to hear it. Roman Catholics were also barred from acting as lawyers or from buying or inheriting land; they also had to pay land tax at double the standard rate. Such manifest inequities tended to be rarely enforced. 'The heirs of the Roman Catholic gentry continued peacefully to inherit their family estates and property was still bought by Papists, though it was sometimes thought wise to use a friendly Protestant as an intermediary'.[38] Anti-Roman Catholic legislation was deliberately focused on 'the moment of succession',[39] to render inheritance by Roman Catholics difficult.

After the death of his wife, William III reigned alone until his death in 1702, and was succeeded by his sister-in-law Anne, whose only son had recently died. In fear of Jacobitism and to ensure the Protestant succession to the throne, the Act of Settlement was passed in 1701. This laid down that in the event of Anne's death without children the Crown was to be vested in a Protestant princess, Sophia of Hanover, a granddaughter of James I, and her heirs. In due time, her son became George I of England. Other claimants were nearer in blood relationships but were disqualified because they professed the Roman Catholic faith.

During Anne's reign, 1702-14, religious feelings seem

to have quietened down, and 'good Queen Anne' personified this welcome and relatively peaceful interlude in domestic politics after the persistent agitations of previous reigns. Heavy penalties against Roman Catholics were still in force but generally not enforced 'if they remained inconspicuous'.[40] Roman Catholics were settling down quietly to practise their religion privately and without harassment. The Roman Catholic aristocracy and gentry had passed through the hostile years of active persecution and deprivation, but had largely managed to survive and keep their faith intact. This treasured inheritance they now passed down to their family and neighbours. By the 18th century, 'the growth of [Roman Catholic] congregations which had been going on under the regime of the gentry had reached a point where a revival of vigour among the clergy would find something substantial to work in... this revival seems... unquestionable'.[41] Even then, religious Tests remained in force until the 19th century; the Church of England exercised its exclusive political and educational privileges to the disadvantage of all dissenters.

In 1753 during the reign of George II (1727-60), the Marriage Act was passed. This was directly offensive to Roman Catholic clergy and laity. Up to then, Roman Catholic rites of baptism, marriage and funerals had been maintained in spite of the penal laws, and Anglican ministers generally co-operated, for example, by entering Roman Catholic baptisms in their parochial registers, although more difficulties were encountered with burials. Roman Catholic marriages had always taken place before a Catholic priest according to Roman rites, and were recognised in law regardless of the existing penal statutes. The new legislation attempted to reform what was admittedly an unsatisfactory state of affairs by declaring null and void any marriage ceremony in England

and Wales not performed in accordance with the ritual of the established Church. Most Protestant nonconformists could accept this requirement without difficulty, but for Roman Catholics the Council of Trent in 1562 made it a serious sin to participate in a Protestant service, and marriage was held to be a sacrament. After considerable discussions, the vicars-apostolic agreed to a compromise solution whereby Roman Catholics attended two ceremonies, one before their own priest and the other before a Protestant minister, in order to satisfy legal requirements. Which service had precedence aroused bitter controversy, and various ingenious solutions were adopted. Not until 1836 was this tendentious Act repealed and marriage in a Roman Catholic church or in a Dissenting chapel, in the presence of a registrar, recognised in law.

Early in the 18th century, a revival of the discreet expansion of the Roman Catholic community which had occurred, as noted, in the later years of Elizabeth's reign, became discernible. A Parliamentary return of 1767 recorded 69,376 Roman Catholics, but according to Norman 'this was rather less than the figure, which was around 80,000... The English Roman Catholic Church, therefore, was not to be regarded – as it sometimes was by 19th century ultramontanes anxious to exult in their effectiveness – as a decaying structure subject to more or less permanent erosion'.[42]

An outstanding personality among Roman Catholic clergy of the 18th century was Richard Challoner (1691-1781). After ordination at Douai and a period as professor, he travelled to London in 1730 and became immersed in missionary work among the poor. In 1741, he was made coadjutor to the vicar-apostolic of the London district and, in 1757, succeeded to this post. His zealous activities over the next four decades included imposing rigorous ecclesiastical discipline and giving inspiring leadership to his clergy, revision of the Douai version of the Bible, and the production of a devotional manual *The Garden of the Soul*, which became a much loved source of Roman Catholic prayer into the 20th century. According to Bossy, 'Almost everything we need to know about the private devotion of English [Roman] Catholics during these decades can be discovered by consulting Challoner's prayer book'.[43] Challoner's distinctive contributions to the Roman Catholic community of the 18th century and beyond are remarkable and diverse. When the Jesuit order was formally disbanded by the Pope in 1773, there were about 120 Jesuits working in England. These were treated most sympathetically by Bishop Challoner. He allowed them to continue their ministry as secular priests and encouraged them to keep in touch with each other.

The accession of George III (1760-1820) received popular acclaim, and the time seemed ripe for Roman Catholics to start negotiations for repeal of the penal laws; such ambitions greatly disturbed the ageing Challoner, who feared that his flock might suffer, if attempts were made modify the law, by a violent backlash from some extreme Protestant quarters. An initiative was taken, however, by a few prominent Roman Catholic laymen, the 'Catholic Committee'. They petitioned the king, negotiated with politicians, and secured the passing of the Roman Catholic Relief Act of 1778. 'Henceforward prayers for the king were said in every Catholic chapel; at last Catholics were recognised as loyal Englishmen.'[44] An oath of loyalty to the Crown was gladly taken by priests and lay people.

Unfortunately, Challoner's fears were not groundless. An outbreak of anti-popery riots was organised by the newly-formed Protestant Association, of which the unstable Lord George Gordon was elected president in

November 1779. In January 1780 the Protestant Association petitioned Parliament for repeal of the 1778 Relief Act.[45] These so-called 'Gordon Riots' were eventually quelled by troops, at the order of George III. Nearly 300 people were officially recorded as having been either shot or died from wounds; of the ringleaders captured, twenty-one were executed. The riots were confined to London, although Roman Catholics elsewhere were greatly alarmed. Norman sums up the event thus, 'The Gordon Riots, as it turned out, had been something of a last gasp from an expiring organism: popular anti-Catholicism indeed survived, for more than a century, but the constitutional spirit and the political will to maintain the penal laws against professions of faith were decaying away'.[46]

The Catholic Committee, which secured the Relief Act of 1778, had been disbanded; a second committee of notable Roman Catholic laymen but also with three clerical members was set up after the disturbances of the Gordon Riots had subsided. Their aim was to extend further the relief measures now enjoyed by Roman Catholics. This time, however, the Roman Catholic bishops intervened and successfully obtained amendments to Pitt's bill of 1791. This second Relief Act gave virtually full religious freedom to English Roman Catholics: it formally recognised Roman Catholic places of worship, where Mass could be celebrated without penalty, although it was laid down that such buildings should not have a steeple or bell, and that the doors were not to be locked, barred or bolted during services. Presumably this provision arose from 'some strange suspicion that Roman Catholics would make use of their chapels for treasonable or some other unlawful purpose'.[47] But the 1791 Act did not confer on Roman Catholics entire equality before the law; they were still barred from Parliament and from holding judicial office or other offices of profit under the Crown, as well as from commissions in the army or the navy. Few Roman Catholics were in the professional classes; the double land tax continued to be demanded of Roman Catholic land owning families.

The initiative taken by the Roman Catholic bishops in negotiations over the 1791 Act indicated clearly that they had reaffirmed their leadership role in the development of Roman Catholic matters in England. 'In so doing, they had pre-empted the Catholic Committee'.[48] Earlier representations by eminent laymen for a role in the appointment of bishops had been firmly rejected by the clerics. This decision coincided with the considered views of many conservatively-minded Roman Catholics, who regarded the challenging proposals of the elite committee as contrary to ecclesiastical prerogative and distasteful to Roman Catholic tradition. Bishop John Milner (1752-1826), a Douai-educated protégé of Challoner (who had died in 1781), became vicar-apostolic of the Midland district in 1803. He was a trenchant opponent of such claims by the aristocracy and gentry. Clerical supremacy was well established by the time of his death. The Roman Catholic landed classes had served the Catholic cause well over several generations, often in times of oppression, but their social privileges and political skills should not lead them to assume that they could continue to exercise the same level of influence as the Roman Catholic Church entered a new phase of its existence in England. 'Milner had anyway been sceptical of the Catholic Committee' and of 'lay interference in the ecclesiastical affairs over the past forty years'.[49] Milner stood steadfastly against what he considered as 'the interfering laity', but he was always a solicitous shepherd of his flock. He had, however, 'a singularly clear-sighted appreciation of all that concerned ecclesiastical prerogative; his filial devotion to the Holy See was always manifest and he had a strong sentiment of loyalty to George III'.[50] In his honest, plain-speaking way he won the solid support of the Catholic middle classes, and had little time for politics or for the wealthy gentry, lawyers and others whom he reckoned to be the 'party of privilege'.[51] 'His episcopal reign marked the beginning of a movement which was to develop through the 19th century. He realised vaguely the great future of Catholicism in the towns'.[52]

Milner did not live to celebrate the Roman Catholic Relief Act of 1829 which concluded the series of legal enactments emancipating Roman Catholics, but his life's work and that of his fellow vicars-apostolic had been dedicated to that end. In his classic study of the period 1781-1803, Bernard Ward referred to the 'turn of the tide' for English Roman Catholics, and states that, 'This period may therefore be appropriately called the Dawn of the Catholic Revival'.[53]

The Jesuit historian, Fr W.J. Amherst, emphasises the debt which English Roman Catholics owe to George III 'in whose reign the repeal of the penal laws first began' and who in his personal dealings with Roman Catholics 'was always kind and amiable'. This 'good old king' had been persuaded, however, by his advisers that to extend full civil and political rights to Roman Catholics 'would be a breach of his coronation oath'.[54]

At the start of George IV's reign in 1820, the English Roman Catholic clergy numbered 'a little over 400... scarcely more than it had been 50 years earlier',[55] in spite of the influx of French émigré priests as well as numerous lay people, including aristocrats, seeking refuge from revolution in France and its spread to other states. Some of these priests remained and established permanent missions in England, particularly London.

Among the lay refugees was Augustus Pugin, a talented but untrained designer, whose son, Augustus Welby Pugin, was, at an early age, to achieve recognition as the foremost interpreter of Gothic design in the 19th century. He was to enjoy the patronage of royalty and also, notably, of the devout Roman Catholic peer, the 16th Earl of Shrewsbury. His benevolence enabled the young Pugin, later a convert to the Roman Catholic faith, to dedicate his exceptional talents and enthusiasm to ecclesiastical architecture for the benefit of the Roman Catholic community.

The English government offered these refugees a safe haven, while English Roman Catholics gave generous alms and, in the case of leading members of the gentry, offered accommodation in their several properties; for example, in 1794 Thomas Weld gave his mansion at Stonyhurst to the Jesuits from Liège.[56]

The French Revolution was instrumental in the return to England of Roman Catholic schools, colleges and seminaries, such as those of Douai and St Omer, which had been established for the education of the sons of the English gentry and for clerical students during the penal years. Most of the French religious communities returned to their country by the second decade of the 19th century, but the English schools and seminaries stayed and put down new roots in their native soil.

The Test and Corporation Acts, which had been in force since 1672, were repealed in 1825, thus removing a degree of religious intolerance for Protestant dissenters and Roman Catholics, and restoring some of their civil liberties. Personal religious convictions were no longer a bar to public office.

In his regency days, George IV had been markedly sympathetic to Roman Catholics, doubtless influenced by his secret marriage to Mrs Maria Fitzherbert, a devout

Roman Catholic and twice-widowed daughter of an English baronet. But, like his father, the king was later to take an unfavourable and even hostile view of the notion of Roman Catholic emancipation. This anti-popery stance of the monarch and many of his leading ministers persisted until, in 1829, Peel secured a Roman Catholic Relief Act; this consolidated and extended the concessions by the earlier Relief Acts in restoring to Roman Catholics civil liberties and freedom to practise their faith, and gave them new confidence and hope. It is notable that English Roman Catholics, including the vicars-apostolic, played virtually no part in getting the measure passed, in which Daniel O'Connell (1775-1847), the Irish patriot and Member of Parliament, was a key negotiator.[57] This historic concession to dissenters and to Roman Catholics was made by Wellington's government, which feared widespread violence leading to civil war in Ireland. According to Leys, however, 'It appears that some of the leading Roman Catholic gentry rather regretted that it was a pugnacious, rampageous Irishman who was really responsible for the grant of their political liberties'.[58] English Roman Catholics did not, however, acquire full freedom; they and Protestant dissenters were excluded from full access to university education, although from 1854 they could take a BA degree, and from 1856 an MA degree at Cambridge which, as Norman notes, 'had always been more liberal in this respect'.[59] It was not until 1871 that the University Tests Act abolished religious tests for university students. Roman Catholic prelates were still forbidden to adopt ecclesiastical territorial titles which were in use by the established Church, a ruling which was re-enacted as the Ecclesiastical Titles Bill of 1851. It tended, however, to become generally disregarded and the prohibition was repealed under Gladstone in 1871.

It has been asserted that after the Emancipation, Roman Catholics could be 'clearly distinguished as "Old Catholics", the "New Catholics", and the "English Catholics". The first party 'were such by heredity, and remembering penal days, wished for no more than to have the benefit of the Act and to go their way in peace'; the second type were chiefly converts 'who had seen the Church of England from the inside... and wanted Rome'. The third type were 'few in number, and they consisted both of hereditary Catholics and converts'. These various types or parties had one aspiration: 'the conversion of England, but they differed sharply about how that should be accomplished'.[60]

Religious orders, such as the Jesuits, Franciscans and Benedictines, were now able to develop their own establishments under the protection of the Roman Catholic Relief Act. In Leicestershire, Ambrose Phillipps (in 1862 he assumed the extra surname of de Lisle which originated from his mother's ancestors), son and heir of a prominent landowner, and a Roman Catholic convert, built a Trappist monastery in Charnwood Forest; this was destined to become the first new monastic establishment in England since the Reformation. In this venture he attracted the enthusiastic co-operation of Pugin, financial support from the vicar-apostolic of the Midland district and, later, generous donations from the 16th Earl of Shrewsbury. Phillipps, Pugin and the Earl were to become virtually inseparable associates in the Roman Catholic revival of the period. Railway contractors, and the owners of stone quarries and lime works also gave generous practical help in the building of the new monastery. Sheer good nature seemed, in some cases, to motivate them.

It is interesting to note that an earlier attempt, in 1820, to introduce a Roman Catholic Emancipation Bill had failed because O'Connell rejected the government's demand that it should exercise a veto over the appointment of Roman Catholic bishops. Nevertheless for all its limitations, Emancipation was an occasion for celebration by the Roman Catholic community in England: no longer were they likely to feel themselves strangers to some degree in their own country. The long struggle for religious freedom and civil liberties was largely won in the last years of George IV's reign, although deep-rooted opposition based largely on bigotry and lack of real knowledge and understanding persisted. In the early 19th century, English Roman Catholics continued to practise their faith discreetly but the 'quiet style' of Catholic observance tended to lead to public suspicions of secretive and in 'some way disgraceful practices'.[61] It was too readily believed that the papacy was still committed to the overthrow of the Crown and Constitution.

Protestant fears and hostilities were then inflamed by what may be considered as the culmination of the transformation of the old Roman Catholic community in England since 1570.[62] This final episode in the 'patient and continuous process of construction', which eventually led to a 'period of take-off for English Roman Catholicism in the early 19th century', was the Restoration of the Roman Catholic Hierarchy in 1850.[63]

On 7th October 1850, Cardinal Nicholas Wiseman (1805-65), flamboyantly and tactlessly, issued his dramatic pastoral *From out the Flaminian Gate of Rome*, announcing that the Roman Catholic Church in England and Wales was, once again, to have its own episcopal hierarchy, replacing the vicars-apostolic who, since the 17th century, had been directly responsible to Rome and were supervised by the Sacred Congregation of Propaganda.

In 1835, when he was rector of the English College

in Rome and acted, as was customary, as agent of the English vicars-apostolic, Wiseman had visited the principal centres of Roman Catholicism in England, given a series of public addresses, and observed that the Roman Catholic gentry still exercised considerable influence in church affairs. Later, in 1840, as coadjutor to Bishop Walsh, vicar-apostolic of the Midland district and president of Oscott, the developing centre for church students, Wiseman decided that it was vital to improve the ecclesiastical organisation of the Roman Catholic Church in England. In his view this necessitated imposing centralised control and stricter discipline on the clergy, and limiting radically the power of lay committees which still operated at a local level. These had evolved from penal times, when lay trustees were devised to protect the ownership of Roman Catholic chapels. Some problems also existed in the relationships between the religious orders and the vicars-apostolic. The secular clergy were beginning to agitate for improved status and recognition of their role in the growing Church, particularly in the fast-developing industrial cities and towns. For several years, in fact, there had been grass-root sentiment for a return to the old form of ecclesiastical government, episcopal hierarchy, and the new confidence in the denomination generated by the Emancipation stirred some secular clergy to seek changes. Because the vicars-apostolic did not possess the full authority of diocesan bishops, parishes were not formally organised, priests acted as missionaries ministering to huge congregations, or as private chaplains to the old Roman Catholic aristocracy and gentry.

Concessions which the vicars-apostolic were willing to make were considered inadequate by Wiseman, who told them that he intended to petition Rome for a diocesan episcopate. To this end he visited Rome in 1847 and successfully negotiated for a restoration of the Roman Catholic hierarchy, which he was appointed to head as Cardinal Archbishop of Westminster. Together with twelve suffragan bishops – the former vicars-apostolic – Wiseman, thereupon, formed the 'undisputed government of the Roman Catholic community',[64] From the penal years through to eventual emancipation and now restoration of its episcopal government, the Roman Catholic community had finally achieved legal recognition, ecclesiastical stability and increasing social acceptability; its members had grown from 80,000 in 1770 to around 750,000 in 1850, mainly in the towns and manufacturing districts. This growth was also experienced by the Church of England and nonconformist churches as the population migrated from the countryside to obtain employment in the rising new industries of the Industrial Revolution.

Although the announcement of the restoration of the Roman Catholic hierarchy had been timed to coincide with the Parliamentary recess and a period when news-gathering was usually at a low ebb, an advance copy of Wiseman's pastoral was published in Paris and became available to *The Times*. This journal quickly seized the opportunity to mount an attack on what was regarded, partly because of Wiseman's ill-chosen rhetoric, as Roman triumphalism. Some leading Roman Catholics, such as the Earl of Shrewsbury, Pugin and Ambrose Phillipps, were deeply disturbed by this unfortunate turn of events. The old battle cry of 'No-Popery' was again heard; effigies of the Pope and prominent English Roman Catholics were burned. In Wiseman's absence – he was travelling back to England at a leisurely pace, unaware of the furore his pastoral had caused – Bernard Ullathorne (1808-89), now Bishop of Birmingham, tried to reassure public opinion by stating that the new hierarchy and its rule was entirely a matter of Roman Catholic Church administration and religious life, and had nothing to do with political or national life. His efforts at reassurance were somewhat frustrated by Newman's sermon at Ullathorne's enthronement on 27th October 1850, when his eloquent phrasing could have been misconstrued as referring to the restoration of the English people to Rome.[65] Ambrose Phillipps wrote pamphlets in loyal support of Ullathorne's sturdy defence of the nature and purpose of the new hierarchical organisation. Virtually as soon as he arrived in London, Wiseman issued a lengthy *Appeal to the People of England*; this was well received, was effective in correcting misconceptions, and also clearly reflected his own personal integrity and powers of leadership. Clerical opposition, which had been evident in the London district and elsewhere to Wiseman's nomination as leader of the hierarchy 'ceased quickly in admiration of the courage and force with which he had overcome the agitation'.[66] Nevertheless, accusations of 'papal aggression', the inflammatory and popular description given to the misconceived papal action, were widespread and 'pulpits of all brands of Protestantism hammered away at the Pope and his English followers' throughout the last months of the year of the restoration of the Roman Catholic hierarchy.[67]

Earlier irritation had been caused to Protestants by the British government's decision, in 1845, to increase the annual grant to Maynooth College, an Irish seminary for training students for the Roman Catholic priesthood. Spasmodic rioting reappeared; Catholic chapels were burnt down, for instance in Stockport, and there were 'No-Popery' demonstrations elsewhere but, as with the notorious Gordon Riots, these largely erupted from residual and rabid anti-Catholic feelings which were unrepresentative of the majority of people's views about the resurgence of Catholicism, evident from the extensive building of schools, chapels and churches. These 'church extension' programmes were, in fact, adopted enthusiastically – and competitively – by all the churches in England and Wales during the Victorian era. In 1850, there were 587 Roman Catholic churches in England and Wales and 788 clergy; by the end of the century these numbers had increased to over 1,500 churches with almost 3,000 clergy.[68]

Since the 18th century, Irish immigration had been significant in enlarging the Roman Catholic community in England. This inflow was inflated by the disastrous famines of the 1840s, from which the starving, indigent people fled in terror. They largely concentrated in the developing cities of Liverpool, Manchester and Bristol, as well as in other industrial centres, and, of course, London. 'Estimates of varying reliability' record that in 1821 Liverpool had a Roman Catholic population of 12,000 which had increased to 60,000 by 1832.[69] In 1881, Irish-born residents were 1.5% of the population of England, but accounted for 12.8% of the population of Liverpool, 7.5% of Manchester, 3.3% of London. Furthermore, 'Leakage from the faith was... largely an Irish phenomenon; but it was on a much less significant scale, proportionately... than lapses by English Protestants from the Protestant denominations'.[70]

Nevertheless, Bossy 'casts doubts' on a 'commonly accepted' view held by historians that 'for all serious purposes the Catholicism of modern England may be taken as a cutting from the Catholicism of Ireland transplanted by emigration into an alien land which had long ceased to have anything worth mentioning to offer in the way of an indigenous Catholic tradition'. He declares that this is a 'respectable historical opinion' which needs to be modified in important and significant respects'.[71] This claim is supported by Norman, who considers that the case has been 'convincingly argued that existing developments within English Catholicism already presaged expansion'. The notion that the Irish influx largely dictated the way in which the Catholic church in England grew in the 19th century requires severe modification. However, he also draws attention to the fact that by the 1850s, around 80% of Catholic congregations were Irish and working-class, and sees this as giving 'a huge impetus to missionary zeal' within the Church..[72]

Best argues that Roman Catholicism was the only major denomination to possess a very solid basis among the urban working classes: 'only the Roman Catholics in England seem to have been, in the lump, proletarian; even lumpen-proletarian... That lump was leavened with the finest social yeast', as reflected in the affluent congregations of some Roman Catholic churches in fashionable parts of London.[73] In addition to members of the 'old Catholic' families, this 'finest social yeast' included celebrated converts like Newman, Manning, Faber, Pugin and Ambrose Phillipps. At the other extreme, a volatile mix of racial bias and religious antipathy, even bigotry, tended to encourage a ghetto-like mentality and behaviour among Irish immigrants in general. Many had come from stricken rural areas. They were relatively unskilled and their families soon fell into abject poverty. Religious differences and suspicions were thus amplified by ethnic and class distinctions.

Although many of the missionary priests who worked in the poorest parts of the industrial towns and cities were of Irish stock, the leadership of the Roman Catholic Church in England was never, as Norman stresses, 'taken over by the Irish'; most bishops came from 'traditional Roman Catholic families and the convert elements'.[74] Clearly, Wiseman was a distinguished exception. Born of Irish parents in Seville, he was sent to Ushaw in 1810 when he was eight years old, and moved to study in Rome ten years later. He did not return to England until 1840. He was a committed ultramontanist and imposed Roman disciplines when he was appointed to head the Roman Catholic hierarchy in 1850.

The 'golden age' of the English mission, Bossy states, lasted perhaps from 1800 to the restoration of the Roman Catholic hierarchy, when it reached 'its formal closure'.[75] In those five decades, the Roman Catholic Church in England built on the firm foundations which had been laid by previous generations of faithful belief and practice. It was to emerge as an integral part of English public life, whose leaders won the respect, and even admiration, of all parties and sections of the public. Their single-minded dedication to both spiritual and temporal welfare, such as care for the poor and sick, and for progressive improvements in education, showed the full extent of their commitment to society in general as well as to pastoral care for their flocks. 'Despite the insistence on Roman authority, it is a notable feature of English Roman Catholic history that it has remained very English. Roman Catholics even in days of severest persecution, as in the reign of Elizabeth I, always insisted on their devotion as Englishmen to the Constitution of the country and to the political values of English liberty'.[76] In the eventful Victorian epoch English Catholics were intellectuals and scholars such as Newman, Ward and Acton, legendary prelates like Wiseman, Manning, Vaughan, Ullathorne and Ilsley, prominent aristocrats and country gentry like the Duke of Norfolk, the Earl of Shrewsbury, the Welds, the Brudenells, and the Leicester squire Ambrose Phillipps.

The scene is so crowded with personalities and issues that any further examination and discussion of the regeneration of English Roman Catholicism in the Victorian period that is not merely superficial requires selectivity and focus. Since, however, the purpose of this book is to consider the role of one of these historic figures and the ways in which he participated and influenced the events and issues with which he became involved, some background knowledge and appreciation has been essential. This introductory chapter has endeavoured to trace the precarious path taken by the Roman Catholic Church in England since the Reformation until, nearly 300 years later, when the restoration of the Roman Catholic hierarchy took place. Of the many leaders from the Victorian era who participated profoundly in intellectual and cultural life, John Henry Newman's contributions to the development of Christian attitudes and beliefs have ensured him a pre-eminent position. The complex nature of his personality, the labyrinthine ways he trod throughout his long life, his astonishing number and range of friends, and other contacts that he cultivated and maintained over many years, as well as his deep personal spirituality, offer many potential opportunities for inquiry.

Several excellent biographies have already been written about Newman, some of which examine to his earliest years; these are listed in the references given at the end of the book. Our aim is to focus on specific aspects of Newman's life and activities related principally to Roman Catholicism during the Victorian era. These particular features cover some of the prominent events and issues in which he became deeply involved. We intend to begin by looking at the significant role he played in the Oxford Movement, and then proceed to his conversion, halfway through his life, to Roman Catholicism; we will then move on to his ordination as a Catholic priest and subsequent foundation of the English Oratory; innovations in the field of higher education whilst he was in Ireland and his ardent commitment to intellectual excellence also reflect Newman's ceaselessly active range of interests. As a controversialist he made an outstanding contribution to religious life in the Victorian epoch; he was a highly skilled polemicist and superb stylist; his writings both as an Anglican and later as a Roman Catholic continue to influence religious and philosophical issues today. Although never a diocesan bishop, Newman's intellectual and spiritual leadership had a unique and pervasive character. He left an indelible mark not only on the Catholic Church in England, but also on the whole body of Christian thought and behaviour.

NOTES

1 Koenigsberger et al., 1963, p.291.
2 Koenigsberger et al., 1963, p.294.
3 Norman, 1986, p.10.
4 Koenigsberger et al., 1963, p.354.
5 Koenigsberger et al., 1963, p.401.
6 Norman, 1986, p.7.
7 Mathew, 1936, p.37.
8 Norman, 1986, p.8.
9 Norman, 1986, p.8.
10 Norman, 1986, p.29.
11 Norman, 1996, p.16.
12 Bossy, 1976, pp.13-18.
13 Cf Norman, 1986, p.15.
14 Cf Bossy, 1976, p.216.
15 Bossy, 1976, p.219.
16 Norman, 1986, p.9.
17 Norman, 1986, p.33.
18 Kenyon, 1972, p.4.
19 Kenyon, 1972, p.3.
20 Cf Norman, 1986, p.34.
21 Cf Leys, 1961, p.85..
22 Mathew, 1936, p.87.
23 Leys, 1961, pp.97-98.
24 Leys, 1961, pp.97-98.
25 Norman, 1986, p.38.
26 Norman, 1986, p.38.
27 Kenyon, 1972, p.200.

28 Norman, 1986, p.39.
29 Kenyon, 1972, pp.203-4.
30 Leys, 1961, p.l04.
31 Kenyon, 1972, p.259.
32 Cf Norman, 1986, p.37; Kenyon, 1972, p.166.
33 Bossy, 1976, p.422.
34 Bossy, 1976, p.70.
35 Norman, 1986, p.45.
36 Leys, 161, p.108.
37 Leys, 1961, p.112.
38 Leys, 1961, p.114.
39 Bossy, 1976, p.158.
40 Leys, 1961, p.125.
41 Bossy, 1976, p.286.
42 Norman, p.30.
43 Bossy, 1976, p.364.
44 Leys, 1961, p.133.
45 Leys, 1961, p.134.
46 Norman, 1986, p.54.
47 Amherst, 1886, p.179.
48 Bernard Ward, l909, p.87.
49 Norman, 1986, p.47.
50 Mathew, 1936, p.151.
51 Cf Mathew, 1936, pp.149-50.
52 Mathew, 136, p.151.
53 Bernard Ward, 1909, pp.ix-x.
54 Amherst, 1886, p.324.
55 Bossy, 1976, p.356.
56 Leys, 1961, p.143.
57 Cf Norman, 1986, pp.64-65.
58 Leys, 1961, p.159.
59 Norman, 1985, p.293.
60 Trappes-Lomax, 1932, p.103.
61 Norman, 1985, p.10.
62 Cf Bossy, 1976, p.5.
63 Cf Bossy, 1976, p.297.
64 Bossy, 1976, p.362.
65 Newman, 1874, pp.121-138.
66 Gwynn, 1946, p.132.
67 Norman, 1985, p.105.
68 Norman, 1986, p.71.
69 Mathew, 1936, p.182.
70 Norman, 1985, p.220.
71 Bossy, 1976, p.297.
72 Norman, 1985, p.7.
73 Best, 1985, p.206.
74 Norman, 1985,p.7.
75 Bossy, 1976, p.322.
76 Norman, 1985, p.2.

2

Newman:
The Oxford Movement and
Tractarianism

ONE of Newman's perceptive biographers, Wilfrid Ward – whose daughter Maisie also wrote an outstanding life of Newman – declared that 'John Henry Newman is indeed himself a remarkable instance of one of his most characteristic contentions, that the same object may be seen by different onlookers under aspects so various and partial as to make their views, from their inadequacy, appear occasionally even contradictory'.[1] There are so many facets to Newman's character. He was a dedicated scholar, an eloquent preacher, a highly talented writer, a religious poet of unusual merit, an ecclesiastical activist, a visionary and also a remarkably powerful protagonist and controversialist. One scholar who has studied Newman concludes that the mind of Newman 'is characterised not by contradictions but by supplementary strengths, so that he may be called, without inconsistency, both conservative and liberal, progressive and traditional, cautious and radical, dogmatic yet pragmatic, idealistic but realistic'.[2]

It is not surprising, therefore, to find that a man so richly endowed stirred the hearts and minds of many and thus exercised considerable influence over those who, like himself, were deeply disturbed about the position and the responsibilities of the Church of England in a society which was experiencing challenges from 'liberalism' and from political unrest emanating from revolutionary France. It has been noted that 'in the 1830s, the Church of England was still closely enmeshed with the nation and its rulers; the great majority of English people were Christian in the sense of never having thought they were anything else'.[3] Religious faith has often been considered to have been behind the moral intensity that was a distinctive mark of the Victorian era; while church-going varied among the social classes, 'Christian values were the central values and all deep individual problems were related to Christian morals'.[4] Of course, personal moral standards were not immune from other influences, and religious beliefs tended to be uncertain in dogma. Disbelief was becoming evident and, indeed, prevalent, among intellectuals.

Newman recognised the emergence of these trends before the Church of England experienced the resurgence that became known as the 'Oxford Movement' or 'Tractarianism'. In 'coming forward as the champion of Revealed Religion', he realised fully 'that his real battle was with "liberalism"'.[5] Newman had defined 'liberalism' as 'a thinking established notions worth nothing – in this system of opinions a disregard of religion is included'.[6]

In an *Essay on the Development of Christian Doctrine*, Newman stressed that 'the search for truth is not the gratification of curiosity'; that liberalism holds truth and falsehood in religion as merely a matter of opinion; 'that one doctrine is as good as another... that there is no truth... that it is enough if we sincerely hold what we profess'.[7] As Trevor puts it, 'By the term Liberalism Newman did not mean the idea of political freedom, but that 'one opinion is as good as another' and that there is 'no objective truth in religion'.[8] When, in his advanced years, Newman came to Rome to be raised to the rank of Cardinal, he made a formal speech of acceptance of the high honour in which he declared that for 'thirty, forty, fifty years I have resisted to the best of my powers the spirit of Liberalism in religion. Never did Holy Church need champions against it more sorely than now'.[9]

But religious concerns were not alone in motivating the Movement; other factors intervened, involving political and constitutional matters, as Nockles has emphasised.[10]

For almost two decades, Sir Robert Peel, in line with Tory policy, had stoutly opposed the principle of Roman Catholic emancipation, but later, in 1828, as Home Secretary, he changed his views in order to avert the imminent danger of civil strife in Ireland following the election of Daniel O'Connell to the Clare constituency. Following this volte-face, Peel formally tendered his resignation as the MP for Oxford University, stating that 'I consider bound to surrender to the University without delay the trust they have confided in me'.[11] However, he also offered himself for re-election. This led to a sharp difference of opinion between the Provost of Oriel, Edward Hawkins, who supported him, and the four Tutors of the College who viewed his re-election as 'far more than a question of politics and political expediency; it was a moral, an academical, an ecclesiastical, nay a religious question; not least it grew to be such with them'.[12] In a long letter to Samuel Rickards, dated 6th February 1829, Newman told him that the previous year the Convocation of the University of Oxford had increased its majority from 3:1 to 2:1 against granting Roman Catholic emancipation: 'this is manly and I like it... It is not *pro dignatate nostra*, to have a Rat as a member'.[13] Newman's objection, which provoked such strongly-worded sentiments, lay in the fact that Peel – as noted – had suddenly switched his views on Catholic emancipation for political advantage, not because of any convictions on the religious issues involved. To his sister Jemima he confided that while, as she knew, he had 'no opinion about the Catholic Question', he was concerned that the way in which it was settled signified the 'encroachments of philosphism and indifferentism on the Church'.[14]

On Peel's defeat by Sir Robert Inglis by a majority of 146 in the by-election on 28th February, Newman exulted openly. In a letter to his mother he declared; 'We have achieved a glorious Victory... We have proved the independence of the Church and of Oxford'.[15] As Gilley comments, 'Newman's fierceness was that of a young man who with his friends has found a cause'.[16] It seems as though there was an almost over-eagerness by Newman and his friends to seize the opportunity offered, unintentionally, by Peel to take a stand against those who would seek to challenge the dominance of the established Church. Indeed, Nockles holds that Peel's repudiation by the University 'deserves to be regarded as an even more appropriate date for the rise of the Oxford Movement than was Keble's Assize Sermon'.[17]

In a postscript to a letter to Samuel Rickards, Newman declared, 'I believe indeed in the doctrine of the *Genius loci*'.[18] It may have been that this dedicated, indomitable belief in the essential and unique quality of Oxford intellectual life caused, as Maisie Ward remarked, early writers on the Oxford Movement to see a 'special strength in the narrowness of its scene... like a Greek republic or an Italian city state of the Middle Ages'. But this, she continues, 'is only partly true'. While Oxford had an 'intense life of its own' it was 'also the intellectual centre of England: in a sense the spiritual centre. The Movement gained from Oxford its historical basis, but Oxford was not isolated'.[19] From the fertile soil of Oxonian intellectualism, enriched by profound religious commitments, grew the Movement which, according to Nockles, was to 'form a chapter in the intellectual history of 19th century Europe, and was in tune with such deep cultural currents as Romanticism'.[20]

Walgrave states that Newman's convictions about the uniqueness of the Church's position in society and of the importance of its independence in fulfilling its sacred mission, derived from the influence of Dr Richard Whately, later Protestant Archbishop of Dublin, whose 'anti-Erastian views (opposing the subordination of the Church to the State) deeply coloured his thought'.[21] This seminal influence was recorded by Newman in his journal; 'On looking back, he found that one momentous truth of Revelation he had learned from Dr Whately, and that was the idea of the Christian Church as a divine appointment, and as a substantive visible body, independent of the State, and endowed with rights, prerogatives, and powers of its own'.[22] From this point of view, the invisibility of the Christian Church was seen as of paramount importance in Church-State relationships. Erastianism, whose roots lay in attempts to impose state control in ecclesiastical affairs, was utterly repugnant to Newman and his associates. They recognised that, from time to time, the Church of England had suffered from what they considered to be this abuse and were determined to do all they could to rid it of this interference. Nockles has thus described the Oxford Movement as 'an anti-Erastian, moral protest against the apparently popular notion that the Church of England was but a human establishment, subservient to the material and secular interests of the State'.[23]

In December 1832 Newman accompanied Hurrell Froude and his father, Archdeacon Froude, on a tour of the Mediterranean which, it was hoped, would improve the health of Hurrell. The voyage was 'entirely uneventful'; Newman's thoughts were fixed on England and what was happening there. He parted company with the Froudes on 9th April 1833, and sailed for 'Naples with Sicily as his objective'. His ambitious travels were to end in an appalling sequence of illnesses, including typhoid fever, from which he almost died; to everyone's surprise he survived and his health gradually improved.[24] Newman came to regard this prolonged period as a 'purifying illness, preparing him for his mission in England'.[25] On his return journey to England, Newman's ship was becalmed for a week in the Straits of Bonifacio during which time he wrote 'the lines "Lead, Kindly Light" which have since become well known'.[26] These entreating words form the opening lines of the poem 'The Pillar of the Cloud', which has been widely adopted as a hymn.

In his *Autobiographical Writings*, Newman records that he had 'three great illnesses' in his life. 'The first keen, terrible one, when I was a boy of 15, and it made me a Christian... My second, not painful, but tedious and shattering was that I had in 1827 when I was one of the Examining Masters, and it broke me off from an incipient liberalism and determined my religious course'. The third illness was that which occurred in Sicily in 1833.[27]

Eventually after exhausting travel, Newman arrived back in England on 9th July 1833, and entered into the fast-erupting controversy over the Irish Church Temporalities Act of 1833. In a letter dated 21st February 1833, Harriet and Jemima had warned their brother about the 'strange things, public and private' which had been happening in his absence, namely 'the mad schemes of Government, and of the despoiling of the poor Irish Church'.[28] The 1833 Act was introduced by the Whig Government in an attempt to rationalise the situation of the established Church of Ireland. Two of the four archbishoprics were abolished as well as eight bishoprics; these were amalgamated with neighbouring dioceses and their stipends removed; revenues of the two wealthiest sees, Armagh and Derry, were reduced; church cess (the tax paid by Roman Catholic families as well as the Protestant minority) was abolished. Owen Chadwick records that these proposals were received in the House of Commons in 'chilly silence'.[29] Such unwelcome legislation was viewed by many High Churchmen as rank Erastianism, which should not be tolerated. It directly challenged the traditional status and authority of an established Church; the freedom of the clergy to preach the Word of God was being imperilled. In un-inhibited letters to his friends, Newman showed clearly that he was outraged by the Temporalities Act. He confessed to Thomas Mozley that it had made him 'hate the Whigs... more bitterly than ever', and he referred to the legislation as 'the atrocious high sacrilege bill'.[30] Of Henry Wilberforce, he requested news of 'what various individuals in England think of this cursed Irish spoliation bill'.[31] In similar vein, he asked George Ryder's opinion of the 'accursed Whig spoliation bill'.[32]

It is widely admitted that the Church of Ireland in the early 1800s was in need of some fairly radical re-organisation: pluralism was rife, absenteeism was common, great endowments were enjoyed by a Church which had relatively few adherents, probably just over 10% of the population. Although the majority of the population were Roman Catholic, they had to pay local taxes to support the established Church. They viewed it as an instrument of British colonialism. Some attempts were made to improve the administration and pastoral standards of the Church of Ireland, but these internal initiatives were inadequate on the whole, and more stringent measures were generally deemed necessary. These were to be imposed by the 1833 Act and under the supervision of the Ecclesiastical Commission of 1835.

The furore caused by the 1833 Act was brought to a head in July 1833 by a celebrated sermon by John Keble, one of the Fellows of Oriel College, whose discussions on ecclesiastical affairs had already attracted wide attention across the University. This elite circle also included John Henry Newman, Edward Bouverie Pusey and Richard Hurrell Froude. Keble, who was Professor of Poetry at Oxford, was invited to preach the annual assize sermon before the University. His theme was 'National Apostasy', which he perceived as aptly describing the sacrilegious intervention by the State in the ecclesiastical concerns of the Church of Ireland. His forthright sermon on the text 'I will teach you the good and the right way', though not intended to be a call to arms, was, nevertheless, a publicly declared expression of the fears felt by High Churchmen over the Whig Government's proposals for reform of the Church of Ireland.[33] Gilley, however, describes Keble's sermon as 'couched in generalities', and suggests that its use of analogies from the Old Testament would have 'delighted a Scottish Covenanter'.[34]

But Gilley also described Keble as 'the most brilliant student of his generation' who had 'resigned his Oriel tutorship in 1823 to become his father's curate' at Fairford.[35] In 1835 he became Vicar of Hursley, Hampshire, where he lived for 30 years. In the *Apologia*, Newman wrote touchingly of this remarkably gifted cleric, who was 'young in years, when he became a University celebrity, and younger in mind. He had the purity and simplicity of a child... He instinctively shut before literary display, and pomp and donnishness of manner, faults which always will beset academical notabilities'.[36]

The precise date on which the Oxford Movement was born has been the subject of debate among historians of that Movement and among Newman scholars. In his journal, Newman records that he heard the Assize Sermon on 14th July 1833 and that 'I have ever considered and kept the day, as the start of the religious movement of 1833'.[37] However, Fr Henry Tristram, a leading Oratorian scholar, adds an editorial comment that Newman 'without a thought of self, assigned the credit to another. But by others an earlier date has been assigned as the birthday of the Movement: 22nd January 1832, the day on which, in his turn as Select Preacher, he delivered the sermon *Personal Influence, the means of Propagating the Truth*. These two views are not irreconcilable with each other. Newman's sermon was an appeal for volunteers in the spiritual combat; Keble's was 'a call to action in the political crisis that seemed to menace the Church of England'.[38] Only after the Whig Government's 1833 Act did the Movement move from expressed concern to organised action.

As noted earlier on page 43, Nockles considers that Peel's repudiation by the University in 1829 could be considered to mark the start of the Oxford Movement even more appropriately than Keble's sermon four years later. Vargish traces the causes of the Movement even earlier, and states that 'in a large measure' it was a 'reaction against what its leaders regarded as the corruptions of the 18th century'.[39]

Hurrell Froude and William Palmer – 'a dry and

learned Irishman from Trinity College, Dublin'[40] – returned to Oxford after enlisting the support of Hugh James Rose, the editor of the *British Magazine*. With Newman and Keble they drew up some guiding principles for their new movement, but not without some conflicting notions about the desirable objectives. 'Both Keble and Newman wanted the campaign to be more religious and less political' than the others did.[41] This is reflected in correspondence between Newman and his close associates.[42] Their concern was to reassert the independence of the Church and to emphasise that its authority is derived from the Apostles; these aims reflect Newman's feelings of personal responsibility. These feelings of personal responsibility were expressed in a letter to Henry Wilberforce.[43] Fr Henry Tristram, as editor of Newman's Autobiographical Writings commented on these feelings as follows: 'When he left England in December, 1832, he was in a state of perplexity about his future course; when he returned in July 1833, he appeared as a man charged with a mission – a mission to save the Church of England from the perils that encompassed her'.[44] In animated correspondence with his former pupil Charles Portales Golightly (who was later to foment anti-Newman feelings in connection with *Tract 90*), Newman declared that 'We have everything against us but our cause',[45] and in a later letter, that 'We have formed a society here for the purposes of rousing the clergy... we have decided to keep most of our views in the background at present... to stir up our brethren to consider the state of the Church, and especially to the practical belief and preaching of the Apostolical Succession'.[46]

The earliest Tracts, Owen Chadwick observes, were 'anonymous and ephemeral sheets of a few pages, privately circulated. Newman conceived them not as regular troops but as sharpshooters'.[47] They have also been described as 'short clarion calls in defence of the Church's independence'.[48] The urgency of the situation spurred Newman to write the first Tract, *The Ministerial Commission* (1833). This was an urgent call to the clergy to recognise and assert the spiritual basis of their authority for this comes from 'our apostolic descent... We have been born, not of blood, nor of the will of the flesh, nor of the will of man, but of God'. (On reflection, this claim might be regarded by some as unwarrantable, if not blasphemous.) The clergy should fulfil their own God-given role. Newman challenged them to '*choose your side*'. This stirring opening to the Tracts for the Times was published anonymously but its authorship was soon recognised. Newman's fiery words asserted the spiritual vocation of the clergy of the Church of England and its inheritance from the earliest days of Christianity, that is, from the time of the Apostles. It was a radical assessment of the Church's position that was to force out into the open, and intensify, internal strifes which had afflicted it for many years. High Churchmen and Tractarians professed the Catholic traditions of the Church of England; Low Churchmen and Evangelicals stressed the significance of the Reformation period and its ecclesiastical implications. In only a few years' time, the Oxford Movement itself was to experience similar internal discord and the departure of Newman with some other leading Anglo-Catholics to Rome.

The writing and dissemination of the Tracts continued apace. By the end of 1833 twenty had been published, of which Newman had written eleven. In addition he had been very active in distributing parcels of the Tracts throughout the district. In his *Instructions for Propagandists*, he stated categorically that 'We have no concern with politics. We have nothing to do with maintaining the temporalities of the Church, much as we deprecate any undue interference with them on external authority'.[49] Clearly, however, as noted already, the origins of the Oxford Movement were rooted in protestations against perceived political interference in the affairs of the Church of Ireland. In this respect Nockles warns that 'The essentially political origins of the rise of the Oxford Movement are too often overlooked. In many ways, Tractarianism represented a revolt of Oxford Toryism at the reforming measures which the Grey ministry brought into parliament in the early 1830s. Yet, historians taking their cue from Tractarian historiography have tended to regard the Movement as always unconcerned with constitutional and political questions. Pusey himself had encouraged this misunderstanding'.[50] Not for the first time in English history, as indicated in Chapter 1, political and religious motivations were so closely meshed and inter-active that it becomes virtually impossible to isolate their individual influences. 'Old fashioned Churchmen were Tories. They loved the Church, but that love was bound up with their hatred of Whiggery, and they had no necessary sympathy with the new Oxford theology'.[51] There was always, of course, the fact that both the Church of England and the Church of Ireland were established by law and that this conferred on them privileges, special status, exclusive rights to university education, entry to the professions, and, until the repeal of the Test and Corporations Acts of 1828 and the Catholic Relief Act of 1829, certain civil and religious freedoms. Disestablishment of the Church of Ireland was still over 25 years away while the prospects of the Church of England being forced to accept the same fate seemed a remote, faintly rumbling threat. When the Ecclesiastical Commission was set up by Sir Robert Peel in response to demands for reform of the administration of the Church of England, the 'threat of disestablishment evaporated just before the Commission was first created'.[52]

In October 1833 Newman felt able to tell Frederic Rogers, an Oxford intimate, that 'We are getting on famously with our Society, and are so prudent and temperate that Froude writes up to me we have made a hash of it, which I account to be praise'.[53] Towards the end of 1833, the Tractarians' efforts were significantly strengthened by Pusey who wrote *Thoughts on the Benefits of the System of Fasting enjoined by our Church'* (*Tract 18*) and appended his initials, EBP, to indicate his tentative association with the other Tractarians. As Dessain suggests, this ruse, however, had an effect 'contrary to his intentions and gave the movement the prestige of his name... The Tracts soon changed their form and developed into small treatises'.[54] From being 'airy missiles' they evolved, as Trevor puts it, into a 'heavy bombardment of scholarly tomes' reflecting the growing maturity of the Movement.[55] Newman himself, however, declined the name 'Newmanites' as referring to 'himself and his ardent band of followers, yet a party they certainly were... He must have enjoyed using his powers of leadership'.[56]

In William Oddie's opinion, Newman was the Movement's strongest intellectual influence through the Tracts, his sermons, and his *Lectures on the Prophetical Office of the Church* (1837)'.[57] Gilley also judges that Newman's voice was the dominant one in the Tracts although, of course, he had many helpers.[58] Nockles claims that Newman at this time can be regarded 'both as a political conservative and a spiritual revolutionary'. He shared with radical Evangelicals 'a belief that political events had necessarily to be interpreted theologically'.[59]

With the valuable addition of Pusey to the Tractarian team, a third way of describing these religious zealots came into use, 'Puseyites'. This term, however, was not in common use until after Newman's secession in 1845 whereas 'Tractarianism' had been a widely adopted alternative for 'Oxfordism' since the early 1840s. The term Oxford Movement was, however, seldom used without inverted commas until the 1880s.[60] The predilection for labelling specific religious affiliations has also been noted by Gilley: 'it was in the 1830s that Newman and his friends gave a novel currency to the terms "Anglicanism" and "Anglo-Catholicism"; it was the first time that the Church of England was to be known as an "*ism*" describing its identity as a third way between Protestantism and Rome'.[61] Whatever appellation was attached to them and their dedicated activities, the important thing to note is that the Tractarians asserted the spiritual independence of the Church from the State, emphasised its apostolicity, and attempted to revive the piety and authority which had supposedly been inculcated by the Fathers of the early Church.[62]

In time, and among themselves, Newman and Froude designated their supporters 'Apostolicals' or 'Ys', whereas 'Zs' or 'Establishment men' were rigid old High Churchmen and 'Xs' referred to ultra-Protestants, 'Peculiars' or Evangelicals, 'of whom there were at first a fair sprinkling in the Associations'.[63]

Celibacy was considered by Newman to be a 'spiritual ideal as opposed to a pragmatic convenience' which provided freedom from marital responsibilities. It impelled the celibate towards total commitment to God's service.[64] However, Newman confided to a close friend, 'Parsons' wives... are useful in a parish, and that in a way no *man* can rival them'.[65] To his sister Jemima, he wrote; 'I am full of work as usual, and trust it may tell... I am not more lonely than I have been a long while. God intends me to be lonely. He has so framed my mind that

I am in a great measure beyond the sympathies of other people, and thrown upon himself... God, I trust will support me in following where He leads'.[66]

As Gilley notes, Newman's commitment to celibacy was an intrinsic part of his personal dedication to God, but he concedes that Newman was for a time under the influence of Hurrell Froude and that he sometimes disparaged marriage, although there is no proof that he was a misogynist.[67] He had, in fact, a circle of women – including his mother and sisters – with whom he kept up a regular correspondence concerned with a wide range of topics apart from family news. He frequently discussed at considerable length sophisticated concepts of religious dogma and observances with them.

In the *Apologia* Newman specifically mentions that in Autumn 1816 he experienced the profound conviction – 'another deep imagination' that it 'would be the will of God that I should lead a single life'. He held this belief firmly, except, as he says in the *Apologia*, for very brief periods up to 1829, but never wavered after that time. He noted that this calling 'strengthened my feeling of separation from the visible world'.[68] In Maisie Ward's opinion, Newman was 'by nature a bachelor, by grace a celibate'. She adds, however, that his 'attitude upon clerical celibacy in general was misunderstood by some even of his most intimate friends'.[69]

Hurrell Froude's health began to give rise to further anxiety and in October 1833, as Newman notes[70] he 'left for good' to travel to Barbados. Newman then had to take on full responsibility for the Tracts. Froude had contributed significantly to Newman's doctrinal insights, such as those concerning the Eucharistic Real Presence and devotion to the Blessed Virgin. These themes came to be reflected in his sermons.[71] Froude had also played a key role in the early stages of developing the notion of writing Tracts, both in giving advice and in his animated views on how the Movement should progress. Newman himself relied heavily on Froude for advice on his projected publications.[72]

In 1834 the first volume of Newman's *Parochial and Plain Sermons* appeared. This eight-volume series covered sermons preached to congregations at Oxford and Littlemore between 1835 and 1841. According to Trevor 'If the Tracts were the fighting front of the Movement, these sermons were the spiritual power behind it, and the real strength of Newman's leadership'.[73] In accordance with conventional Anglican practice, the sermons were read. Hence they were meticulously written and sensitively structured. Trevor holds that 'Few of Newman's sermons were controversial; they are psychologically penetrating applications of Christian teaching which could appeal to Christians of every tradition, and still do'.[74] These *Parochial and Plain Sermons* were, in fact, the first of Newman's Anglican works to be republished in 1878, the year before he was created a Cardinal by Pope Leo XIII. Then, at his request, the volumes were edited by W.J. Copeland, who had once been his curate at Littlemore. In a letter to Copeland, Newman expressed his gratitude: 'You have been of the greatest use to me in the matter of the Sermons... Unless you have broken the ice, I could have re-published nothing which I wrote before 1845,6. The English public would not have borne any alterations and my own people would have been much scandalised had I made none. They murmured a good deal at the new edition of the Sermons, as it was – but, since you, not I, published them, nothing would be said about it'.[75] In a draft of the 'Advertisement' for the Sermons which, in 1877, he sent to Copeland for clearance, Newman stated that 'the author has been careful to follow faithfully the text as it stands in Mr Copeland's edition of them. At the same time he is glad to be able to state that they do not contain a word, which, as a Catholic, he would wish to alter'.[76] In a long letter to Hugh James Rose, editor of the *British Magazine*, Newman gave his reasons for supporting the continued imposition of subscription to the Thirty-nine Articles demanded of entrants to Oxford University.[77] He signed the 'Oxford Declaration against the Admission of Dissenters', which was enthusiastically championed by eighty-seven university dons.[78] When the bill to admit dissenters was defeated, he openly rejoiced. But the protest by Oxford University teachers was challenged by Renn Dickson Hampden, Principal of St Mary's Hall, who published a pamphlet, *Observations on Religious Dissent*, in which he advocated the total abolition of religious tests. Newman expostulated strongly to Hampden: 'While I respect the tone of piety which the pamphlet displays, I dare not trust myself to put on paper my feelings about the principles contained in it, tending as they do in my opinion altogether to make shipwreck of Christian faith'.[79] Newman received from Hampden a courteous dismissal: 'I think the same candour and good motives should induce you to wait rather for a full discussion of a question, and a fair hearing of parties on both sides'. He would be 'quite ready' to hear any arguments that may be brought.[80] Newman's reaction to Hampden may have been partly influenced by the fact that when Dr Hawkins, Provost of Oriel, took from Newman his tutorship, it had been given to Hampden. In his journal, Newman admits that 'ever since [he] had unfriendly feelings towards Hampden'.[81] These feelings were to be aggravated further when he was unsuccessful in securing the Chair of Moral Philosophy, which was awarded to Hampden who had been 'put up' by Hawkins 'at the last moment'.[82] Hostile feelings were rekindled when, in 1836, Lord Melbourne appointed

Hampden Regius Professor of Divinity, to the disgust and alarm of the High Churchmen. Protests were made without avail, and Convocation had to be content with passing a public vote of no confidence in the allegedly 'unorthodox' appointment.[83] Newman considered that the way things had turned out 'was a lesson for both Church and State… Erastianism dies a natural death… the State casts us off. The Clergy will be forced back upon the truth by the pressure of circumstances'.[84]

Meanwhile the Oxford Movement was steadily growing and Newman's reputation had been enhanced by the *Parochial Sermons* and by *The Arians* 'which had caused a stir among the learned of the University'.[85]

The Arians has been described as 'a young man's book, written with enthusiasm but without the rhetorical grace and effortless flow of Newman's later books'.[86] Newman himself referred to it critically; 'As to *The Arians*, except that the matter of it is true, I have long thought of it the most imperfect work that was ever composed… I once asked Froude, if it was not pompous. thinking that a sin of it, but he said decidedly no'.[87] Some forty years later, Newman told a correspondent that his book on the Arians should not be referred to 'as "great", it is not even little. It was to have been in Mr Rose's intention, the beginning of a Manual on the Councils, and the gun went off in quite another direction, hitting no mark at all'. He explained that he had to finish it by 'a fixed day, and had to hurry through the last pages especially, till I knocked myself up'.[88] In his eighties, Newman reflected that considering that *The Arians* was his first book, 'that my reading up to then had not got as far as the Nicene Council and that I had but a year to do it in, and that I was in weak health, I do not wonder that it was not worse… Yet with all its defects I think it has some good points in it, and in parts some originality'.[89]

In Ker's opinion, although *The Arians* was 'far from being a history of the principal Councils...there was no question, however, about the distinction of the work'.[90]

The principle of reserve or 'economy' was identified by Newman as important in communicating religious knowledge in terms that are comprehensible to the receiver. According to Selby, 'Since we are at a distance from truth and can only apprehend it by means of economical representations, words themselves are economies... Words do not transmit the essence, but afford a partial insight into truth; they demand the participation of the reader.'[91] Ker notes that Newman's treatment of the principle of economy 'is perhaps the most interesting aspect of the book'(*The Arians*).[92] A similar point is made by Nockles: 'Reserve became a distinctive element of the Tractarian spiritual ethos'.[93]

In September 1835, Newman wrote to Bowden that 'we have determined to commence a series *against Popery*, i.e., to devote next year at length to the subject. Many advantages will follow from this. Two years since the cry was against the Dissenters this helped us – now Popery is the popular alarm'.[94] He also wrote in similar vein to Henry Wilberforce[95] and to H.E. Manning.[96] His motives in the decision to attack Rome seem to have been mixed. In a long letter to Mrs William Wilberforce (but marked 'not sent' in his papers), Newman disclosed that 'the more I examine into the RC system, the less sound it appears to me to be; and the less safely could I in conscience profess to receive it'. He listed his objections: they were to the doctrine of Transubstantiation, to the 'polytheism' associated with 'saint-worship', to the 'praying to images', and to the 'frightful doctrine of purgatory'. He ended his letter in a rather more relaxed manner: 'Surely we shall be judged according to our conscience, and if we have a clear sight of what is wrong with Rome, we must not follow our inclinations, because Rome has what is attractive in some part of her devotions'.[97]

At the same time, Newman was becoming increasingly aware of the charge that his views and actions could be perceived as indicating that he was drifting towards Rome. Bowden had warned him 'the world accuses you of popery'.[98] This so shocked Newman that he decided to devote three Tracts (38, 40 and 71) to the 'Roman question'. However, Maisie Ward maintains that the need to clear his reputation was not a major motive; rather he considered that it was necessary to attack Rome 'because the *via media* could not be justified unless Rome were shown to be wrong'.[99] To this task Newman applied himself with characteristic commitment and enthusiasm. He affirmed that the 'glory of the English Church' lay in having taken a *via media* '*between* the so-called Reformers and the Romanists', but it had 'fallen away from its principles and is in need of a second reformation'.[100] Two of these Tracts consist of a dialogue between 'Laicus' and 'Clericus'.

To clarify his thoughts Newman gave a series of lectures in St Mary's during 1834-36; from these, *Lectures on the Prophetical Office of the Church, viewed relatively to Romanism and Popular Protestantism* was published in 1837. In the lectures he expounded the distinctive character of the Church of England as a *via media*: 'Anglican theology against Liberalism and Protestantism on the one side and Popery on the other.[101] The lectures had largely originated from controversies with Abbé Jean-Nicholas Jager in 1834–36. During them he once confided to Bowden that 'The Abbé has replied to me – and the controversy is getting interesting. He is so weak that so far it is not fun. But it is an object to make known our opinions'.[102] Just over ten years later, however, Newman revealed to Henry Wilberforce that his belief in the 'theory of the *Via Media*' was so strong 'in the year 1834 or 1835' that he feared his arguments might have unsettled Abbé Jager. He also confessed that the arguments were not, in fact, his own but were evolved from works by Laud, Stillingfleet and others. 'I do not think I had that unhesitating belief in it in 1836-7 when I published my *Prophetical Office*, or rather I should say that *zeal* for it – for I believed it fully or at least was not conscious that I did not. It is difficult to say whether or not a flagging zeal involves an incipient doubt...As time went on and I read the Fathers more attentively, I found the *Via Media* less and less satisfactory. It broke down with me in 1839'.[103] As Walgrave notes, Newman's study of the Fathers and of the great heresies and schisms of early Church history gradually led him to views about 'the ancient Church as it really was and the positions taken over by both sides in the controversies of the patristic era'.[104]

In the *Apologia*, Newman admitted that the *via media* 'was an impossible idea; it is what I have called "standing on one leg"; and it was necessary, if my old issue of the controversy was to be retained, to go further either one way or the other'.[105] According to Gilley, the *via media* 'was an attempt by Newman to justify the existence of the Established Church as a separate Christian Communion besides the Churches of the Reformation and Rome'.[106] In 1877, Newman produced a new edition of the *via media*, as discussed in Chapter 7.

Newman had already indicated something of his increasing spiritual anguish in a long letter to Hugh James Rose in May 1836. In this he confessed that 'You have spoken the truth, I do *not* love the "Church of England"'. Rather, he loved 'the old Church of 1200 or 1600 years... I cannot love the "Church of England" commonly so designated – its very title is an offence... for it implies that it holds, not of the Church Catholic but of the State... Viewed *internally*, it is the battlefield of two opposite principles; Socianism and Catholicism – Socianism fighting for the most part by Puritanism its unconscious ally... Luckily, none of the Articles are positively Calvinistic... what is wanting in one is supplied in another... but there are grave omissions... My heart *is* with Rome, *but not* as Rome, but as, and so far as, she is the faithful retainer of what we have practically thrown aside'.[107]

Despite his worries, Newman was able to assure his sister Jemima, in April 1837, that his *Prophetical Office* was selling very well. 'It only shows how deep the absurd notion was in men's minds that I was a Papist; and how they are agreeably surprised'.[108] Nockles comments on this that 'up until 1839, as he later confessed, Newman remained secure and confident in his Anglicanism... yet, even in the *via media* phase... one can sense that Newman's concept of Anglicanism was nebulous and somewhat theoretical... Viewed in retrospect, Newman's *via media* phase seems but a temporary staging-post in his religious odyssey, but at the same time it was held and propounded with a conviction, passion and fierceness which could not have been excelled'.[109]

As we have seen in Chapter 1, in 1835 the future Cardinal Nicholas Wiseman had delivered a series of public addresses on his visits to some of the principal centres of Roman Catholicism in England. These attracted considerable attention and were 'the first public presentations of Catholic doctrines in England'.[110] Wiseman harnessed his considerable intellectual and dialectical skills in co-founding with Daniel O'Connell, in 1836, a journal, the *Dublin Review*, for which he wrote many articles, including one on the *Schism of the Donatists*, which was published in August 1839, and was to have a major influence on Newman. In it he made 'his famous comparison between the Anglicans and the Donatists, which, according to Newman... absolutely pulverised the Anglican theory of the *via media*'.[111] According to Wilfrid Ward, furthermore, 'Newman never really recovered from the blow inflicted by Wiseman's article... The isolation from the rest of the Church Catholic – a commonplace of the controversy – had suddenly got hold of him... He never returned to the old *Via Media*'.[112] The Donatist schism of the 4th and 5th centuries had been condemned by St Augustine in the celebrated utterance *securus judicat orbis terrarum*. Wiseman had been following closely the development of the Oxford Movement, respecting and sympathising with Newman and his associates, but, according to Gwynn, his appeal to the voice of ancient authority 'threw a bombshell into their camp by pointing out the analogy between the claims of the Donatists and what the Tractarians were now attempting... In each case, a local church asserted the [Roman] Catholic Church was in error, while it alone retained the title to be called Catholic'.[113]

The famous saying of St Augustine 'pricked Newman's mind... because suddenly he wondered about his national Church, the Church of England, i.e. its differences from an international Church'.[114] *Securus judicat orbis terrarum* might be interpreted either to indicate that 'if everyone agrees, the verdict must be right', or it 'could be stretched to give a very authoritarian meaning – the international Church is the see of Rome, bow to its solitary edict... it was this second meaning that was present in Newman's mind'.[115] Ker states that Newman's own (free) translation runs: 'The universal Church is in its judgements secure of truth'.[116]

In the *Apologia*, Newman confessed that the 'palmary words of St Augustine' had escaped his observation; they 'absolutely pulverised' the theory of the *via media*.[117] During a walk with Henry Wilberforce in October 1839, Newman told him that for the first time since he began the study of theology 'a vista has opened before me, to the end of which I do not see'[118]

Newman confided to his friends the intensity of his shock at reading Wiseman's hard-hitting article: 'I have had the first real hit from Romanism which has happened to me… I must confess it has given me stomach-ache… I seriously think this is a most uncomfortable article on every count… How are we to keep hotheads from going over?'.[119] He was, however, increasingly reluctant to 'attack the Roman Church as a sister Church'[120] and wrote an article for the *British Critic*, of which he became editor in 1838, entitled: *The Catholicity of the Anglican Church*, in an effort to console himself and his friends. But, as Owen Chadwick observes, 'he was not quite the same. He said later that he had seen the shadow of a hand on the wall… He discovered in himself a growing dislike of speaking against the Church of Rome'.[121]

Newman was still engrossed in delivering lectures and in developing these into published works. His *Lectures on the Doctrine of Justification* were given in the Adam de Brome Chapel in St Mary's during 1837 and published the following year. He had dedicated these lectures to Bishop Bagot of Oxford but, unexpectedly and to his dismay, he had to face a charge from the bishop who, in gentle but firm words, warned that some of the language used in the Tracts 'might lead people into error'.[122] Newman, ever mindful of the sacredness of episcopacy, was perplexed, although willing to withdraw any Tract that was judged to be offensive or even to suppress all of them, as he indicated to his friends.[123] He stressed to Bowden that what Bagot said 'was very slight indeed, but a Bishop's lightest word *ex Cathedra* is heavy'. As it happened, the bishop himself was much disturbed by the intensity of Newman's reaction. According to Trevor 'he was alarmed by such apostolical submission'[124] and the issue was quietly set to rest. But the matter clearly rankled with Newman, as may be judged from a letter to F.W. Faber in which he commented that people 'will always lag a little behind in order to be safe and moderate, and to have the satisfaction of abusing you'.[125]

In 1838, another troublesome matter involved Newman. Hurrell Froude, his close friend since undergraduate days, had died on 28th February 1836, leaving Newman stricken with grief, as he intimated to another close friend, John William Bowden.[126] Hurrell Froude's father, the Archdeacon of Totnes, sent to Newman the many papers left by his son, including published articles, sermon manuscripts, a few private letters and, more dramatically as it was to prove, remnants of his private journal. The Archdeacon told Newman and his associates that they had freedom to publish whatever they wished. This fragmentary assortment of papers – known as the 'Remains'– contained material that was to cause Newman and Keble, who were, somewhat reluctantly, acting as literary executors, far more trouble than they had ever anticipated. They circulated the papers among their friends and sought their advice on how to deal with some of the highly sensitive issues involved. Newman told Frederic Rogers that 'Keble, Pusey, Williams, Copeland, Wood and you are for publication of F's papers'.[127] At the end of the month, apparently still wavering for a time, he then wrote to Keble stating clearly why publication should go ahead.[128] It was not until 31st August, however, that Newman was able to tell Rogers[129] that he had just received from Archdeacon Froude Hurrell's private journal (1826-27), of which he was not previously aware. The entries included details of fastings, faults and temptations over that period. These intimate spiritual revelations, together with details of some of Hurrell's private and personal views on aspects of religious belief and practice, began to make Newman nervous. He wrote to Keble that 'I do wish *you* would seriously think of the objection which will be made to dear Hurrell's papers, which the Journal I shall send you on Tuesday will confirm'.[130]

Newman's anxieties persisted, as may be seen from a letter to Bowden the following January: 'Anxious I have been, and am very, about several things. Froude's volumes will open upon me a flood of criticism, and from all quarters'.[131] His fears were to be fulfilled when the papers were eventually published. He was beset on all sides by Evangelicals, Low Churchmen, and moderate Anglicans who fiercely attacked the views of Froude, now made public. Froude had written, for instance, 'I am becoming less and less a son of the Reformation'[132] and 'The Reformation was a limb badly set; it must be broken again to be righted'.[133] Such sentiments were presumably not intended by Froude for publication but they provoked furious feelings and added to the strong suspicion that Tractarianism was full of 'Romanist tendencies'.[134] Owen Chadwick comments that 'the repudiation of Protestants appeared before the public in a new and shocking light. Newman's Tracts disliked the word Protestant, Froude disliked Protestants. Newman wanted to reform the Reformation, Froude seemed to want to destroy the Reformation'.[135]

In addition to inflaming the opinions of many High Churchmen, the *Remains* disconcerted some Tractarians; Newman and Keble might perhaps have exercised more discretion in their responsibilities as literary executors. 'The controversial publication... represented a landmark and a turning point in the history of the Oxford Movement... it brought into the open the first rumblings of official disapproval of the Movement'.[136]

In spite of the earlier uncertainties about publishing Froude's papers that were expressed to his confidants, Newman seems almost to have shrugged off the belligerence of his critics. This is reflected, for instance, in a letter to Edward Churton, a High Churchman who was sympathetic to the Oxford Movement: 'As to the passages in the *Remains* you speak of, I never have repented publishing them one single moment, and though I cannot imitate your language and say "I *never* shall regret", yet I have no reason to suppose I ever shall'.[137] He declared that he fully believed that Keble and he had 'acted on the truest and wisest view of what is *expedient*'. According to Maisie Ward, he did not doubt that 'Froude, Keble, Pusey and himself were Catholics, and that the Protestant attack on the *Remains* had been a furious attack on its Catholicism'.[138] While, however, Newman, Keble and many other Tractarians upheld the principles of antiquity, Pusey himself retained his respect for the English reformers even though he gradually took a more critical view of the Reformation.[139]

It was popularly believed that publication of the *Remains* caused Golightly to ferment the anti-Tractarian feelings which resulted in the erection in Oxford, by public subscription, of the Martyrs' Memorial to the memory of Cranmer, Latimer and Ridley. According to Gerard Tracey, 'The testimonial was certainly seen as a test for Newman and Pusey, and suspicions increased when they did not subscribe'.[140] Newsome notes that apart from wanting to demonstrate against Froude's *Remains*, the 'notorious skirmisher' Golightly had schemed 'to split the Oxford Movement by his project for the Martyrs' Memorial' and he had enjoyed some measure of success.[141] Tractarianism was, however, strengthened in 1839 when William George Ward joined it. His book *The Ideal of a Christian Church* was condemned by the Convocation of Oxford University in 1845 because of its perceived 'Romish' doctrines. With Frederick Oakeley, a former Fellow of Balliol, Ward infused new life into Tractarianism. The Wardites, who also included J.D. Dalgairns and F.W. Faber, discarded the historical rhetoric and preoccupation of early Tractarianism, enthusiastically promoting a 'Romanising' of the liturgy and introducing other pious practices. As Nockles puts it, 'an ideological watershed had been reached in the Movement'.[142]

In January 1840, Newman told Rogers that he had received a visit from 'Mr Spencer, the RC priest'. Originally he had refused to meet him because he was in *loco apostatae*, but later he was persuaded to see him. Newman wrote that he found this aristocratic convert to Roman Catholicism to be 'a gentlemanlike, mild, pleasing man, but sadly smooth. I wonder whether it is their habit of internal discipline, the necessity of confession, etc., which makes them so'.[143] Although Newman had declined an invitation to meet Spencer over dinner, he met him privately when they discussed the desirability of praying for unity among the Churches. While the proposal appealed to Newman, it was received suspiciously by Manning and Pusey.[144] Spencer's visit and his own apparent distinctly reserved response to the suggestion of some form of mutual prayer for Church unity, clearly lay on Newman's mind. A few weeks later he put forward the rationale of his views to Spencer in a long and courteous letter.[145]

Newman felt he needed some peace and quiet. He advised Henry Wilberforce that he would be 'going up to Littlemore on Saturday week to stay there till Easter

Eve, – and wish to have as little to do as I can'.[146] During this period he imposed on himself a very strict regime of fasting and penance, as recorded in his journal[147] and also completed writing the account of his illness in Sicily, recovery from which had been a turning-point in his life.[148] Newman's preoccupation with religious problems and his despondency at this time about the Church of England can be seen in a letter to his sister Jemima: 'I begin to have serious apprehensions lest any religious body is strong enough to withstand the league of evil, but the Roman Church'.[149]

Littlemore life consoled Newman and he drafted a memorandum giving reasons for staying there; he would need a library and might well set up a '*Monastic* house' which 'could train up men for the great towns'. He would not give up the University and could continue his Sunday afternoon duties at St Mary's. It might be possible to be considered a 'head of a hall offspringing and in a way dependent upon Oriel as in old times at St Mary's Hall'.[150] He also mentions these aspirations to Pusey and S.F. Wood.[151] A few weeks later Newman told his sister Harriet that a field of nine acres had been purchased in Littlemore; where it was planned 'to build a retreat'.[152] On the same date, he asked Harriet's husband to give him 'some hint about building' and specified the accommodation needed.[153] Committing himself still further, Newman wrote to the Provost of Oriel, Edward Hawkins, enquiring whether 'the college would be likely to consent to my resigning St Mary's in Oxford and keeping Littlemore.[154] On the following day he told Tom Mozley that he had made what may seem to be 'a sudden resolution, but is not' to relinquish editorship of the *British Critic* after the April issue, and asked if he would take over the journal for him.[155]

To Keble, Newman wrote an extended explanation

of why he was considering resigning from St Mary's. His reasons included the impossibility of creating a truly pastoral ministry, the influence he knew he exerted on young Oxford students who were not his responsibility, and the fact that his sermons were considered to be 'disposing his hearers towards Rome'.[156] Keble replied that it would be virtually impossible for Newman to avoid such problems in 'any other place' where his 'net was cast'. In his opinion, the Heads of Houses 'did not have the smallest authority over you as Vicar of St Mary's'. They might forbid undergraduates to attend but Newman was free to preach. He could not see how giving up St Mary's would help in the least.[157] Newman willingly accepted this down-to-earth advice and, in thanking Keble, commented that 'fair trial' had not yet been made 'of how much the English Church must be able to tolerate 'infusions of Catholic truth'.[158] About three weeks later he wrote to another confidant, Frederic Rogers, mentioning his discussions with Keble about St Mary's: 'The upshot is, whether I continue so or not, that I am much more comfortable than I have been. I do not fear at all any number of persons as likely to go to Rome, if I am secure about myself. If I can trust myself, I can trust others. We have so many things on our side, that a good conscience is all that one wants'.[159]

Newman returned to vigorous controversy in seven spirited letters, signed 'Catholicus', in *The Times*. The last of these appeared on 27th February 1841, and the collection was published later as *The Tamworth Reading Room*. In these letters Newman attacked Sir Robert Peel who had made a speech at the opening of a new library and reading room at Tamworth. The speech had attracted considerable attention on account of its decidedly utilitarian emphasis. Newman was alerted to the speech and seized the opportunity to strike against a politician for whom he had slight regard (see pp. 43/4). According to Ker, 'Apart from their political and social interest and the ways in which they anticipate the *Idea of a University*, the letters constitute the one sustained work of satire that Newman wrote as an Anglican'.[160] Trevor comments, however, that Newman 'certainly only wished to attack the notion that education makes people morally. He did it with ridicule and was at the top of his form'.[161]

On the same day as the last of his letters to *The Times* appeared – 27th February 1841 – *Tract 90* was published. As usual it was anonymous but its authorship was an open secret. Newman, who was experiencing a personal religious crisis, argued with singular skill that although the Thirty-nine Articles were drawn up for the establishment of Protestantism, they may also be interpreted as compatible with Catholicism; 'While our Prayer Book is acknowledged on all hands to be of Catholic origin our Articles also, the offspring of an uncatholic age, are, through God's good providence, to say the least, not uncatholic, and may be subscribed by those who aim at being catholic in heart and doctrine '.[162] Latitude of interpretation was held to be a vital characteristic of the Thirty-nine Articles. Thus while the Articles were intentionally written to establish Protestantism, Newman argues that 'they are not framed on the principle of excluding those who prefer the theology of the early ages to that of the Reformation'. The framers so worded them that 'those who did not go so far in Protestantism as themselves' might be able to subscribe to them. 'The Protestant Confession was drawn up with the purpose of including Catholics; and Catholics now will not be excluded. What was an economy in the reformers, is a protection to us. What would have been a perplexity to us then, is a perplexity to Protestants. We could not then have found fault with their words: they cannot now repudiate our meaning'.[163] Newman's reference to 'Catholics' never 'Roman Catholics', reflects his care to avoid associating the term 'Catholic' exclusively with the Roman Catholic Church. It was, rather, an attempt by the Tractarians to emphasise the inherent Catholicity of the Church of England, and to make the claim that Anglo-Catholics are indeed some of the people which the framers of the Articles had in mind. Newman, a theologically conservative Anglican, believed that the Articles were intended to include various parties within the Church of England. Dessain comments that *Tract 90* propounded two main arguments for this Catholic interpretation: (1) the historical point that the Articles were drawn up 'early in the reign of Elizabeth I in such a way as to induce Roman Catholics to subscribe to them', and (2) that 'since the Anglican Church was a branch of the Catholic, its formularies must admit of being interpreted in accordance with what the Church Catholic had held from primitive times'. Further, according to Dessain, there was 'an underlying irenical purpose' in *Tract 90*.[164] However, the reaction to the Tract was decidedly different, although Trevor has described it as a 'short treatise, not a polemic'.[165] It was subtly argued and some might have considered it to smack of sophistry. But, Gilley comments that Newman discussed only fourteen of the 'Articles', and shocked his readers 'by extracting from a number of these 'a sense which contradicted their obvious literal meaning'.[166]

Newman's hopes that it would be an instrument of reconciliation were dashed. In a letter, dated 14th March 1841, R.W. Church told Frederic Rogers of the furore caused by *Tract 90*: 'He [Newman] did not think it would be more attacked than others, nor did Keble or H. Wilberforce. Ward, however, prophesied from the first that it would be hotly received, and so it proved'.[167]

On 12th March 1841, Newman wrote to his sister Harriet: 'I fear I am clean dished. The Heads of the Houses are at this very moment concocting a manifesto against me'. On the following day he told J.W. Bowden that he expected 'the very worst, that is, a condemnation will be passed in Convocation upon the Tracts as a whole'.[168] Meanwhile *Tract 90* was being widely read – 2,500 copies were sold within a fortnight. The ever-active Golightly, in attempting to discredit Newman, had disseminated copies of the Tract, and sent it to all the bishops.[169] Newman, however, had suspected Golightly would make mischief for him and called him the 'Tony-fire-the-faggot' of the resulting agitation.[170] Nevertheless, he remained 'pretty cheerful', as Church reported to Rogers.[171]

With Golightly's connivance, four senior tutors had been scrutinising *Tract 90* and, on 8th March 1841, they wrote to the editor of the Tracts for the Times that *Tract 90* 'opened the door to the teaching of Roman Catholicism in the University'.[172] Meantime Newman had been producing a pamphlet. He also told his sister Jemima, in a letter of 15th March 1841, 'What will be done I know not. I try to prepare myself for the worst'.[173] On the same day he wrote to J.W. Bowden saying that he believed the Heads had 'just done a violent act: they have said that my interpretation of the Articles is an *evasion*'. But, he assured his reader, 'Do not think that this will pain me – no *doctrine* is censured, and my shoulders will bear the charge'.[174] The Heads' decision had overtaken his pamphlet which, in the custom of the time, was in the form of a *Letter addressed to the Rev. J.H. Jelf*, who was a Canon of Christ Church and an old and impartial friend of Pusey's. The *Letter* was largely rendered redundant by the Heads' action but it gives an insight into Newman's defensive posture.

73

In a letter to Keble of 25th March 1841, Newman said that Bishop Bagot wished him to write a letter saying that 'at his bidding, I will suppress *Tract 90*. I have no difficulty in saying and doing so if he tells me, but my difficulty is as to my *then* position'.[175] He felt, as Meriol Trevor puts it, that he was 'being driven into a corner where he must either defy his Bishop or deny his principles – for to suppress the Tract would imply its censure'.[176] His predicament was made even worse because Episcopal condemnation was virtually unanimous. What crippled Newman, as David Newsome points out, was 'a broadside from the Bench of Bishops – a succession of hostile charges, which threw him into a position from which not even his most skilful casuistry could rescue him'.[177] His consistent exaltation of episcopal authority compelled him, in the end, to retract what he had written. In Nockles' view, Newman had misconceived the episcopal response and, 'never slow to sense a personal affront, in human terms [he] found the Episcopal disowning' of *Tract XC* 'a humiliation'.[178]

Eventually Newman agreed with the compromise offered by the kindly and troubled Bishop Bagot, distasteful though it was to have to write of 'Roman corruptions' in his letter to the bishop. This settlement was mentioned in a letter, dated 30 March 1841, to his ever solicitous sister Jemima: 'The Tract affair is settled on these terms, which others may think a disappointment, but to me is a very fair bargain. I am now publishing a letter to the Bishop at his wish stating that he wishes the Tracts to be discontinued, and he thinks No. 90 objectionable as tending to disturb the Church. I am quite satisfied with the bargain I have got, if this is all – as I suppose it will be'.[179] On 4th April 1841, Newman told Bowden that 'The Bishop sent me a message that my Letter had his unqualified approbation'. As for himself, he declared that he had 'not had one misgiving through-out and he trusted that 'what had happened will be over-ruled to subserve the great cause we all have at heart'.[180]

Newman records in a memorandum in his *Auto-biographical Writings*, dated 26th October 1863: 'In September, 1833, I began the series called Tracts for the Times. In 1838 I became editor of the *British Critic*. In 1841, on occasion of the publication of No.90 of the Tracts, the Board of Heads of Houses brought out a censure of the doctrine contained in it as an evasive interpretation of the Thirty-nine Articles, and at the wish of Dr Bagot, Bishop of Oxford, I brought the series to an end. At the same time, I retired from Oxford to Littlemore, a hamlet two miles from Oxford, which was an integral part of St Mary's parish, where I had built a church'.[181]

Newman, as Owen Chadwick observes, had 'coura-geously essayed to treat the catholicity of the Articles in *Tract 90*,[182] but he had been forced to retract and sought consolation in his beloved Littlemore. Earlier Newman had abandoned the *via media*; he was now on the *via crucis*, on his pilgrimage towards Rome.

In 1843, another notable Tractarian – E.B. Pusey – was also to undergo a distressing experience as the result of a sermon he had preached on 'The Holy Eucharist as a comfort to the Penitent'. In the sermon he spoke with marked fervour about the Real Presence. His sermon was delated to the vice-chancellor as being heretical; a uni-versity court was set up and found against Pusey, who was suspended from preaching within the precincts of the University for two years. Newman worried about the effect that this would have on his friend, who was still suffering from the death of his wife a few years earlier. In a letter, dated 24th May 1843, to his sister Jemima, he expressed this concern: 'Do you know that the Vice-Chancellor has taken to a sermon of Pusey's preached last Sunday at Christ Church, and that six doctors (of divinity) are about to sit on it?... I am not without anxiety as to its effects on him personally'.[183] However, Pusey bore his suspension stoically and, according to Gilley, 'His faith was untroubled by the disgrace, and it was as Puseyites, not Newmanites, that the Anglo-Catholics were to remain within the Church of England'.[184]

Newman continued his largely reclusive life at Littlemore 'for some days quite alone, without a friend or servant'.[185] At his cottage, according to Maisie Ward, he lived ascetically, studying the Fathers, praying intensely, and meditating deeply on spiritual matters, including the possibility of 'having to join the Church of Rome'.[186]

On 29th December 1842, Newman had written to Bowden that 'I am publishing my University Sermons, which will be thought sad, dull affairs; but having got through a subject, I wish to get rid of it'.[187] He also told his sister Jemima, on 23rd January 1843, that his University Sermons 'are not theological or ecclesiastical, though they bear immediately upon the most intimate and practical religious questions'.[188] A little later, on 7th March 1843, he was to tell the Rev S. Rickards that 'my University Sermons which have been published little more than a fortnight, have come to a second edition. I cannot think that they have been bought for their contents'.[189] These fifteen sermons of Newman's Anglican ministry, preached in the University Church of St Mary the Virgin from 1826 to 1843, are occasionally described by Newman as 'Discourses'. He never repudiated their contents.

In a memorandum of 26th October 1863, Newman recorded succinctly the sequence of major events in his life, including his eventual retirement from active involvement in the Oxford Movement. On this he writes that 'In

1843, I published a retraction of the strong charges I had made against the Church of Rome'.[190] This retraction, although appearing anonymously, was published in the *Conservative Journal* on 28th January 1843, and he confided to J.R. Hope, on 25th January 1843, that his conscience had goaded him to 'eat a few dirty words of mine'.[191]

Newman consulted Keble again about his possible retirement from St Mary's and Keble assured him in reply that provided he could continue his ministry at Littlemore, the decision could be taken. Newman then confessed that his feelings for Rome had been getting stronger, whereupon Keble urged him to retain his active ministry, otherwise he would be exposed to the dangers of secession from the Church of England. Apparently Newman was now experiencing a stressful conflict of loyalties to the Church of England, to the Oxford Movement in which he was so closely bound up, and now to the pressing demands of his conscience that he should abandon these treasured affiliations and become a Roman Catholic. In a revealing letter to James Mozley, dated 1st September 1843, Newman conceded that 'The truth is, I am not a good son enough of the Church of England to feel I can in conscience hold preferment under her. I love the Church of Rome too well'.[192] Throughout his life Newman insisted on the supremacy of conscience – an authoritative moral dictate within him, which praised, blamed and issued command.[193]

Newman remained at Littlemore, absorbed in translating St Athananius and with his mind wracked with conflicting emotions surrounding the decision he had taken as to whether he should stay in the Church of England, to which he was intimately attached, and continue to enjoy its protective environment and the opportunities for preferment, or should he join the Church of Rome and accept a chaotic upheaval of his whole life with all the uncertainties that this would involve.

On 7th September he sent his resignation from St Mary's to Bishop Bagot, fearing that he would 'cause much pain', but assuring him that the decision was made only after considerable reflection. His resolution, he told the bishop, 'is already no secret to my friends and others', and he heartily thanked him for all the past 'acts of friendship and favour' he had received from him.[194]

On the seventh anniversary of the consecration of Littlemore church – 25th September 1843 – Newman preached his last Anglican sermon: *The Parting of Friends*. His text was 'Man goeth forth to his work and his labour until the evening'. In Maisie Ward's poignant words: 'Like the singing of the Reproaches, or the Lamentations in Holy Week, the little church was filled with the clear voice making audible every word of Christ's lament over the holy city that had rejected Him'.[195]

Following his resignation, Newman exchanged several letters with Archdeacon Manning and also Gladstone. He set out firmly his views to the former: 'I must tell you then frankly, unless I combat arguments which to me, alas, are shadows, that it is from no disappointment, or, impatience, that I have, whether rightly or wrongly, resigned St Mary's – but because I think the Church of Rome the Catholic Church, and ours not a part of the Catholic Church, because not in communion with Rome, and I felt I could not honestly be a teacher in it any longer'.[196] Such clearly-stated convictions 'thoroughly alarmed' Manning who, despite his warm feelings of friendship towards Newman, felt compelled to deliver his relentless *No-Popery* sermon on Guy Fawkes Day, 1843, in Oxford.[197]

On the following day, Manning called on Newman at Littlemore who refused to see him. As Gilley notes: 'It was Manning's first experience of Newman's inability to separate persons and principles, and of his unforgiving strain, when as a rival cardinal, he came to embody the alternative to Manning's own unbending Ultramontanism'.[198] On the other hand, Manning displayed some degree of insensitivity in attempting to see Newman almost immediately after preaching an anti-Catholic sermon. Deeply shocked, Manning returned to Oxford – but in just over five years, he himself was destined to tread the path to Rome.

Newman now immersed himself in the task of preparing a philosophical treatise, *Essay on the Development of Christian Doctrine*, which, according to Trevor, 'was germinating all through the painful year that followed his resignation'.[199] For many years, Newman had been gathering thought on this topic, that is, that the doctrine of the Church had been gradually defined. The idea had been first aired publicly in his last University sermon, given on the Feast of the Purification of the Blessed Virgin Mary in 1843. This hagiographic discourse Ker describes as 'the most brilliant of the University Sermons and one of the most original and penetrating of his writings'.[200] Newman postulated that a principle of development could be discerned by which the Christian Church from its early days was able to define its doctrines 'by making explicit that which had been implicit'.[201] As Dessain points out, Newman's *Essay on the Development of Christian Doctrine* was published fourteen years before Darwin's *Origin of the Species* appeared, and Newman experienced no problem in accepting the idea of evolution 'as long as it was theistic'.[202] He had produced a theory of the development of religious doctrine which, not unexpectedly, attracted sharp criticism from various quarters, but was to become accepted and applied in the historical study of the development of ideas and institutions. His essay was essentially an exploration in which he involved himself deeply and through which he clarified his own thoughts about where his future lay. On 8th June 1844, in a letter to Keble, Newman made a long statement about his state of mind and conscience from his boyhood years down to the present time. He referred to Keble's stirring sermon on 'National Apostasy', which was 'the beginning of the Movement', his own growing feelings that the 'Roman Communion is the only true Church' which came from his intensive study of the Fathers, and his attempts 'to resist such urgent and imperative' thoughts by his writings and 'great efforts to keep others from moving in the direction of Rome also'. But, he confessed, the time for argument was past: 'I have been in one settled conviction for so long a time, which every new thought seems to strengthen'.[203]

Just over a year later, on 11th July 1845, Newman wrote to Richard Westmacott, an acclaimed sculptor and old friend, that 'it is morally certain I shall join the RC Church... It has been the conviction of six years – from which I have never receded, and (for which) I have waited patiently a long time'. He explained that his conviction was founded on study of early Church history, and that he had come to the conclusion that the Church of Rome (was) in every respect the continuation of the early Church. 'I think she is the early Church *in* these times, and the early Church is she *in* these times. They differ in doctrine and discipline as child and grown man differ, not otherwise'.[204] In this remarkable and explanatory letter, the influence of Newman's theory of doctrinal development is evident; in a few months' time he would make his historic decision, but 'it was with no anticipation of human happiness that Newman approached his journey's end'.[205]

NOTES

1   Wilfrid Ward, 1913, p.2.
2   Ker, 1990, p.viii.
3   Trevor, 1996, p.46.
4   Briggs, 1990, p.155.
5   Dessain, 1980, p.71.
6   *LD* II.264, Simon Lloyd Pope, 15 August 1830.
7   Newman, 1989, p.357.
8   Trevor, 1996 p.26.
9   Ward, 1913, II, p.460.
10 Nockles, 1997, p.67.
11 *LD* II.117 *footnote*.
12 Newman, 1956, p.97.
13 *LD* II.118.
14 *LD* II.120, 8 February 1829.
15 *LD* II.125,1 March 1829.
16 Gilley, 1990, p.73.
17 Nockles, 1997, p.69.
18 *LD* II.372, 30 October 1831.
19 Maisie Ward, 1948, p.224.
20 Nockles, 1997, p.324.
21 Walgrave, 1960, p.31.
22 Newman, 1956, p.59.
23 Nockles, 1997, p.53.
24 Newman, 1956, pp.111-120.
25 Dessain, 1980, p.34.
26 Newman, 1956, p.119.
27 Newman, 1956, p.268.
28 *LD* III.186.
29 Chadwick, 1971, p.56.
30 *LD* III.242, 11 March 1833.
31 *LD* III.247, 9 March 1833.
32 *LD* III.249, 14 March 1833.
33 Cf Newsome, 1993, p.163.
34 Gilley, 1990, p.111.
35 Gilley, 1990, p.63.
36 Newman, 1993, p.388.
37 Newman, 1956, p.119.
38 Newman, 1956, p.119.
39 Vargish, 1970, p.91.
40 Chadwick, 1971, p.70.
41 Chadwick, 1971, p.72.
42 *LD* IV.20-22, 25 August 1833.
43 *LD* IV.9, 16 July 1833.
44 Newman, 156, p.120.
45 *LD* IV.13-14, 30 July 1833.
46 *LD* IV.28-29, 11 August 1833.
47 Chadwick, 1971, pp.74-75.

48 Dessain, 1980, p.35.
49 *LD* IV.78, Autumn 1833.
50 Nockles, 1997, p.57.
51 Gilley, 1990, p.119.
52 Chadwick. 1971, p.l26.
53 *LD* IV.56, 2 December 1833.
54 Dessain, 1980, p.37.
55 Trevor, 1996, p.52.
56 Maisie Ward, 1948, p.315.
57 Cf Oddie, 1993, p.vii.
58 Cf Gilley, 1990, p.130.
59 Nockles, 1996, p.100.
60 Cf Nockles, 1997, p.38.
61 Gilley, 1996, p.65.
62 Cf Vargish, 1970, p.97.
63 Maisie Ward, 1948, p.242.
64 Cf Ker, 1990, p.132.
65 *LD* V.346 Frederic Rogers, 29 August 1836.
66 *LD* V.313 Mrs John Mozley, 26 June 1836.
67 Cf Gilley, 1990, pp.19-25.
68 Newman, 1993, p.92.
69 Maisie Ward, 1948, p.272.
70 *LD* IV.72, 26 October 1833.
71 Dessain, 1980, pp.26, 29.
72 *LD* IV.38-40, 2 September 1833; *LD* IV.47-49, 9 September 1833.
73 Trevor, 1996, p.51.
74 Trevor, 1996, p.51.
75 *LD* XXVI.293-94, 20 April 1873.
76 *LD* XXVIII.190, 7 April 1877.
77 *LD* IV.239, 25 April 1834.
78 *LD* IV.239, 25 April 1834.
79 *LD* IV.371, 28 November 1834.
80 *LD* IV.372, 28 November 1834.
81 Newman, 1956, p.98.
82 Trevor, 1996, p.52.
83 *LD* V.265, 'Declaration', Oxford, 10 March 1836.
84 *LD* V xiv.
85 Maisie Ward, 1948, p.255.
86 Gilley, 1990, p.89.
87 *LD* V.399, Henry Wilberforce, 29 December 1836.
88 *LD* XXVIII.172 Robert Charles Jenkins, 27 February 1877.
89 *LD* XXX.240 William Bright, 25 July 1883.
90 Ker, 1990, p.48.
91 Selby, 1975, p.67.
92 Ker, 1990, p.49.
93 Nockles, 1997, p.198.
94 *LD* V.142, 11 September 1835.
95 *LD* V.142, 9 September 1835.
96 *LD* V.136, 8 September 1835.

97   *LD* IV.367-9, 17 November 1834.
98   Dessain, 1980, p.39.
99   Maisie Ward, 1948, p.258.
100 Dessain, 1980, p.39.
101 Wilfrid Ward, 1913, p.59.
102 *LD* V.25, 5 February 1835.
103 *LD* XI.100-1, 27 January 1846.
104 Walgrave, 1960, p.38.
105 Newman, 1993, p.203.
106 Gilley, 1990, p.156.
107 *LD* V.303-5, 23 May 1836.
108 *LD* VI.61, 25 April 1837.
109 Nockles, 1991, pp.38-39.
110 Norman, 1985, p.123.
111 Norman, 1985, p.148.
112 Wilfrid Ward, 1913, p.69.
113 Gwynn, 1929, p.330.
114 Chadwick, 1990, p.43.
115 Chadwick, 1990, p.43.
116 Ker, 1990b. p.35.
117 Newman, 1993, p.174.
118 Bacchus, 1913, p.14.
119 *LD* VII.154, Frederic Rogers, 22 September 1839.
120 Gilley, 1990, p.184.
121 Chadwick, 1971, p.180.
122 *LD* VI.265-6, 'Bishop of Oxford's Charge', 14 August 1838.
123 *LD* VI.286-8, John Keble, 14 August 1838; and *LD* VI.292, J.W. Bowden,
     17 August 1838.
124 Trevor, 1996, p.64.
125 *LD* VI.320, 25 September 1838.
126 *LD* IV.249-50, 2 March 1836.
127 *LD* VI.76 1 June 1837.
128 *LD* VI.96-97, 30 June 1837.
129 *LD* VI.120-21.
130 *LD* VI.118, 27 August 1837.
131 *LD* VI.188, 17 January 1838.
132 *Remains* VI. 336.
133 *Remains* VI, 433.
134 Wilfrid Ward, 1913, p.60.
135 Chadwick, 1971, p.175.
136 Nockles, 1991, pp.35-36.
137 *LD* VI.325, 3 October 1838.
138 Maisie Ward, 1948, p.337.
139 Cf Nockles, 1997, pp.126-27.
140 *LD* VI.xviii.
141 Newsome, 1993, p.284.
142 Nockles, 1997, p.143.
143 *LD* VII.205-6, Frederic Rogers, 8 January 1840.
144 *LD* VII.214-5, H.E. Manning, 15 January 1840.

145 *LD* VII.233-5, 9 February 1840.
146 *LD* VII.246, 27 February 1840.
147 Newman, 1956, pp.217-8.
148 Newman, 1956, pp.121-38.
149 *LD* VII.245, 25 February 1840.
150 *LD* VII.263, 17 March 1840.
151 *LD* VII.264, E.B. Pusey, 17 March 1840; *LD* VII.267, S.F. Wood, 17 March 1840.
152 *LD* VII.328, 20 May 1840.
153 *LD* VII.328, Thomas Mozley 1840.
154 *LD* VII.409, 20 October 1840.
155 *LD* VII.411, 21 October 1840.
156 *LD* VII.416-8, 26 October 1840.
157 *LD* VII.431-2, from John Keble, 3 November 1840.
158 *LD* VII.433, 6 November 1840.
159 *LD* VII.449-51, 25 November 1840.
160 Ker, 1990, p.206.
161 Trevor, 1996, p.72.
162 'Introduction' *Tract 90*, Newman, 1841, pp.4-5.
163 *Tract 90* 'Conclusion', pp.83-7.
164 Dessain, 1980, p.74.
165 Trevor, 1996, p.74.
166 Cf Gilley, 1990, p.199.
167 Mozley, 1891, p.329.
168 Mozley, 1891, pp.326-7.
169 Mozley, 1891, p.329.
170 Trevor, 1996, p.74.
171 Mozley, 1891, p.330.
172 Ker, 1990, p.217.
173 Mozley, 1891, p.335.
174 Mozley, 1891, pp.335-6.
175 Mozley, 1891, p.338.
176 Trevor, 1996, p.76.
177 Newsome, 1993, p.284.
178 Nockles, 1997, p.295.
179 Mozley, 1891, p.314.
180 Mozley, 1891, pp.344-5.
181 Newman, 1956, p.12.
182 Chadwick, 1971, p.183.
183 Mozley, 1891, p.413.
184 Gilley, 1990, p.218.
185 Wilfrid Ward, 1913, p.75.
186 Maisie Ward, 1948, p.391.
187 Mozley, 1891, pp.405-6.
188 Mozley, 1891, p.406.
189 Mozley, 1891, p.409.
190 Newman, 1956, p.12.
191 Mozley, 1891, p.406.
192 Mozley, 1891, p.423.

193 Cf Dessain, 1980, p.145.
194 Bacchus, 1917, p.262.
195 Maisie Ward, 1948, p.402.
196 Bacchus, 1913, p.276.
197 Bacchus, 1917, p.280.
198 Gilley, 1990, p.221.
199 Trevor, 1996, p.94.
200 Ker, 1989, p.XIX.
201 Griffin, 1993, p.6.
202 Dessain, 1980, p.81.
203 Bacchus, 1917, pp.313-18.
204 Sugg, 1983, p.70.
205 Maisie Ward 1948, p.448.

3

Newman:
Roman Odyssey

ON 6th September 1843, Newman, as mentioned in the preceding chapter, had resigned as Vicar of St Mary's, the University Church, a post to which, in 1828, he had been 'presented by Mr Hawkins, Provost of Oriel'.[1] After resigning he lived in seclusion at Littlemore, immersed in writing and battling against growing convictions that would, eventually, lead him to take the further step of severing his official links with the University. But he was able to reassure his old friend, R.W. Church, in a letter dated 3rd April 1845, that 'I have never for an instant had even the temptation of repenting my leaving Oxford... How could I remain at St Mary's, a hypocrite?'.[2]

He had secured on 12th April 1822 – at the early age of 21 – a Fellowship at Oriel College, 'then at the height of its literary fame'.[3] The young Newman described this conspicuous achievement 'as a turning-point and most memorable event', declaring that he never wished for anything in life 'better or higher than to live and die a Fellow of Oriel'.[4] Such youthful elation is understandable; so also can his distress be realised when, some 23 years later, he became aware that he would have to resign his post in the college, to which he was so deeply attached. It was at Oriel that Newman had benefited greatly, according to Chadwick, from 'intellectual osmosis', the most important influence being exercised by 'the sweet-natured, godly pastor and poet John Keble'.[5]

On 21st November 1844, Newman, in a lengthy letter, confided that 'I scarcely was ever present at a Roman service even abroad. I knew no Roman Catholics. I have no sympathies towards them as an existing body... I am setting my face absolutely towards the wilderness'.[6] Three days later, he wrote almost identically to his sister Jemima, adding, 'I am not conscious of any resentment, disgust or the like, to repel me from my present position: and I have no dreams whatever – far from it indeed. I seem to be throwing myself away'.[7] He viewed with some trepidation the prospect of abandoning the assured and comfortable life of an Anglican cleric and Oxford academic in order to associate himself with those who professed a religion which largely lacked acceptance in the polite society of the period, and of whose members he knew virtually none.

In a moving letter to his sister Jemima, dated 15th March 1845, Newman confided his inner thoughts about what he believed he was 'called to do... I am making myself an outcast, and that at my age... I may be wrong, but He that judgeth is the Lord'.[8] In her reply of 21st March, Jemima wrote firmly but tenderly, 'But yet I have no bias towards Rome, nor see any compensation in Rome to make up for the defects of our Church'. She also assures her brother that 'I am not conscious of a bitter feeling towards Rome; we seem to have enough to do with sorrow and humiliation at home without quarrelling with other Churches'.[9] She shared his confidences while remaining a member of the Church of England, even though she was aware of her brother's likely influence over her religious convictions.[10]

In a letter of 20th April 1845, Newman alerted James Mozley that 'By November I expect to have resigned my Fellowship'. He added: 'I don't mind your telling this in confidence to anyone you please'. Not surprisingly the news soon circulated, as Newman no doubt expected it would.[11]

Just over six months later, on 3rd October 1845, Newman wrote officially to Hawkins, the Provost of Oriel, resigning his Fellowship. He received a cold, formal acknowledgement, with the hope expressed that Newman would be spared some of the worse errors of Rome.

On 6th December 1845, Jemima (Mrs J. Mozley) wrote to her sister-in-law Anne Mozley (who was to edit Newman's correspondence during his life in the Anglican Church)[12] that 'I have had a letter which I have been expecting and half dreading to receive, this week from JHN to say that he has written to the Provost to resign his Fellowship. He adds that now anything may be expected any day'.[13] In fact the resignation from Oriel was the necessary step towards finalising his long-maturing plans to submit to Rome. This action had already been taken, in September 1845, by W.G. Ward, a member of the Oxford Movement since 1839. Ward, as noted in Chapter 2, had incurred the wrath of the University because of alleged 'Romish doctrines' in his work *The Ideal of a Christian Church*, and it was proposed to penalise him heavily. Newman had written to James Mozley, on 5th January 1845, protesting against the harsh treatment given to Ward, particularly when 'atrocious heresies' had been published elsewhere without apparent censure.[14] At the same time as Ward's case was being considered, the Convocation of the University had a proposal before it to censure Newman's *Tract 90*. Such an ill-conceived measure was robustly denounced by Charles Marriott,

Fellow and Dean of Oriel, and a close friend of Newman. He asked 'If the tract was to be condemned by the University, ought it not to have been condemned in 1841' instead of four years later and 'thus call for a fresh and gratuitous infliction of pain when no single fresh act on the author's part has occurred to warrant such repetition?'.[15]

The proposal aroused Newman's friends and they rallied to his aid, determined to veto the censure on him. At a meeting of Convocation on 13th February 1845 to hear the cases against Ward and Newman, the former was deprived of his degrees by only a narrow majority, while the censure on Newman's *Tract 90* was vetoed by the Proctors. Ironically, in a few months' time both of these leading members of the Oxford Movement would be received into the Roman Catholic Church. Around this time, two of Newman's Littlemore community also changed their religious allegiance: J.D. Dalgairns travelled to Aston Hall, Staffordshire, to be received by Fr Dominic Barberi, Superior of the Passionist monastery; and Ambrose St John, a former curate of Henry Wilberforce who was to become Newman's closest friend during his Oratorian years, was received into the Roman Catholic Church at the Catholic College of Prior Park on 30th September.

Dalgairn's visit to Barberi seems to have motivated Newman to invite the missioner to break his journey to London, en route for Belgium to attend a meeting of his Congregation, and stay overnight at Littlemore. Newman confided to Wilberforce about the proposed visit by Barberi that 'He does not know of my intentions, but I shall ask of him admission into the one true Fold of the Redeemer. I shall keep this back till all is over'. Newman added that Barberi 'is a simple quaint man, an Italian; but a very sharp clever man too in his way'.[16] On the evening of 8th October 1845, Barberi arrived at Littlemore after an exhausting four-hour coach ride in torrential rain. Newman recorded in his diary for that day, 'Father Dominic came at night, I began my confession'.[17] He completed his confession the following day and, with two other members of the Littlemore community, Frederick Bowles and Richard Stanton, was received into the Roman Catholic Church.[18] The Passionist missionary left Littlemore the next day and reported to his superiors that Newman was 'one of the most humble and loveable men I have met in my life'.[19] Newman had, in fact, already met Father Barberi, although briefly, in the summer of 1844 when he was giving a mission in Oxfordshire and, as a friend of Dalgairns, had visited Littlemore.

Subsequently he was always reluctant to discuss his reasons for becoming a Catholic,[20] and some time later he told an old friend that 'Catholicism is a deep matter – you cannot take it up in a teacup'.[21]

Dessain observes that 'a considerable number' had preceded Newman into the Church and that over the next few years 'several hundred University and educated men followed his example'.[22] Meanwhile, Newman had written to many of his wide circle of friends to tell them about his conversion to Catholicism. To his sister Jemima he wrote that 'I must tell you what will pain you greatly… This night Father Dominic, the Passionist, sleeps here. He does not know of my intention, but I shall ask him to receive me in what I believe to be the One Fold of the Redeemer'. The text of this letter is virtually identical to that sent to Wilberforce the day before.[23] He wrote similar letters to several close friends, such as R.W. Church, Mrs Bowden, Mrs William Froude, Miss Giberne, H.E. Manning, Pusey, Faber and Charles Russell.[24] The latter, who was Professor of Ecclesiastical History at Maynooth College, Co. Kildare and co-editor with Wiseman of the

Dublin Review, had corresponded with Newman and sent him books since April 1841.

Russell had read *Tract 90* and was deeply disturbed by references to Article XXVIII relating to Transubstantiation, which reflected misunderstandings of this important Roman Catholic doctrine. After much hesitation – he was a comparatively young seminary professor, under 30 years of age – he wrote to Newman on 8th April 1841,[25] giving a scholarly account of this 'precious doctrine' and 'most earnestly remonstrated' against the treatment given to our 'belief of the Eucharist'. With great respect, Russell imitated that Newman had 'completely misconceived us'.[26] In his urbane reply, Newman assured Russell: 'I do *not* accuse your Communion of holding Transubstantiation in the shocking sense we both repudiate, but I impute that the idea of it to our Articles which, I conceive, condemn a certain view of it which some persons or party in your Church have put forward against the sense of the sounder portion of it'.[27] Newman acknowledged Russell's influence in these remarkable words: 'He had, perhaps, more to do with my conversion than any one else'.[28] Newman's journal for 1st August 1843, had recorded a visit from 'Mr Russell'.[29] According to Gilley, his friendship with Newman 'is notable as Newman's sole warm connection with a Roman Catholic before he himself became one'.[30] Russell wrote congratulating Newman on his conversion and sent him a translation he had made of *The Moral Tales* written by Canon Carl von Schmid, for which Newman thanked his warmly.[31]

From Keble, Newman received a reply on 3rd October 1845, typical of his gentle and gracious friend. He told Newman that he had been a 'kind and helpful friend' in a way 'scarce anyone else could have been; and you are so mixed up in my mind with old and dear and sacred thoughts that I cannot bear to part with you, most unworthy as I know myself to be. And yet I cannot go along with you. I must cling to the belief that we are not really parted: you have taught me so, and I scarce think you can unteach me'. He sent Newman his blessings and hoped he 'would have peace where you are gone'.[32] 'Poor Keble', as Gilley describes him, had never been troubled with the kinds of doubt that had agonised Newman. 'He needed all his love of Newman to show an exquisite tact and tenderness for a tortured frame of mind for which he felt no sympathy'.[33]

Before his own conversion, Newman had expressed strong feelings about those who converted to Catholicism, such as William Lockhart, who had joined the Littlemore community in July 1842 and, realising that Newman had doubts about exercising his sacramental powers of confession, had promised that he would, nevertheless, remain for three years. Later, however, he felt unable to stay and, in just over a year, visited Fr Gentili, the Italian Rosminian missioner, at Loughborough and became a Roman Catholic. This defection clearly upset Newman and appears to have accelerated his decision to resign the living of St Mary's. In a letter to Keble about Lockhart's abrupt departure he stated that 'You must fancy how sick it makes one'.[34] He also told his sister Jemima that Lockhart's departure 'will very likely fix the time of my resigning St Mary's'.[35] Following this correspondence, Newman had sent Bishop Bagot his resignation on 6th September.

Not everyone was as kind to Newman as his old friends Pusey and Keble; the latter's gentle reaction has already been noted. Pusey had expected Newman's conversion, preparing himself and others for the blow, and had benignly developed a theory that Newman was responding to a divine call – 'a mysterious dispensation', as he described it in correspondence with Keble and Woodgate.[36] Pusey thought that Newman would be working in 'another part of the vineyard' of Christianity. Newman, however, had argued, particularly in *Tract 90*, that 'there was a Catholicism that was not Roman'. Therefore, when he seceded to Rome, many of his former associates treated him as a traitor. He was regarded 'as a crypto-Romanist' while he was in the Church of England and, on his conversion, he was also thought of as 'a crypto-Protestant' by many.[37]

Suspicions about the 'new arrivals' tended to persist among Roman Catholics, particularly among many of the 'old Catholics' (see chapter 1, page 30). Also, Chadwick observes that when Newman left the Church of England, he thought himself repudiated by that Church; prejudices about 'Romanists' lingered; historical associations with the Marian Martyrs, the Armada, Jacobotism and 'Popish plots' tended to flavour popular perceptions and attitudes. The eminent philosophers and historians of the 19th century 'resented Newman's departure and tried to forget him'.[38] His conversion had 'sent a *frisson* of alarm through English Protestantism, leading some to suppose that the Church of England really was liable to disintegration'.[39]

Newman's dominant influence in the University was no longer felt. Trevelyan puts it that 'as if a spell had been snapped, Oxford swung round to more secular interests and more liberal thought... what had been the Oxford Movement went out into the world and became a pan Anglican movement... to penetrate the general body of the clergy'.[40]

The Oxford Movement regrouped after Newman's secession; 'Pusey assisted by Keble and Marriott, took over the mantle of leadership'.[41] This new era of the Movement was, as noted already, characterised by a diffusion of its ethos and activities by parochial clergy inspired by its principles and practices. From its intellectual and religious roots, via Littlemore, a second generation Tractarianism spread its influence far beyond the pulpit of St Mary's or the 'monasticism' of Newman's haven at Littlemore, into the East End of London and the industrial cities and towns. Finding themselves generally disbarred from established areas of church activities, these second-generation Tractarians moved out into the suburbs. As a result, the Church of England tended to become 'polarised into two rather uncommunicative groups: High Church men who looked longingly, though not submissively, to Rome as the acknowledged leader of Catholic Christendom, and Low Church men who continued to stress the 'serious Roman aberrations from fundamental beliefs'.[42] This 'grass-roots tendency was, perhaps, developed through force of circumstances, but it certainly echoed Newman's own devotion to ministering for the spiritual needs of not just Oxford intellectuals but also for those who lived on a less exalted level in the hamlet of Littlemore.

On the morning of 31st October 1845, Newman accompanied by Ambrose St John and Walker, went to Oscott at Wiseman's invitation to receive the sacrament of confirmation on All Saints Day. It was only the second occasion that Newman had met Wiseman who, since 1840, had been President of Oscott College and also Coadjutor to the vicar apostolic of the Midland District. The first time they met was in Rome in 1833 when, as Anglican clerics, Newman and Hurrell Froude called on Wiseman, then rector of the English College in that city. They were told forthrightly by Wiseman 'that not one step could be gained without swallowing the Council of Trent as a whole'.[43]

This uncompromising utterance did not discourage

Newman from replying that he was sure 'God had some work for me to do in England'.[44] On meeting at Oscott, twelve years later, Newman offered Wiseman a draft copy of his book on the *Development of Christian Doctrine*, which Wiseman had 'the breadth of mind to insist it should be published as it stood; Newman, therefore, brought it out on his own responsibility'.[45] Wiseman's toleration of the book was remarked on approvingly by Newman in a letter to James Hope, written from Oscott on 2nd November 1845.[46]

At one stage in his life, after leaving St Mary's, Newman, as mentioned already, passed through a period of wracking uncertainty about his religious faith and also about what to do with his life. He speculated whether he should live as a layman but Wiseman, who had great insight into Newman's troubled mind, persuaded him that he should enter the Roman Catholic priesthood. Newman demurred at first because, as Trevor puts it, he 'had so long been a teacher in a Church he now felt to be in schism'. This initial concern was soon cleared, however, as also was the question of second ordination, which 'was customary if there was any doubt of authenticity'.[47]

During his stay at Oscott Newman was shown a building by Wiseman, which was in use as a boys' school and owned by Oscott: it had been a centre of Catholic activities since the 17th century. 'Bring your friends here', he was told by Wiseman, 'and carry out your studies for the priesthood with the help of our professors from Oscott'.[48] Newman accepted the offered accommodation which he was to call Maryvale in place of its existing title of Old Oscott College. Part of Wiseman's strategy was to keep the Roman Catholic converts from Littlemore together under his protective care and, eventually, he planned to nurture the development of a new infusion of Roman Catholic life into England through the establish-

Newman and Ambrose in Rome in 1846

Birmingham Oratory: Italian Renaissance style. The domed Oratory
was added as a memorial to Cardinal Newman

Pope Leo X111: 'I have always had a cult for Newman'

ment of an Oratory of St Philip Neri in England. (This plan is discussed in the next chapter.)

Newman wrote to Dalgairns telling him of Wiseman's offer and shrewdly assessed its suitability for the Littlemore community. He thought it was impossible for them to remain in their present accommodation 'unless we are simply to be literary laymen... Fr Dominic wishes us to be a congregation... It grows on me more and more that I must go to Rome, even if I move first to Oscott'. He reflected astutely that if he 'ultimately went into orders... there would be decided advantages for going to Rome, to avoid an individual bishop [e.g. at Oscott] appropriating me'.[49] He secured the agreement of his associates at Littlemore for this move.

In response to many invitations, Newman paid visits to Catholic centres in Ware, Stonyhurst, Prior Park, London and elsewhere during the next few months and was most hospitably received. Gilley suggests that 'Newman's treatment by his new co-religionists was at first one of pride'.[50] From London he wrote to Ambrose St John, reporting that he had – an hour's talk with Dr Griffiths, the vicar apostolic of the London District 'who is a very amiable taking person – not at all what I expected'.[51] Newman also told St John of his visit to St Edmund's College, Ware, where he had discussions with Dr Edward Cox, the President and found him 'a very pleasing man'.[52] On the same day Newman wrote to Frederick Faber, who had earlier intimated that he was bringing forward the date of his reception into the Roman Catholic Church, that 'I have just returned from St Edmund's, where my news about you... caused great joy'. He hoped that they would meet before Faber's intended overseas trip.[53]

In between his visits, Newman wrote to Wiseman, thanking him profusely for all the kindness and help he was giving the Littlemore community in offering them a new base at Old Oscott – 'Littlemore continued'. However, he expressed some concern about taking steps which would 'implicate others besides myself... They are so different from each other, and their calling so uncertain that I should be very loth to do anything to commit them absolutely to a particular course in a particular place, any more than myself, though I have every wish to bring them for their own sake under your Lordship's influence'.[54] Newman's letter reflects his cautious approach to the idea of moving to Oscott although, as he conceded in a letter to Fr Dominic Barberi, 'there are a great many difficulties in the way of our remaining here... and besides this and other things, I suppose the Bishop's wishing it is a strong reason for moving'.[55] Wiseman had followed Newman's activities closely over some time, and the planned move of the Oxford Movement converts to his district was all part of his scheme.

That Newman had an informal and growing friendship with Fr Dominic may be seen from a letter to him about an impending visit to the Passionists at Aston Hall: 'But as to my speaking to your people, please put that out of your thoughts. It is not in my line. Nor would it be becoming. And I come to enjoy your society, not to have any work put on me'.[56]

On Christmas Eve 1845, Newman wrote to tell Henry Wilberforce that 'Yesterday we came to the conclusion of leaving this place and availing ourselves of an offer which has been made to us under the highest sanction... It is a sad thing to leave poor Littlemore – but one has no function, position, or occupation there – and one cannot stand all the day idle.[57]

Early in 1846 Newman entered in his diary a memorandum of discussions he had with Dr John Briggs, vicar apostolic in Yorkshire, on whom he had called during his travels around the country, about the imminent move to Old Oscott: 'Dr Briggs seemed quite prepared for what I had to say, nay he went on to tell me that it was an old plan of Dr Wiseman's, which he did not see his way to follow'. He stressed that such 'local institutions' (as the proposed community at Old Oscott) 'must be subject to the Bishop of the district'; every one should be 'either under the Bishop of his birthplace, or of his domicile – he would have us at once get formal leave of our respective Bishops to go to Old Oscott'.[58]

A letter to Faber – who was about to go abroad – gives a revealing insight into Newman's evolving and marked interest at this time in the Oratorian way of life. He writes: 'I have long felt special admiration for the character of St Philip Neri... I wish we could all become good Oratorians, but that, I suppose, is impossible'.[59] An editorial footnote by Fr Charles Dessain states that 'The plan of joining the Oratory, hinted at by Dr Wiseman, was discussed at Littlemore, and Newman produced a copy of the Rule of St Philip, published in 1687'.[60] Wiseman's influence had encouraged Newman's own growing interest in Oratorianism, and he was quietly considering with his Littlemore associates its essential nature and suitability for their future way of life in the Catholic Church.

In February 1846, members of the Littlemore community departed for Old Oscott, leaving Newman, as he told Ambrose St John *Solus cum solo*.[61] He advised Mrs Bowden that his new postal address would be 'Mary Vale, Oscott, Birmingham', and confided that the plan of quitting this place was eased by the 'pleasant memory which attaches to it... it has been the happiest time of my life, because so quiet. Perhaps I shall never have such quiet again... I shall have a great many anxieties of various kinds in time to come'. He ended his letter, 'I must go over to the poor house before the fly comes'.[62] Maisie Ward remarks on Newman's 'real clinging to Littlemore village as well as the parish', seeing his solicitude as part of the same tender affection shown to his family, to memories of his childhood home, and to Oriel.[63] Some of the villagers of Littlemore recalled his kindnesses in visiting them and comforting them in their times of distress, even though he himself experienced many trials.[64]

Newman stayed the night of 22nd February with an old friend, Manuel Johnson, observer at the Radcliffe Observatory, where several old friends, including Pusey, came to say farewell.[65] He left Littlemore on the following morning, in the company of Bowles, and full of melancholic memories; he was not to be in Oxford again for over thirty years.[66]

Newman told James Hope – who was to change his name to Hope-Scott following his marriage in 1847 to the granddaughter of Sir Walter Scott – that he was 'to go to Rome at the end of June, and become a student at the Propaganda'. (The College of Propaganda was concerned with preparing students from across the world for the priesthood.) 'As you may suppose, it is simply my own act. I first mentioned to Dr Wiseman my wish for a regular education – and when he opened the subject today, he asked if I was of the same mind as before… He is going on business to Rome… and will introduce and settle me'.[67] Wiseman's continued commitment in helping to smooth Newman's path as he entered a new phase of his life is reflected in this correspondence.

While at Maryvale, Newman kept up his regular correspondence with his wide circle of friends, among whom was W.J. Copeland, who, as mentioned in Chapter 2, had been his curate at Littlemore and had stayed on after Newman's departure. 'As you suppose', Newman wrote, 'it was, of course, a very trying thing for me to quit Littlemore – I quite tore myself away… I have been most happy there, though in a state of suspense… I cannot help thinking I shall one day see Littlemore again; including yourself'.[68] But they were not to meet for about sixteen years when, in a London street, they had a chance encounter.[69]

In a diary entry for 6th June 1846, Newman recorded that he, Ambrose St John and others received the tonsure and minor orders at Oscott.[70] Another interesting diary entry[71] notes that Newman, in company with St John and Bowles, went to Coventry for Dr Ullathorne's consecration as vicar apostolic of the Western District. Ullathorne was transferred to the Central District in 1848 and made the first Bishop of Birmingham two years later when the Catholic hierarchy was restored in England and Wales. Ullathorne was to be Newman's bishop for many years after the Oratory was established in Birmingham. Their destinies, as will be discussed in the next chapter, were to become closely linked in their care for the spiritual welfare of Roman Catholics in this rapidly expanding industrial centre.

From a long and frank letter to Dalgairns, it can be gathered that Newman and St John found life at Oscott quite trying at times. To some extent this was due to its mixed function. It was both a boys' school and a seminary. They felt that the two student bodies should be separated, Oscott being a boys' school and Maryvale for clerics. The former is a 'bustling place – divines require something more strict, more monastic… all is disorder at Oscott… consequently the clerical "slip away" to other places such as Stonyhurst'. Newman concedes that Dr Wiseman 'is a punctual precise man… but Oscott is a bustling thoroughfare'.[72] After the serenity and privacy of Littlemore, the hectic environment of Oscott was obviously unwelcome to Newman and his group.

Newman's feelings are revealed in this plaintive entry in his journal: 'How dreary my first year at Maryvale... when I was the gaze of so many at Oscott, as if some wild incomprehensible beast, caught by the hunter, and a spectacle for Dr Wiseman to exhibit to strangers, as himself being the hunter who captures it!... I was made a humiliation at my minor orders and at the examination for them; and I had to stand at Dr Wiseman's door waiting for Confession amid the Oscott boys. I did not realise these as indignities at the time, though, as I have said, I felt their dreariness'.[73] For Newman it was, as Meriol Trevor puts it, 'a difficult time, for Oscott was the show-place of English Catholics and the illustrious convert the showpiece'.[74]

On the lighter side, Newman was invited by the 16th Earl of Shrewsbury to visit his ancestral seat, Alton Towers, for the consecration of the new Roman Catholic church in Cheadle, Staffordshire, on 1st September, 1846. This invitation was 'gladly accepted'.[75] John Talbot, the 16th Earl, a devout and munificent benefactor, spent a substantial part of his wealth on patronising the highly talented Gothic-revivalist architect, Augustus Welby Pugin, who considered Cheadle church to be his ecclesiastical masterpiece. Together with Ambrose Phillipps de Lisle, a Catholic landowner in Leicestershire, this triumvirate made a conspicuous contribution to the Roman Catholic parishes of Victorian England (see Chapter 1). For instance, they fostered the missionary work of Luigi Gentili, the Italian Rosminian priest, who became chaplain to Ambrose Phillipps' household. Phillipps had also donated land from his estate for the foundation of the first post-Reformation Cistercian abbey in England; the Passionist priest, Dominic Barberi, received hospitality and encouragement in his ardent missionary activities. Pugin worked frenetically in designing Catholic churches and chapels, with the liberal financial support of the Earl of Shrewsbury and the collaboration of Ambrose Phillipps. Newman was drawn into this potent fellowship, and later on negotiated with the 16th Earl in connection with the Oratorian foundation. (This will be discussed in the next chapter.) Some time before, Phillipps had written to Newman congratulating him on becoming a Catholic and invited him to his Leicestershire home. Newman thanked him, but regretted that pressure of work precluded him from accepting the invitation.[76] About four years before this date, Newman was composing *Tract 90*, and Phillipps had 'written enthusiastically to his friends about the impending revolution of religious attitudes'.[77] In that short time much had also happened in Newman's life affecting his religious beliefs and practices, as already discussed.

It was not until September 1846 that Newman and Ambrose St John left Maryvale to study theology at the College of Propaganda; they stayed there for just over a year. As they travelled to Rome, Newman and St John received warm welcomes and generous hospitality. On arrival they found that the College did not have their rooms ready for occupation so they were accommodated in a nearby hotel. Eventually, in early November 1846, their rooms were available. 'They are certainly very nice rooms, and everyone is very kind', Newman wrote in a long letter to Richard Stanton, who had been received into the Catholic Church by Fr Barberi at the same time as himself. He added that he had contacted the Jesuits at the Collegio Romano and went on to say that 'There is no doubt the Jesuits are the real men in Rome... We hope to hear something of the Oratorians – but at present I see nothing except seculars and Jesuits – the Oratorians may prove a middle point between them'.[78] In a letter to Dalgairns a week or so later, Newman again refers to

Jesuits: 'with no persons do we get on so well. Not that I mean to be a Jesuit or to persuade you – but I really think we should leave ourselves open to everything'.[79]

To Dalgairns, he had also mentioned that criticisms of his theory of development were being made. 'The Theologians of the Roman College, who are said to sway the theology of Rome, are introducing *bits* (without having seen the whole book) *bits* of my Essay into their lectures to dissent from'. He had complained but had been assured that the professors were 'not speaking against my book'.[80] However, he felt that he had finally been able to convince the chief theologian at Rome, Fr Giovanni Perrone, Professor of Dogmatic Theology, of the soundness of his beliefs.

In November Newman and St John had a private, informal interview with the Pope. Newman reported that 'He is a vigorous man, with a very pleasant countenance and was most kind'.[81]

Towards the end of the year, Newman felt able to tell Henry Wilberforce: 'I was happy at Oriel, happier at Littlemore, as happy or happier still at Maryvale – and happiest here' in the College of Propaganda at Rome.[82] In a rather self-deprecating aside, Newman said he was little known in Rome 'both because I am so slow at the languages and because I am so bashful and silent in general society... Rickards had apparently said of me, that when my mouth was shut, it seems as if it would never open and when open as if it would never shut. So that I don't expect people will know me'.[83]

Some aspects of Roman life disconcerted him. He was, for instance, appalled to discover, during a conversation with a Jesuit priest, the low level of studies in philosophy and theology at the College; 'Aristotle and Aquinas are out of favour'. When Newman voiced his astonishment that the Pope had not intervened to put

104

right this serious omission, his informant 'shrugged his shoulders and said that the Pope could do nothing if people would not obey him... the Romans were a giddy people, not like the English'.[84] While, however, the education at the College failed to impress Newman, the range of nationalities certainly did: 32 languages were spoken there.

In another lengthy letter to Dalgairns, Newman wrote about Roman life and the possibilities of various religious orders, for example, the Dominicans, the Jesuits and the Redemptorists. The latter 'are said to be like the Jesuits, only less military, at least so I understand it'. He described a visit that St John and he had paid to the Chiesa Nuova – St Philip's Church: 'If I wished to follow my bent, I should join them, if I joined any – They have a good library, and handsome sets of rooms apparently. It is like a College with hardly any rule. They keep their own property, and furnish their own rooms. It is what Dr Wiseman actually wishes, and really I should wonder, if at last I felt strongly inclined to it, for I must own I feel the notion of giving up property [would] try my faith very much'.[85] Wiseman's pervasive interest and Newman's reluctance to abandon some degree of personal freedom, are factors which seem to have influenced the type of religious vocation chosen by Newman and his associates.

As Dessain states, 'The Oratorians were free subjects, who had few rules and must learn to live together by means of tact, self knowledge and the knowledge of others. Each had his own work and was to rely on personal influence rather than discipline in pursuing it. This was Newman's way, and the fact that he and his companions had learned to live together at Littlemore and Old Oscott meant that their work of preparation was already half done'.[86]

Writing to Dalgairns in January 1847, Newman put forward 'an idea' on which he wanted an opinion: 'The more we see, the more we seem to think that our choice lies between being Jesuits and seculars... The Oratorian Rule seems a sort of *Deus e Machina* here; and so Dr Wiseman wished it to be. Well then, we have said to ourselves, let us see what the Oratorians are like'. He proceeded to a fairly detailed analysis of the Oratorian life and duties, which he believed, would need some alteration 'in order to adapt it to the state of England, and this would be in favour of study'.[87]

Newman's views on his religious vocation were beginning to clarify, and after a prolonged period of introspection and uncertainty, it seemed to him that the way in which he and his companions could best serve the Church was becoming evident. He had studied the Rule of St Philip diligently and, according to Ffinch, 'in many ways, St Philip reminded him of Keble'.[88] When still at Littlemore, Newman had, as noted earlier, secured a copy of the Rule of St Philip and discussed it with his friends.

On 17th January 1847, Newman wrote to Wiseman that 'it is curious and very pleasant that after all the thoughts we can give the matter, we come round to your Lordship's original idea, and feel we cannot do better than be Oratorians.[89] In a further letter to Dalgairns, Newman intimated that the Oratorian Rule 'was almost in all its parts perfectly unsuited to a country of heretics and Saxons'. However, he was having discreet enquiries made about what, if any, alterations might be tolerated to enable an English Oratory to be founded.[90] Later Newman wrote again, and at some length, to Wiseman about developments in Rome related to the Oratorian concept. He confessed difficulty in communicating at a distance of 1,400 miles, particularly when so much change was taking place, but he hoped that matters would, in the end, allow them to proceed with 'your written sanction than only in the belief that we have it'.[91] In discussions in Rome Newman's patience and diplomatic skills were well tested, but he was soon to reap the reward. Just over a week later, he was able to inform Wiseman that the Pope had 'taken up' the proposed plan for an English Oratory with a Rule adapted to suit that environment. The Holy Father wished more aspiring Oratorians to come to Rome at once, and he would provide a novitiate. (This extended letter was added to by Ambrose St John, in Newman's absence on a visit to Rome for further negotiations.) St John himself stressed that the Pope had 'at once expressed his approbation for an adaptation of St Philip's rule'.[92]

Writing to Mrs Bowden from Rome, Newman was able to report enthusiastically that 'there is a great stir here for the Catholic Church in England... The Pope will not rest till he has put Catholic affairs on a better footing, but it is very difficult to make changes without the thorough good will of English Catholics, through whom they are to be carried out'.[93] To the priest who received him into the Church, Newman was delighted to tell him, 'We are to be Oratorians. The Pope has been very kind to us'.[94] In thanking Faber for his congratulations, Newman reassured him that there was 'not a chance or your and our interfering with each other. England is large enough'.[95] In retrospect, this was a rather over-optimistic opinion of the way in which their relationship would develop.

Newman told his former Anglican curate, whom he held in warmest regard, that 'one very prominent reason' for founding an Oratory in England 'has been that it admits of *so many different sorts of minds*'.[96] Newman also remarked to Mrs Bowden that 'The more I understand it, the more the Oratory seems the proper thing for England at this moment... the object of St Philip was to educate a higher class of priests for parish work – most of his followers were highly educated men, corresponding precisely to the fellows of English universities. There is an abundance of piety and zeal in the English priests at present, but they want education'.[97] To another correspondent, Newman pronounced that 'We [the Oratorians] are the Athenians, the Jesuits Spartans. Ours is in one respect more anxious and difficult – we have no vows, we have fewer rules – yet we must keep together – we require a knowledge of each other, which the Jesuits do not require. A Jesuit is like a soldier in the phalanx – an Oratorian like a legionary – he fights by himself by *carita* [sic] – which means tact, self-knowledge, knowledge of others. This requires a specific training'.[98] This classically-inspired statement of the distinctive nature of Oratorianism summarised, imaginatively, the essential appeals he had discerned in his new vocation. The recipient of this letter became, in due course, Fr Francis Knox of the London Oratory.

On the feast of St Philip Neri, 26th May 1847, Newman and Ambrose St John were ordained subdeacons by Cardinal Fransoni, and on the following Saturday, at St John the Lateran, the cathedral church of the Pope as Bishop of Rome, they were ordained deacons. On Trinity Sunday, 30th May 1847, they were raised to the priesthood in the Propaganda Church.[99]

In the retreat he made at St Eusebio, the Jesuit Retreat House, before ordination, Newman declared that he had in his mind a 'wound or cancer' that prevented him from being a good Oratorian. He reflected earnestly and deeply on his life, and admitted that for some years he had 'had many things to oppress him...'. 'In the Church of England I had many detractors; a mass of calumny was hurled at me; my services towards the Church were misrepresented by almost everyone in authority in it'.

He shared with certain of his friends an exile 'but not even in that retreat was I safe from those who pursued me with their curiosity'. He felt oppressed and lost hope, and the cheerfulness he used to have almost vanished. He felt acutely that he was no longer young – he was then 46 – and that his best years were spent: 'I see myself to be fit for nothing, a useless log'. When he became a Catholic, he 'lost not a few friends', and death claimed others most dear to him. Religious observances were faithfully followed in his 'retreat' at Littlemore, but now he felt a reaction against such practices. 'I am always languid in the contemplation of divine things, like a man walking with his feet bound together'.[100]

Such self-analysis reveals something of the inner torment which, over the years, had afflicted Newman. His feelings of rejection and persecution, and his declarations of uselessness arose from a period of intense reflection on his life so far – and yet, if he had but known, he had just passed the halfway mark in his long life, and was still to make his historic and unique contributions to the regeneration of the Roman Catholic Church in England, through his pervasive intellectual, theological and spiritual leadership.

After ordination, Newman and members of the Maryvale community spent five months in the Oratorian noviciate for English students at Santa Croce, Rome. Before the College of Propaganda, Newman had communicated to the rector the 'general discontent among English-speaking students'.[101] They were not allowed outside visits, their reading was greatly restricted, and mature students like Newman and his group felt keenly the lack of opportunities for philosophical and theological discussions. To his sister Jemima, Newman confided his concern about the 'conservatism' which seemed to stifle intellectual progress at the College of Propaganda:

'it is astonishing, with my recollections of Oxford, 16 or 17 years ago, how exactly they resemble the Kebles, Perceval, etc., etc., and Froude before his eyes were opened to see through the hollowness of the then so called Toryism... There is a deep suspicion of *change*, with a perfect incapacity to create anything *positive* for the wants of the times'.[102] Newman found such an intellectual environment directly antipathetical to his own restless, searching spirit, and committed belief in intellectual and religious development. (Newman's pre-eminent contributions to the theories of university education are discussed in Chapter 5.)

While in Rome, Newman had the opportunity for discussions with Wiseman, as he noted, for example, in his diary for 11th and 31st July, and 17th August 1847.[103] On 9th October Newman wrote from Rome to Wiseman, saying he had hoped to tell him that they had been given a brief to found an English Oratory but this was delayed 'until after the Congregations meet again in November'. But he was able to report that the Pope had appointed him to be 'first Superior', with power to choose the 'four Deputies'.[104] Wiseman sent a 'long reply' in which he mentioned that although he had 'considered Maryvale in every respect the proper place for Noviciate, House of study and retreats, and central house', Newman might bear in mind the opportunities by 'having a house in London'.[105] Among Newman's diary entries is one recording that, on 1st December 1847, he 'called on Manning and walked with him'.[106] The latter was still a senior Anglican cleric and it was not until 1851 that, like Newman, he entered the Roman Catholic Church and later became a Catholic priest, eventually being created Cardinal Archbishop of Westminster.

On 6th December 1847 Newman, with St John, began the journey back to England and thence to Maryvale. They went via Loretto, where both said Mass at the Holy House.[107] As they travelled, Newman managed to keep up the flow of his correspondence, including a letter to his sister Jemima telling her that, 'We had one or two very nice interviews with him [the Pope] before parting... There is every appearance of his being as firm as he is kind'.[108] The weary travellers at last reached London on Christmas Eve and stayed there over Christmas, visiting various friends and also having lunch with Wiseman. On Friday 31st December, they travelled on to Maryvale where they were greeted as Catholic priests and Oratorians.

NOTES

1   Newman, 1956, p.86.
2   Mozley, 1891, p.465.
3   Newman, 1956, p.10.
4   Newman, 1956, p.63.
5   Chadwick, 1990, p.14.
6   Bacchus, 1917, p.351.
7   Mozley, 1891, p.445.
8   Mozley, 1891, pp.459-61.
9   Mozley, 1891, pp.461-2.
10 Maisie Ward, 1948, p.438.
11 Mozley, 1891, p.464.
12 Mozley, 1891
13 Mozley, 1891, p.467.
14 Mozley, 1891, p.453.
15 Mozley, 1891, p.454.
16 *LD* XI.3, 7 October 1845.
17 *LD* XI.4.
18 Ker, 1990, p.316.
19 Trevor, 1996, p.101.
20 Cf Dessain, 1980, p.84.
21 *LD* XI.110 J. Spencer Northcote, 8 February 1846.
22 Dessain, 1980, p.89.
23 *LD* XI.8, 8 October 1845.
24 *LD* XI.3-16.
25 Bacchus, 1917, pp.118-122.
26 Bacchus, 1917, pp.120-121.
27 Bacchus, 1917, pp.122-123.

28 *LD* XI.9 *footnote*; Newman, 1993, p.237.
29 Newman, 1956, p.242.
30 Gilley, 1990, p.206.
31 *LD* XI.53, 7 December 1845.
32 Mozley, 1891, pp.471-73.
33 Gilley, 1990, p.216.
34 Mozley, 1891, p.417.
35 Mozley, 1891, pp.417-78.
36 Maisie Ward, 1948, p.454.
37 Trevor, 1996, p.47.
38 Chadwick, 1990, pp.76-77.
39 Norman, 1986, p.209.
40 Trevelyan, 1948, p.280.
41 Nockles, 1997, p.302.
42 Pawley, 1974, p.136.
43 Reynolds, 1958, p,39.
44 Newman, 1956, p.136.
45 Trevor, 1996, p.102.
46 *LD* XI.23.
47 Trevor, 1996, p.102.
48 Meynell, 1890, p.51.
49 *LD* XI.29-31, 9 November 1845.
50 Gilley, 1990, p.245.
51 *LD* XI.37, 20 November 1845.
52 *LD* XI, 22 November 1845.
53 *LD* XI.38-9, 22 November 1845.
54 *LD* XI.54, 8 December 1845.
55 *LD* XI.61-2, 14 December 1845.
56 *LD* XI.77, 23 December 1845.
57 *LD* XI.79, 24 December 1845.
58 *LD* XI.89-90, 10 January 1846.
59 *LD* XI.105, 1 February 1846.
60 *LD* XI.105.
61 *LD* XI.124, 21 February 1846.
62 *LD* XI.126, 22 February 1846.
63 Maisie Ward, 1948, p.426.
64 Trevor, 1996, p.104.
65 *LD* XI.125, Henry Wilberforce, 21 February 1846.
66 *LD* XI.125, diary entry 23 February 1846.
67 *LD* XI.152, 18 April 1846.
68 *LD* XI.132-3, 10 March 1846.
69 Newman, 1956, p.261.
70 *LD* XI.173.
71 *LD* XI.179.
72 *LD* XI.193-5, 6 July 1846.
73 Newman, 1956, p.255.
74 Trevor, 1996, p.104.
75 *LD* 225, Earl of Shrewsbury, 18 August 1846.
76 *LD* XI.l9, 19 October 1845.

77 Norman, 1985, p.209.
78 *LD* XI.267-70, 6 November 1846.
79 *LD* XI.275, 15 November 1846.
80 *LD* XI.281, Feast of S. Cecilia 1846.
81 *LD* XI.285, F.S. Bowles, 26 November 1846.
82 *LD* XI.294, 13 December 1846.
83 *LD* XI.295, 13 December 1846.
84 *LD* XI.279, J.D. Dalgairns, Feast of S. Cecilia 1846.
85 *LD* XI.303-7, 31 December 1846.
86 Dessain, 1980, p.92.
87 *LD* XII.16, 15 January 1847.
88 Ffinch, 1992, p.146.
89 *LD* XII.19-20, 17 January 1847.
90 *LD* XII.22, 22 January 1847.
91 *LD* XII.43-4, 14 February 1847.
92 *LD* XII.50-4, 23 February 1847.
93 *LD* XII.59, 7 March 1847.
94 *LD* XII.62, Fr Dominic Barberi, 14 March 1847.
95 *LD* XII.66, 31 March 1847.
96 *LD* XII.69, 23 April 1847.
97 *LD* XII.101, 21 July 1847.
98 *LD* XII.113, T.F. Knox, 10 September 1847.
99 *LD* XII.84-5, Mrs J.W. Bowden, 30 May 1847.
100 Newman, 1956, pp.245-8.
101 Ker, 1990, p.331.
102 *LD* XII.102-4, 28 July 1847.
103 *LD* XII.92; 106; 108.
104 *LD* XII.124-7, 9 October 1847.
105 *LD* XII.126, 29 October 1847.
106 *LD* XII.131.
107 *LD* XII.131, diary, 10 December 1847.
108 *LD* XII.137, 21 December 1847.

4

Newman:
Oratorian Vocation

THE seed of Oratorianism had lain in Newman's mind for some time; he had shown his Littlemore group of close friends a copy of St Philip Neri's Rule, as noted in the preceding chapter. His mind had been further stimulated by Wiseman's sympathetic interest in the Oxford Movement and by his readiness to offer practical help when Newman and several of his close associates seceded from Anglicanism and became Roman Catholics.[1] At this critical convergence of events, Wiseman offered accommodation and opportunities for the converts to continue to share fellowship, to reflect on their future lives, and to discuss ways in which they might pursue an active ministry in their new environment. From discussions at Littlemore, they had become familiar with the general nature of the Oratorian way of life and had reflected on its relevance to their religious aspirations and experiences.

This process of evaluation and assimilation of Oratorianism continued in Rome until Newman himself had become convinced that the Rule of St Philip Neri was the one which was most likely to give him and his associates the best opportunities for developing their religious vocations. In the autumn of 1847 he wrote from Rome saying that the Brief for setting up the English Oratory had been effected; it was 'made out for Birmingham – and Maryvale will be the mother house of the whole kingdom'. This historic and welcome news was given in a letter to Mrs J.W. Bowden, an old family friend. Newman added, perceptively, that 'it is certain, important changes are about to take place in the state of Catholicism in England, and we must in some way or other be brought nearer to London, even if my home continues to be Maryvale'.[2]

Now, with Papal authority, Newman and his associates were back in England, after ordination in Rome, with the mission of opening an Oratorian House. For the time being, they would, once again, be living at Maryvale where, on 2nd February 1848, the Feast of the Purification, Newman formally established the first English Oratory, of which he was the Superior. According to Ward, Newman chose that day deliberately. It was the Foundation Day at Oriel. He also wished his new Oratory to benefit from the blessings of this special feast day of the Blessed Virgin Mary.[3]

Dessain stresses the importance of the Oratory for Newman: 'It was his chosen vocation; to found it in England was the first commission he received from the Catholic authorities; it was the framework for the rest of his long life, and, as has so often been the case with founders, through it some of his cruellest trials came'.[4]

In his Anglican years, Newman had experienced many tribulations but these were by no means over when, approaching fifty years of age, he became a Catholic priest and member of the Congregation of the Oratory. Some of the turbulence and trials which Newman endured arose from his publishing and polemical activities, others from challenging educational aspirations, while several involved clashes of personality and arose from differences of perception of what should be done. Newman's early years as an Oratorian Superior were, unfortunately, made stressful by members of his own community, in

116

particular Frederick Faber. Newman had, in fact, been told by Wiseman, when they met in London over Christmas 1847 as Newman was returning from Rome, that Faber and his community of 'Wilfridians' wished to join the Oratory. Newman at once wrote to Faber that 'You may fancy the joy with which St John and I heard the news that you proposed we should be one... I cannot say more till I know your precise wishes and intentions – I will but say that, from the very wish I have that we may come to an understanding, I am anxious you should try if you have fully mastered *what* Oratorianism is. In many important aspects it differs from what you are at present. It is not poetical it is very devotional'.[5] Newman's welcoming words were thus tempered by his concerns about Faber's realisation of the essential nature of Oratorianism. In a letter to Dalgairns in Rome, Newman informed him that 'Faber has offered himself and his to me, simply and absolutely – his house, his money, his all. The proposal came through Dr Wiseman – but, as I wanted his own words, he has written to me this morning on the subject... I need counsel. The sooner you can come the better'.[6] On the same day, Newman wrote to Faber, inviting him to visit and talk over the whole matter.[7] In a diary entry for 6th January 1848, Newman recorded that Faber and two of his community visited Maryvale and stayed until Saturday 8th January.[8] The visit 'went off very well', as Newman was able to tell Richard Stanton. It was agreed that the entire Wilfridian community should be received as Oratorians.[9] On 14th February, Newman travelled to Cheadle and fulfilled this agreement. But he was soon to discover that he had taken on 'more than the responsibility for Faber and seventeen young men'.[10]

These enthusiastic young converts, led by the mercurial Faber, were to cause Newman many heartaches. As he confided to Ambrose St John, 'my great trouble is some of the giovani [Newman's habitual way of describing the members of this young community] – not that any thing new has occurred, but they have so repelled any thing between us but what is external, shown so little confidence, as to throw me back upon myself – and now I quite dread the fortnightly chapter'.[11]

As an undergraduate, Faber had heard Newman preaching in St Mary's, Oxford and, like many of his generation, had been enthralled, so much so that he became known as 'Newman's acolyte'. His University career was not remarkable, although he became a Fellow of University College, and in 1843 he secured the beneficiary of a College living as rector of Elton in Huntingdonshire. Almost immediately, with letters of introduction from Wiseman, he then visited Italy, paid homage at the shrine of St Philip Neri, and had a private audience with the Pope. On return to England in 1845, Faber – who was a bachelor – transformed his household of men servants, together with some of the village boys, into a quasi-monastic community. Very soon after Newman's conversion to Roman Catholicism in 1845, Faber, six boys and one woman from his parish were also received into the Roman Catholic Church. His next move was to set up his community in Birmingham and, later, at Cotton Hall, Cheadle, Staffordshire, where the devout and generous 16th Earl of Shrewsbury was their patron. Here Faber established the community of the 'Brothers of the Will of God', or 'Wilfridians' as they came to be called.

It has been said that Newman, while welcoming Faber and his Wilfridians as Oratorians, stressed that their earlier aspirations to monasticism would no longer be relevant if they were to adopt the Rule of St Philip Neri. While still at Littlemore, Newman had been approached by Faber, suggesting that the two 'communities' might be merged, but he had firmly discouraged the proposal. He suggested that should Faber's plan fail, then he might prolong his stay in Rome and 'give some months to the discipline of some seminary'. Further, he shrewdly observed that 'I shall not be surprised, even though you join us... you would find yourself ultimately called elsewhere. I cannot help thinking you should be a distinct centre of operation and collect people about you'.[12]

Just over a year later Newman was to write again to Faber, who had sent his congratulations on 'the news of your becoming an Oratorian', and commenting that his own community had been discouraged by Wiseman from 'making an Oratory'. Newman's response was cordial but carefully worded. 'Do not for an instant fancy our plans will clash, there is no chance of it. You have your own ways and powers, which no one can rival, of working out your object, even if our object were precisely the same, which is not the case. At the same time I am surprised to find our general plans are more the same than I thought at first.'.[13]

However, on Christmas Day 1847, Newman wrote in his diary that 'There is great difference at present between us, that he (Faber) is much more *poetical* in the largest sense of the word than the Oratorians. In devotions, in asceticism, on obedience, in dress, in names, etc'.[14] These views were enlarged in a letter to Faber quoted on page 117.[15] Newman was becoming more and more aware that although he and Faber shared much in common in that they were both Oxford men who had changed their religions affiliation to the rather suspect Roman Catholicism and had attracted others to follow them in a life of profound religious dedication, nevertheless there were distinct differences in their personalities which affected the ways in which they developed their Oratorian vocations. These markedly divergent developments were almost constant sources of irritation between them. Newman disliked Faber's enthusiastic adoption of Italianate forms of devotion, of sermons laced with miraculous legends, and of a fervent religiosity that fitted uneasily into contemporary England. He specifically advised Antony Hutchinson, who had joined Faber in 1848, to 'avoid everything extreme'. Stories introduced into sermons should be relevant and edifying, 'not such as are likely to surprise or offend people, as some miraculous accounts would do'.[16] Newman's dislike of religious 'excesses' epitomised his own essentially restrained, reflective approach to his pastoral activities in the expansion of Roman Catholicism in Victorian England. Faber's exaggerated pious practices, his predilection for ornate vestments, exuberant 'Roman' church architecture, and Ultramontanism tended to alienate the 'old Catholics', who were more comfortable with Newman because of his 'Englishness' which was in direct contrast to the Italianate religion of the Ultramontanes. It seems that they sensed in him views and practices which fitted in happily with the more moderate way in which they and their forbears had, particularly in penal times, observed their Faith. Newman's published opinions on the position of the laity in the Church must also have influenced their perceptions of him.[17]

While Faber played an important role in the growth of Oratorianism in England he had made no contribution at all to the initial stages of developing its Brief in Rome or to the choice made by Newman and his close companions of the Oratorian vocation.[18] When, in the end, Faber followed the path taken by these early 'pioneers', his behaviour oscillated between deep affection and reverence for Newman, and a nearly nonstop flow of criticisms and complaints about various aspects of Oratorian life and other matters. After a noviciate of only one month, Newman had appointed Faber to be novice-master. Trevor remarks that this 'was a great mistake... Faber and his novices had nothing to do except worry Newman and blame him for everything they did not like'.[19] Friction between them became so unbearable, that, later on, separate communities had to be established in Birmingham and in London.

This, however, was in the unseen future. For the present time Newman was trying to solve the problems which had been brought about by Faber's ardent and sudden desire to join the new English Oratory. The Oratorians were now split between two sites – one in Birmingham, the other in a remote part of rural Staffordshire; added to this was the obligation to continue to provide pastoral care for Catholics living within the vicinity of Cotton Hall which, together with the Church of St Wilfrid, largely donated by the Earl of Shrewsbury, had been the original centre of Faber's Wilfridian community.

To Newman's dismay he discovered from Faber that St Wilfrid's was in financial difficulties,[20] and he asked him to consider alternative ways of ridding themselves of this 'so little an Oratorian place'; he also requested Faber to provide an account of the expenses incurred in living there.[21] Lord Shrewsbury's chaplain was assured that they would 'take into our best considerations the views expressed about Cotton Hall' which, although well placed as a missionary centre 'is not quite the place for an *Oratorian*'. Newman explained that 'Our brief speaks expressly of *urbes ampliores* [large towns]'.[22] Extended correspondence arose from attempts to satisfy the expectations of the Earl of Shrewsbury regarding continuation of Catholic pastoral care in the neighbourhood of his estate, and his view that abandonment of the monastery he had provided for Faber's Wilfridians would be a breach of contract.[23]

Newman had already told Lord Shrewsbury of the conflicting pressures he was experiencing: 'We see our way so little at present, that I am not able to speak about Cheadle. Certainly the wish at Rome was that we should place ourselves in large towns, such as Birmingham, London and Manchester'.[24] Two weeks later, he firmly re-stated 'the case... as we view it: – We come to England Oratorians; the Oratorians are notoriously, even more than the Jesuits, inhabitants of cities; the community of St Wilfrid's proposes to join us, and... I am expressly told that [their application] has your Lordship's sanction'. He repeated that the Oratorian Brief 'expressly destines us for *urbes ampliores* and for the *nobilior splendidior, doctior* class of society' [the more educated and wealthy upper classes].[25] The unsuitability of the rural location was again emphasised in another letter to the Earl: 'We do not think Cheadle is a place which would answer the purpose of an Oratorian Mission'.[26]

From time to time, misunderstandings and a note of exasperation creep into both sides of this extensive correspondence, to which Newman was a harassed and rather reluctant contributor. A viable solution still seemed to be remote; Newman's time and energy were being exhausted and costs were rising. As a result, in the autumn of 1848, all the English Oratorians became centred at Cotton Hall and it was agreed to maintain pastoral care in the district, as requested by the Earl of Shrewsbury.

In a memorandum dated 18th September 1848, Newman recorded that he had been informed by Dr Ullathorne, vicar apostolic of the Central District, that he wished the Oratorians to be in Birmingham, and he hoped to find premises suitable for a chapel and accommodation for a small community in a short while.[27] On 29th September Newman wrote another short memorandum: 'We decided by vote to leave this place (Maryvale) for

Birmingham, the residue going to St Wilfrid's. This is the only way in which by the Brief we could give up this House'.[28] He also wrote to Ullathorne confirming their conversation and the agreement to move to Birmingham, provided suitable accommodation for 'as many of our community as shall live there would be available'.[29]

Meanwhile the Oratorians were clustered at Cotton Hall, in a community numbering around forty, which Newman considered far too large for the Rule of St Philip Neri to be followed faithfully. An authentic Oratorian community was comparatively small – perhaps no more than ten – where a small group of secular priests and lay brothers 'learned to live together by means of tact, self-knowledge and the knowledge of others' and relied 'on personal influence rather than discipline in pursuing their specific duties'.[30] The situation at Cotton Hall put the whole ethos of an Oratory at risk, apart from the fact that the rural location was directly contrary to the traditions of Oratorianism and to the special Brief which Newman had received from Rome. To find himself and the English Oratory in such an unacceptable situation, and at so early a stage in their development, may be presumed to have been very worrying. Ullathorne's intervention was, there-fore, timely as well as challenging, and it gave Newman an opportunity of disentangling himself, to some extent, from the immediate problems of the Cotton Hall com-munity. In following Ullathorne's request, Newman doubtless realised that he would, in fact, be conforming to the Papal Brief, which specifically referred to a Birmingham Oratory.

But Faber – known as Fr Wilfrid in the Oratorian community – was to be, once again, a source of anxiety to Newman. Worries arose over translations of Italian, French and Spanish *Lives of the Saints* which Faber had been working on since 1847. With typical care for his community, Newman warned Faber that 'There is a row blowing up. Now, if we are advocates of doctrines, however true, with no *authority* to back us, it is the story of the Oxford Tracts over again – we shall be in a false position, and the harm and scandal done to religion, and the mischief to the Oratory, will be incalculable'.[31] A row certainly did blow up and lasted for two months. Some 'old Catholics' were affronted by Faber's vivid account of miracles and austerities, as well as revelations about ecclesiastical scandals in some continental countries, and they sharply criticised his publications. When Faber joined the Oratorians in February 1848, it had been agreed to defer for a year the decision as to whether the Oratory should take over the Series but Newman hesitated about informing the publishers of the possible suspension. The September issue of *Dolman's Magazine* contained a ferocious review by Fr Edward Price, a London priest, of Faber's translation of the *Life of St Rose*, accusing him of promoting 'gross, palpable idolatry'.[32] Newman quickly realised the perilous position, and told Faber that 'the question of the *Lives of the Saints* had been submitted to the Bishops assembled at Ushaw' as 'it would be unfair to the Oratory, ungrateful to the Pope, to plunge the Oratory on its commencement here into a controversy, where dogmatic correctness was on the side of its opponents'.[33] In the postscript to a further letter, four days later, Newman added, with typical subtlety, that for a long time they should limit themselves to publishing 'such *Lives* as have no startling forms of worship, etc., in them – or if this cannot be, then the *Lives* not of *contemplatives* but of those who have *done some work* in their life-time: St Vincent of Paul, St Francis de Sales, St Vincent Ferrer, etc., etc.'[34] Newman also wrote to Wiseman, Newsham and Ullathorne seeking their support and defending the heavily criticised *Life of St Rose*.

However, Ullathorne ordered publication of the Series to be stopped forthwith. Newman told Faber that the decision 'took me quite by surprise' but, he assured him 'I will stand by you, and no reproach shall fall on you, which does not fall on me'.[35] Two days later he advised Faber that, after consulting the Fathers of the Oratory, it had been unanimously concluded that the Series should be suspended at present since 'we are given to understand that the Lives of foreign saints, however edifying in their respective countries, are unsuited to England, and unacceptable to Protestants'.[36]

In the lengthy correspondence over this contentious and irritating matter, Ullathorne had, as Newman readily remarked, been 'very kind and easy in his manner', but also very firm in his views about the possible disservice such publications might do to the Roman Catholic Church in England.[37] Newman was not, however, content to let the bluff Yorkshire prelate's remarks pass without comment: 'I conjecture that you would not dislike, or rather would wish, to hear of my opinion on the subject. I fear then, I must say, with deference to your Lordship, that my own experience as a Protestant leads me to an opposite conclusion to that which your Lordship has so clearly expressed. Protestants are converted by high views, not low ones... Having been one of a party who were led on to the Catholic Church by her stronger doctrines, and who despised half measures and uncertain statements, of course I am justified in speaking for that party, though I may not be a fair representative of other sets of Protestants'.[38] Ullathorne replied by return, thanking Newman for the 'straightforward expression of your sentiments which is always so satisfactory'. But he warned that 'we must guard against mistaking each other'. He suspected their viewpoints tended to be different. *The Lives of the Saints* had been one of the 'principal enjoyments' of his life and he reflected on how 'hard and toilsome and full of pain are the unseen labours of a Bishop in a country like this' where, for twenty years, he has had to deal with the virtues and vices of laymen and clergy. From this long pastoral experience, he confessed that whenever he committed a blunder exercising his ministry, it had arisen 'from assuming the existence of a higher degree of the habit of the cardinal virtues in individuals than they possessed'.[39]

This frank and intimate exchange of views between two of the leading Roman Catholic churchmen of the period presaged the close relationship that developed over the next four decades or so, as both Newman and Ullathorne grew increasingly to respect, value and, eventually, to hold each other in affectionate regard.

To his confidante Mrs J. W. Bowden, Newman wrote forcefully that 'There is an old timid party among the Catholics who fear them [*The Lives of the Saints*] – and we are determined that if they are to go on, they shall go on without the carpings and criticisms of men who do, or can do, little more *than* carp... no one ever began a good work without ten thousand oppositions and trials, as the *Lives of the Saints* abundantly show'.[40]

Newman stuck like a limpet to the hard core of the criticism made of Faber's translation as 'gross, palpable idolatry'. This serious charge against a priest of his Oratory had not, he informed Wiseman, been condemned outright by his vicar-apostolic.[41] A few days later, Ullathorne conceded that 'though negative in form, the disapproval [of the reference to Faber] is very positive in substance. And the words of a Catholic Bishop, spoken publicly, in direct censure of a particular act, even mildly expressed, fall on the public ear with great weight'. He took the opportunity to state that he was 'pained to witness the acute sensitiveness which several little matters have been viewed of late... this cannot be without a hidden ingredient of self-love a most subtle spirit, and the object of the fears and combats of the humble saints of God'. After this gentle rebuke, Ullathorne expressed a hidden concern: 'I have often in my secret heart regretted that the course of events has tended [sic] to isolate the fathers of the Oratory from the body of Old Catholics in this country. I am not solitary in that feeling which is a most kind one'. He closed his lengthy personal letter by reflecting sensitively that 'I know that your lives have been lives of warfare and contest, and that you have had painfully to controvert the authorities under which you were brought up. We have not had that fierce trial. Habits still cling in hidden ways and will come back unknown to us in this poor restless nature of ours'.[42]

The next day, Ullathorne was able to send Newman 'an apology from Mr Price to Mr Faber... written at the intimation of his bishop' i.e. Wiseman.[43] This was a welcome end to the long-drawn, frustrating matter into which, once more, Newman had become involved so personally, although Dessain notes that 'Ullathorne seemed not to allow for Newman's being the Superior of a religious community, with the obligation of protecting those under him'.[44] Newman warmly thanked Fr Edward Price for his 'kind and generous letter to Mr Faber, which was most touching', and invited him to call at St Wilfrid's 'to allow us to show... the love and respect we feel for you'.[45] *The Lives of the Saints* resumed publication in January 1849.

Early in 1848 Newman had been involved in another commitment which he had found troublesome, as he recorded, idiosyncratically, in his journal: 'to please Dr Wiseman, I made the wretched throw off in London, against my will, of the Oratorian Lent-preaching 1848 at Passiontide – a blunder and failure, which even now I cannot think of without a raw sensitiveness'.[46] Few attended the sermons given by Newman and his fellow Oratorians: according to Ward 'it was a fortnight of complete failure'.[47] Newman had, in fact, told Lord Adare, who was later to become a Catholic, that 'It is a great trouble to me to preach at all, and this kind of preaching does not suit me. I can preach to people I know, but any thing like a display is quite out of my line... Others of my party will preach much better'.[48] Newman left London dejected. His next task was to be setting up an Oratory in Birmingham, which was the wish of Ullathorne, as mentioned already.

The search for suitable premises in Birmingham was under way. A disused gin distillery in Alcester Street, in a run-down working class district was discovered. Newman commented that it would suit them 'very well' as it had space sufficient for a chapel, library and living accommodation. He declared that 'We shall throw ourselves on the piety of the Catholics of Birmingham for all our expenses... [although] there is hardly a Catholic, and hardly a wealthy person'.[49] About three weeks later, Newman reported to R. A. Coffin, rector at Cotton Hall, that, 'As to the gin shop they grant us a lease for those three year but it is doubtful whether they can promise a renewal, if we want it. This is a difficulty, but I suppose not a serious one... It is magnificent, but *will take a mint of money to get into it*, at least a £200 touch'.[50] Towards the end of the year Newman asked Ullathorne to 'mark down the streets which we consider to be our boundaries'. But he pointed out that 'an Oratory in its proper idea is not a *Mission*, and ought not to have any district attached to it. Its work is simply within its own homestead for those who choose to come, whether for the sermons, for Confession, or for its Exercises; but in the *present* state of Birmingham, we wish, as I mentioned to

128

Bust of Newman by Sir Richard Westmacott, a school fellow and lifetime friend.

your Lordship, with your permission, to undertake a mission, leaving the future to take care of itself.[51]

When the matter of the renewal of the faculties of the Oratorians arose i.e., episcopal authority to fulfil specific priestly offices in a diocese or defined area, Ullathorne requested 'certain information... needed for my guidance'.[52] Newman responded at once, and confirmed that they always considered the faculties for hearing confession *within the Community* to be derived from the Bishop, but they also claimed certain exemptions in accordance with their rule and as bestowed in the Papal Brief to the English Oratorians, which privileges are enjoyed by all Oratories.[53] This information satisfied Ullathorne who declared that 'I have no other object in view simply to understand the precise relations which canonically exist between the English Oratory and the Vicar apostolic'.[54] This correspondence typifies the directness with which Ullathorne and Newman dealt with each other in setting Newman's spheres of influence. At the same time, Newman was aware of the sensitivities of the situation, as shown in a letter to Mrs Bowden, in which he states that 'there has always been a rivalry and opposition between regulars and seculars and though we are not regulars quite, and our Bishop *is* (strange to say) a regular' (Ullathorne belonged to the Benedictine Order), 'it is showing itself in the mutual intercourse of him and ourselves. However, we have so kind a patron in the Pope himself, and so strong a Brief that we are not *very* anxious – though all disputes are anxious'.[55]

On a more mundane level, Newman was able to tell Ullathorne at the end of December 1848 that 'the house in Alcester Street is at least made over to us, and we have sent whitewashers and char-women in forthwith. It is still uncertain when it will be tenable, for workmen are not very quick in their operations in an empty house'. He reminded Ullathorne that they proposed 'simply to set up an Oratory… not to undertake a Mission or formally to commit ourselves to its duties'. The three parts of an Oratorian's day were: prayer, sacraments, and preaching: 'where by prayer are meant our peculiar exercises, and by sacraments those of Holy Eucharist and Penance. Our confessionals, where there is need of it, could be open a good part of the day'.[56]

In his diary for Friday, 26th January 1849, Newman wrote, 'set off for Birmingham [Alcester Street] for good with Fr Frederic' and on the next day, 'An altar was set up for Mass'.[57] Formal opening of the new Oratory was on 2nd February, the Feast of the Purification, on which same feast-day the Oratorians had been first established in England at Maryvale in 1848. At this opening ceremony, Newman preached a sermon, *The Salvation of the Hearer the Motive of the Preacher*; this was to become Discourse I of his collection of twenty-eight *Discourses addressed to Mixed Congregations*, which was his principal publication during 1849 while he was immersed in ministering to the poor who came in hundreds to Alcester Street. Some months later he admitted that these sermons were 'more rhetorical' than his earlier ones.[58] Ian Ker considers their rhetoric to be 'often more Italianate than Newmanian', although he allows that Newman's 'characteristic genius is not altogether absent'.[59] In these sermons dedicated to Wiseman, Newman deliberately chose to speak in terms that would be intelligible and appeal to his 'mixed' congregation, largely made up of poor, working-class people. With them he shared his thoughts about the divine mysteries of the Catholic faith. According to Ffinch, 'Even Benjamin Jowett, that great bulwark of Broad Church Anglicanism, admitted that "Romanism had never been so glorified before"'.[60] Dessain observes that these sermons of

Newman's were 'much more elaborate and ornate than the Anglican sermons, and contain many passages of eloquent beauty, although there is nothing above the head of his mixed audience. They are genuine Newman, but not typical'.[61] The reception given to Newman's Birmingham sermons was certainly very different from that of those he had delivered in London the previous year. His listeners were by no means the educated upper classes – the *nobilior splendidior, doctior ordo* of the Papal Brief – but they thronged to hear Newman's 'discourses', as he preferred to call these sermons. Such activities reflect the ways in which Roman Catholicism was being spread in an industrial city by an Oxford intellectual and convert, whose natural inclinations seemed more inclined towards scholarship than a pastoral apostolate. He was not indifferent to the pressing material problems of the poor but he regarded social conditions as of less immediate hazard than the spiritual needs of the people around him. Norman states that, 'As a matter of ordinary Christian duty, of course, he offered succour to the afflicted if he could', and it is said that he used to pay the medical bills of the poor living in the neighbourhood of the Oratory.[62]

Wiseman was still wanting the Oratorians to open a House in London, but Newman reported to him in January 1849 that his brethren had unanimously agreed that 'we must set the Birmingham House well before we think of London'.[63]

Newman told Mrs Bowden that 'We are trying to put our house to rights, but what weary work that is – I have had a clearing out from Oriel, a clearing out from Littlemore – a getting in to Maryvale, a getting in and out at Rome, a getting in to St Wilfrid's, and now a getting in to Birmingham. I intend to be here for good – but what can one promise oneself?'.[64] His weariness was aggravated by Faber's complaints, including a long letter about an alleged 'gap' between the novices at Cheadle and Newman, their dislike of Ambrose St John, and Faber's impatience about the opening of a London Oratory.[65] Newman dealt patiently with the novices' perceptions, allowing that particular friendships had, apparently, existed between some of the Apostles, and suggesting that separate congregations might be the solution.[66] He agreed that 'Fr Ambrose had great influence with me, but it is in *certain* things, and I give as full influence to others in other certain things'.[67]

As Newman continued his correspondence with Faber, he put forward the proposal that some members of the Birmingham Oratory could go to London and, after five or ten years, might be constituted as a separate London House. Until then, however, they would remain members of the Birmingham Oratory and he would remain their Father Superior.[68] He rejected outright Faber's argument that the founding in Birmingham of the first English Oratory was accidental: the plan had been carefully worked out during his noviciate in Rome, 'after a minute study of the origins of the Oratory'.[69] In another letter, Newman reminded Faber that 'since mutual *carita* [sic] is the basis of St Philip's Rule, an Oratory must necessarily be of a size that would encourage the development of a family ethos' and 'We are at least too many by half for one Oratory'.[70] As Dom Placid Murray puts it, 'Newman never wavered in his preference for a small Oratory, feeling that one cannot really love (intimately) a large number of persons with the supernaturalized but still human affection traditional in the Oratory'.[71]

Newman also found it necessary to reject other misconceptions about Oratorian life. Finally Faber assured him that 'all was now plain and every one seems to understand how matters are',[72] but he was unhappy at the prospect of leaving Newman's immediate charge.

Newman even considered, briefly, the possibility of himself going to London to avoid such problems of separation.[73] But he put aside the idea of being based in London. He would have to leave his library behind and it would be 'impossible to read or write in London'. The choice lay between the 'exclusively missionary [London] and the partly theological [Birmingham]'. London was at the centre of political and cultural life where many of the upper and educated classes could be reached, whereas Birmingham was a grim manufacturing town with distinctly limited cultural interests. He was, however, also mindful of his responsibilities to the Pope for developing the Birmingham House, which was expanding despite all the problems of being virtually in a slum area. An evening school of 100 children was being run, and other missionary activities were being planned. Newman had been able to get the lease extended to fifteen years, which enabled certain alterations and repairs to be undertaken. Nevertheless, in the midst of all these activities, Newman's thoughts were never far from his Oxford days: 'It is this day 27 years that I was elected Fellow of Oriel – what a changed state of affairs I find myself in'.[74]

The decision to open a London House was taken; Newman divided the Oratory into two teams, as recorded in the Decree Book of the Birmingham Oratory for 28th May 1849.[75] Faber was to be rector of the new community; Newman was to be the overall Father Superior of the Birmingham and London Houses. Premises in King William Street (later called King William IV Street), off the Strand, in London, were obtained. Like the Birmingham House, the London one was to start in 'another gin shop' – not a distillery, however, 'but a place of entertainment'.[76] Once again, Newman was embroiled in battles with builders and also the owner of the property who was refusing to let it to the Roman Catholics on the grounds that the 'organ would be a great nuisance', and that a Roman Catholic chapel attracts the 'lower classes' and 'beggars'.[77] These difficulties were overcome and the building was made suitable for Oratorian use. It was opened on 31st May 1849, when Newman preached on *Prospects of the Catholic Mission* (Discourse XII of *Discourse to Mixed Congregations*). Faber was in his element in London society, preaching and converting all whom he could reach and persuade. Newman was anxious, however, about Faber's flamboyancy, particularly in view of his erratic behaviour at Cheadle and over the *Lives of the Saints*. Faber was a prolific and talented writer of devotional treatises and hymns, some of which achieved ready acceptance by Catholics and Protestants alike. These frequently displayed sentimentality and emotional appeals which, although influential at that time, often seem over-exuberant today. But, as Norman expresses it, 'his writings were of quite outstanding importance', redolent of Italianate poetry and particularly related to Marian devotions.[78] Faber was to receive a Doctorate of Divinity from Pope Pius IX in 1854. By this time his health, never sound, was in serious decline and led later to his extended absences from the London Oratory.

As was his custom, Newman drew up a memorandum on the 'Birmingham and London Communities' in which he recorded the pension arrangements and financial contributions to be made by the members of the two Houses.[79] This detailed attention to pecuniary matters reflects Newman's conscientious approach to all issues – spiritual and mundane alike. It may even have been imbibed from his early years when his father was a banker.

Gilley points out that Newman's mind was still preoccupied with 'the encumbrance of St Wilfrid's, which brought him into conflict with both Ullathorne and

Shrewsbury'.[80] He had to remonstrate sharply with Faber about the irresponsible attitudes that he had displayed and that had caused great offence to these leading Catholics as well as to 'old Catholics'; Newman felt that he had been left to sort out a problem that, largely, was not of his own making. Faber and the London Oratorians showed little interest and gave virtually no help to Newman in this frustrating task. After protracted negotiations, it was reluctantly agreed that the Oratorians should 'place two Fathers there i.e., at St Wilfrid's in Staffordshire, one from Birmingham, the other from London House, with the provision that each of the other Fathers should be bound to reside there as much as a month each year. Moreover, that in addition to the Mission, a College should be established there, the age of the youths received being for the present undetermined'.[81] In an earlier letter to Miss Giberne, Newman had mentioned that 'We want to form a little school of possible Oratorians there (Cheadle) but can't find the boys. Our married friends will not turn Catholic'.[82] For the time being, however, the burden of St Wilfrid's had been lessened although it was not until the summer of 1850 that 'Newman succeeded in handing over St Wilfrid's to the diocese'.[83]

On 18th January 1850, Newman listed the various responsibilities of the members of the London Oratory. These would be in force until the Feast of the Purification, 1851 'at which time, I suppose, I cease to be superior, and my authority is at an end'.[84] The position of Father Superior relates to a specific Oratory and its Congregation and, as noted earlier, Newman had fulfilled this responsibility at both establishments. On the London Oratory's achieving independence from Birmingham, Newman would then relinquish the post of Superior of both Oratories.

135

Newman's persistent financial worries were significantly reduced by a liberal endowment brought by Edward Caswall when he joined the Birmingham. He was a former Anglican clergyman who had been influenced by Newman's *Development of Doctrine*. After the death of his wife from cholera, he had studied in Rome. Following ordination as a Catholic priest and having no family, he became an Oratorian. His donated wealth enabled Newman to buy, for £1,800 in May 1850, the site in Edgbaston on which the present Oratory was built.[85]

During May 1850, Newman delivered a series of lectures at the London Oratory. These were published as *Certain Difficulties felt by Anglicans in Catholic Teaching*, and together with Sermons to *Mixed Congregations* have been described as belonging, to the 'honeymoon period of his Catholic life, having a 'tone of exultant optimism which we find at no other moment of his life either as an Anglican or as a Catholic'.[86] He had been persuaded by Wiseman to involve himself but did so with marked reluctance, not wishing to rake up old fires and possibly offend some of his old Anglican friends. At the same time, he realised that it would be extremely hard not to do so if he were to talk openly about the undeniable differences between the adherents of these faiths. He did so with devastating irony. In the end – and in Owen Chadwick's opinion to his discredit – Newman wrote the only one of his books 'which many Anglicans found it impossible to forgive'.[87] Even Newman's benign biographer, Wilfrid Ward, described the first seven lectures as the 'only instances among his writings of what might be called aggressive controversy... they are an attack... addressed to the Tractarians who remained in the Anglican Church – the friends he had left behind him'. But he added that Newman had expressly stated that it was not his wish 'to weaken the hold of the Anglican

Church on the many, but only on those who he believed ought to join the Church of Rome'.[88] Newman himself confessed that in preparing the lectures, he had never written before 'so intellectually against the grain'.[89] Dessain says that Newman always insisted that in writing these lectures 'he was not acting in direct hostility to the Anglican Church as such, but merely carrying the Oxford Movement to its legitimate conclusion'.[90]

The lectures were planned to coincide with the trial of the Reverend George Gorham, an outspoken Low Churchman who had been presented to a living by the Crown in the diocese of the High Church Bishop Henry Phillpotts of Exeter. After exhaustive enquiries, Phillpotts alleged that Gorham regarded baptism merely as a *symbol* of regeneration and refused to institute him to the living. On appeal the ecclesiastical Court of Arches' judgement against Gorham was set aside by the Judicial Committee of the Privy Council. Thus a secular court of appeal overruled a Church court: a civil court had asserted its supremacy in spiritual affairs, namely those to do with doctrine. The decision evoked considerable debate in certain quarters, and resulted in several defections from the Church of England to the Roman Catholic Church; they included H.E. Manning. The Gorham Case (1850) revealed, according to Newman, 'that Erastianism held sway in the Church of England'. Newman had followed the trial, and its outcome influenced his decision to focus in these lectures on the Oxford Movement in the hope of attracting the remaining 'Puseyites' to Roman Catholicism.[91]

In the same year, and soon after the publication of Newman's *Difficulties of Anglicans*, the newly appointed Cardinal Archbishop of Westminster – Dr Wiseman – issued a tactless pastoral letter announcing the restoration of the Catholic hierarchy. This resulted in violent

'No-Popery' agitation against what became known as the 'Papal Aggression'. Anti-Catholic feelings were fanned by *The Times, Punch*, and other journals. The latent anti-Catholicism which had last raised its head during the notorious Gordon Riots (see Chapter 1, pages 31-34 above) again became very visible, and resulted in some mob demonstrations and damage to Catholic chapels by a few fanatics. Newman was spurred to writing once more and, from the Birmingham Oratory, produced what some twenty years later he 'ever considered' to be his 'best book'.[92] In *Lectures on the Present Position of Catholics in England*, he sought to refute with energy and irony the misrepresentations of Catholicism deliberately fostered by some fanatical Protestants. In a letter to Canon Estcourt, Newman commented that 'In my lectures on Catholicism in England I oppose, not the Anglican Church, but National Protestantism, and Anglicans only so far as they belong to it'.[93] Throughout his life, Newman never lost affection for the Anglican Church, but he maintained that these lectures were aimed at 'the misconceptions concerning Catholicism which generally occupy the English mind'.[94]

The nine lectures which constitute *The Present Position of Catholics in England* were delivered at the Corn Exchange in High Street, Birmingham, to packed audiences in 1851, a year in which the Ecclesiastical Titles Bill was passed to reimpose prohibitions on the use of ecclesiastical territorial titles by Roman Catholic bishops which duplicated those used by the established Church (see Chapter 1, page 29). Each lecture was printed and made available in the week following its delivery. Chadwick puts it that in his lectures Newman 'intended to expose the more ludicrous and revolting forms of anti-popish prejudice. He mocked the number of the Beast, and John Bullism, and tried to expose "Maria Monk" and the ex-priest Achilli'.[95] The last of these targets, however, resulted in Newman being involved in a long and unpleasant libel action, which was brought about by Achilli with the support of the Evangelical Alliance (see Chapter 6).

Newman's Birmingham lectures were not solely for the purpose of dismissing popular myths about Catholicism; he also called his Catholic listeners to accept that they had a duty to live their lives in such a way that their Protestant critics would see with their own eyes what Catholicism really meant. He stressed the importance of the laity, i.e., themselves, in becoming well informed about their religion so that they, in turn, would be able to give insights to enquirers about the nature and practices of their faith. He declared that 'Catholics ought to know Catholicism better than other men'.[96] In these lectures Newman deplored that 'more use was not made of married converts, like clergymen, who, I have said and truly, viewed together have an amount of talent, which the unmarried clergy converted have not'. He went on to suggest to J. Spencer Northcote, an old Oxford friend and Catholic convert, that 'One most interesting series of lectures would be, if every one of you gave his *own* ground of conversion' and he reminded him that 'many of the early apologists were lay men'.[97] Dessain notes that one of the weaknesses of the Church was its clericalisation and the consequent inferior position of the laity, and claims that Newman was 'keenly aware that the Church was not merely the clergy but all who had received the Holy Spirit'.[98] Newman, in fact, formally 'addressed' the Corn Exchange lectures, when they were published, to the 'Brothers of the Oratory' who were a confraternity of laymen attached to an Oratory. He viewed the *Orat. Parv.* (Little Oratory) as 'more important than anything else', for without it the Oratory itself 'would have failed'.[99]

Newman had distinct reservations about the need at that time for the restoration of the Catholic hierarchy. He stated that 'We want seminaries far more than sees. We want education, *view*, combination, organisation'. There should be a concerted effort to encourage young Catholics to band together to go out and tell the people about their faith, and to start up journals for this purpose'.[100]

In a further letter to the editor of the *Rambler*, Newman expressed his support of his activities in organising lectures in London and other cities, given by laymen in defence of Catholicism.[101] However, a few weeks later one such layman, J.M. Capes, was warned by Newman that 'our bishop [Ullathorne] is a cautious man' and he doubted whether Capes' lectures would be liked by Ullathorne 'in his heart'.[102] The bishop had a strong aversion to laymen involving themselves in some kind of 'lay preaching'. Capes was advised to avoid misapprehensions of his activities; he should make clear that there was no intention that these lay efforts should be regarded as preaching with authority, which remained the exclusive province of priests. But Newman reassured Capes that 'I am sure that they [laymen] may be made in this day the strength of the Church'.[103]

In the summer of 1850 Newman declined an invitation from Archbishop Cullen to preach at the dedication of a church in his diocese of Armagh, pointing out that the Fathers of the Oratory 'do not commonly preach out of their own church, and the Father Superior in particular does not quit the town where he is situated during the period of his office'. He likewise declined requests from other prelates and religious organisations.[104] In his journal, Newman records that 'I first knew Dr Cullen at Rome in 1847, when he was very civil to me... When the University was to be founded for Catholics in Ireland, he wrote to consult me on this subject'.[105] (In the next chapter, extended discussion of Cullen's negotiations with Newman over the University occurs.)

Ullathorne sent Newman the Rescripts by which Pius IX had conferred on him a Doctorate of Divinity; Newman acknowledged them with a 'hasty line' expressing his 'extreme gratification'. He was already attracting admiration in Rome through his responses to the Gorham affair.[106] It was, therefore, perceptive of Ullathorne to choose Newman to give the sermon in St Chad's Cathedral on the occasion of his, Ullathorne's, installation as the first Bishop of Birmingham, for Newman was (and remained), as Norman observes 'an isolated figure, yet always at the centre of men's perception of English Catholicism but at the periphery of the institutional Church'.[107]

According to Ian Ker, Newman's celebrated sermon *Christ upon the Waters*, delivered on 27th October 1850, 'contained all the elements of his satirical genius, not least the kind of imagery typical of this period of his writings'.[108] Newman pilloried the materialism of a provincial society which had no sense of moral purpose and had shown disregard of moral values. In flowing phrases he glorified the regeneration of the Roman Catholic Church in England, 'coming out of prison as collected in her teaching, as precise in her action, as when she went into it… she seeks, she desires no temporal power, no secular station; she meddles not with Caesar; she obeys him in his place, but she is independent of him. Her strength is in her God; her rule is over the souls of men; her glory is in their willing subjection and loving loyalty'.[109] Of course *The Times* and other publications took up their customary carping attitude towards Catholic events, and Newman's rhetoric was picked at gleefully. It was even said publicly that he deserved to be 'kicked out' of the country – for which offensiveness an apology was later made.[110] Newman told Philip Howard, a Catholic MP, who reported a speech by the Reverend A.C. Tait, Dean of Carlisle (formerly one of the Tutors who had denounced *Tract 90*), and who now denounced his sermon *Christ upon the Waters*, that for seventeen years he had been the subject of so much daily misrepresentation, in the public prints and at public meetings, that 'I never think at all about whatever is said against me in the one or at the other'.[111]

When, as noted already, a site in Edgbaston had been bought through Fr Edward Caswall's generosity, it was decided in May 1850 to build a house for the community and to collect funds for the erection of a church. (Early in the 20th century, a widespread appeal would be made to build the present Oratory church as a memorial to Newman.) The Oratorians then vacated Alcester Street and moved to their new home in Hagley Road, Edgbaston, on Low Sunday 1852.[112]

Apart from being preoccupied with appealing for funds and in writing lectures and sermons, Newman had continuous worries about London Oratory, and particularly about their joint responsibilities for the mission at St Wilfrid's, Cheadle. In a long letter to Faber he 'unburdened' himself and urged him to 'put his shoulder to the wheel' and to provide 'some plan' to clarify the position.[113] Faber's response was not helpful: 'I have relinquished the task as hopeless... As to what we are to do now, I cannot at all see; and as superior we must look to you to propose something'.[114] Newman was thus left to negotiate with the Earl of Shrewsbury to find an acceptable solution.[115] After protracted discussions, which also involved the Redemptorists, the Passionists eventually took over St Wilfrid's from the Oratorians.[116]

This tedious business being settled at last, Newman gave his attention once more to the relative positions of the two Oratorians. He told Faber that he was 'decided on their separation... it was impossible to be a non-resident Superior, or to govern an absent House'. He also dismissed rumours that he would be made a bishop: 'no one can seriously wish it, who is loyal to St Philip; and there are no limits to which I would go to prevent it'.[117] Matters now moved quickly to a head and on 9th October 1850 a Decree was issued formally setting up a London Congregation of the Oratory.[118] On 12th October, Faber was elected the first independent Superior of the London Oratory.[119]

These events had virtually coincided with the restoration of the Catholic hierarchy, and Newman felt worried about possible repercussions in society at large. According to Trevor, 'the London Oratorians were in the thick of it... Birmingham too was not without its excitements'.[120]

As already noted, there were marked differences in personality and temperament between Newman and Faber. The result was a degree of incompatibility that led to mutual frustration and misunderstanding. The separation of the two houses resulted in these differences being reflected in the ways in which their communities developed and reacted to one another. Faber tended to be erratic and unreliable; Newman was cautious and disciplined, yet in his scholarly approach he was also capable of challenging beliefs and behaviour if an issue of importance sufficiently aroused him. Both men tended to suffer bouts of illness. Newman, apart from his near fatal illness in Sicily during 1833, was particularly prone to colds and toothache, although he must presumably have had a remarkably strong constitution, since, until a venerable age, he kept up an exacting routine. Faber, on the other hand, suffered at a relatively early age from a degenerative disease that brought on his early death at the age of 49 years. Nevertheless, despite their psychological and physiological differences, the two men also displayed from time to time fraternal feelings of touching concern for one another. These spasmodic occasions seemed, however, insufficient to temper their habitual reactions to each other.

Faber's failing health and extended periods of convalescence and Newman's prolonged absences in Dublin during the time he was connected with the Catholic university, also contributed to some degree of instability within their communities.

In October 1850 when the London House formally became independent of the Birmingham House, Faber had proposed that Newman should keep up some measure of supervision over them. Newman declined this proposal but did agree that he should be consulted on important matters for a period of three years. Both Houses had become well-established by 1855; the Birmingham House had moved in 1852 from a slum area of the city to the attractive environment of Edgbaston, and the following year the London House migrated from their insalubrious building off the Strand to fashionable Brompton.

Relationships between the Houses reached a crisis point in 1855 when the London Oratory applied to Rome for relaxation from the Oratorian Rule that forbade the hearing of nuns' confessions. This prohibition dated back to the time of the founder, St Philip Neri, who considered that Oratorians should not be diverted from their principal duties by undertaking the spiritual direction of nuns. When Newman had made certain modifications to St Philip's Rule so that an Oratory could be effective in the conditions of Victorian England, he had retained the original ban on Oratorians becoming involved in giving spiritual direction to nuns.

The origins of the problem in 1855 arose from a

request by Wiseman to the London Oratorians to take charge of the spiritual care and direction of nuns. After doing this for some time, they decided to ask Rome 'for an interpretation or suspension of the particular rule which forbade it'.[121] This was done by Faber without consulting Newman. The Congregation of Propaganda in Rome assumed that Newman would have been consulted and, after conferring with the bishops in Birmingham and London, prepared to issue the necessary dispensation. Newman first became aware of this matter when Ullathorne told him that he was glad to hear 'a rescript from Rome was coming to dispense them [the Oratorians] from this provision of the Rule: Dalgairns [at Birmingham Oratory] had undertaken similar work for the nuns at Stone, which they had felt some qualms about, but which the bishop encouraged'.[122] In his journal Newman noted, perhaps a little unfairly, that 'All that sad quarrel with the London House was owing to Fr Dalgairns thinking he might do what he pleased in my absence'.[123] Newman and the Birmingham community were deeply shocked to discover that London, unilaterally, had decided to seek Rome's permission to change the Rule without the knowledge or consent of the other English House. The special nature of the Oratorian vocation was governed by their Rule; independent attempts to alter it threatened the whole way of life by which they had chosen to serve God. In their judgement, the London Oratorians' action was not merely a matter of legalistic niceties: it had profoundly disturbing implications which could strike at the heart of Oratorianism.

From Dublin Newman wrote to Ambrose St John as Father Rector. He set out at considerable length the problems arising from London's independent action. He warned the Birmingham community that 'If one part of our Rule is suspended, while we sleep, so may another.

We may wake in the morning, and find that the Fathers at Brompton have demanded a virtually *new* Rule, and impose it, through Propaganda, upon us'.[124]

Newman decided that he should visit Rome and present personally to Propaganda his concerns about the misunderstandings that had arisen as a result of Faber's arbitrary action. In a diary entry for 26th December 1855, he records that Ambrose St John and himself 'set off for Rome'. He told Mrs Bowden that, as he passed through London, he would 'tell the Cardinal' who 'is prepared for some one of the Birmingham House going to Rome – but not me'.[125] In fact, Newman sent a letter, dated 27th December, to Wiseman to inform him of his visit and plans to 'lay before Mgr Barnabo and others the real state of the difficulty about the Oratory, which will be greater, I am sure, as time goes on'. He also requested Wiseman's opinion of two resolutions which he had sent to him earlier: namely, that any decision by Propaganda for one House should apply solely to that one; and that any request to come for an interpretation of the Rule should be submitted to other Houses for their opinion.[126] Newman's statement thus indicated that his aim was to preserve the future independence of his own House, not to oppose the granting of permissions to London Oratory.[127]

Newman's letter was immediately sent to Faber by Wiseman, who explained that he had received a letter from Cardinal Fransoni intimating that Propaganda 'could not imagine' that Faber had not consulted Newman before making his original application. The London Oratory at once circulated the Italian Oratories and also Propaganda, giving their account of the breach with Newman, and accusing him of wanting to exercise a '*generalate* over the whole Congregation'.[128]

On 12th January 1856, Newman and Ambrose St John arrived in Rome. On the way they had had discussions with various Oratories, among which were Verona, Turin and Florence, about their respective ways of observing the Rule of St Philip Neri, particularly as related to the spiritual direction of nuns. In an interview with Mgr Barnabo on 17th January Newman thought he 'seemed defensive', appeared to have 'some idea or other of me, which we could not get to the bottom of'. But Newman added that 'a long interview with the Pope was most satisfactory'.[129]

Newman and Ambrose St John had a long and most satisfactory interview with the Pope on 25th January. According to Newman, 'He wished to *hear our side*, having heard the other. I suppose he got part of his information from the Bishop [Ullathorne], but the greater part came from the London House... Then he went on to speak *in extenso* of various things, as if to put us on our ease'. After some time, Newman stated, the Pope referred to the letter from the London House, and St John gave a clear account of the trouble which had arisen because London had made an application for a faculty to hear the confessions of nuns without Birmingham's knowledge which, if granted, 'would make the Oratory seem to be one order'. A few days later, Barnabo recommended to Newman not to pursue his official supplication that 'nothing done by the Holy See by one Oratory might affect another... because the grant of it would *diminish* my power, inasmuch as I was *Deputato Apostolico* for setting up the Oratory in any part of England. (He said that our brief was to be extended by Rescript to Ireland, where I suppose I should have the same office.)' Newman confessed that he was puzzled by Barnabo's information and could only suppose that 'Propaganda overrides Canon Law'; it seems, he thought, 'that, in setting up a House, I may make *conditions*, if not inconsistent with the Brief and Rule. And this seems to be Barnabo's meaning...

that for the Pope to rule any thing about the existing independent *action* of Oratories, is to limit my existing powers'.[130]

Trevor suggests that the original Brief Newman had been given by the Pope conferred on him powers greater than he had realised.[131] This opinion presumably rests on the fact that Newman, as noted, had the status of *Deputato Apostolico*. Birmingham would not, therefore, be compelled to follow London's lead in the matter in question. This was reassuring and some reward to Newman and his loyal community. Partial success was better than downright failure; but it did little to reduce the friction between the two Houses.

Newman now thought the time was right to recapitulate the essential nature of an Oratory and the Oratorian vocation. He did so in seven letters written from Dublin to Birmingham in March 1856. They were later published as *Remarks on the Oration Vocation.*[132] Each of these seven letters focuses on one particular point and the argument is then taken forward through the succeeding letters as follows: Letter I: The Oratory is not a religious body, and yet is like one; its members aim at perfection, yet at a perfection different in its circumstances and peculiarities from that of regulars; Letter II: Certain qualifications attaching historically to Fathers of the Oratory, by which they are distinguished from ordinary secular priests, that is, the breeding of a gentleman, the mental elevation and culture which learning gives, the accomplishments of literature, the fine arts and similar studies; Letter III: The literary qualifications and liberal knowledge traditional in the Italian Oratory; Letter IV; Various characteristics of a Father of the Oratory, both in how he differs from the ordinary run of secular priests, and how he differs from the type of a regular; various counsels (of perfection) he does not pursue; Letter V:

The precise instrument of Oratorian perfection, is that he is 'a secular priest'; but not only so, but a secular priest 'living in community'; Letter VI: The duty of obedience to the Rule; Letter VII: Obedience to the Superiors. According to Murray, 'The kernel of the whole matter is Letter V on community living as the precise instrument of Oratorian perfection'.[133]

Newman's afflictions were added to by a rather tactless letter from Wiseman in June 1856 saying that he proposed to write a dedication to Newman and Faber jointly in his 'poor panegyric of St Philip' that was to be published under the auspices of the London Oratory. Newman responded that he 'rejoiced to hear' about the publication, and would accept the honour of a dedication provided that 'his name was included with those of the Birmingham Fathers'.[134] Wiseman showed Newman's letter to Faber, and through him to various persons, and commented on it 'in most disrespectful terms… and, without a word of explanation to me, immediately proceeded to publish the Dedication to Fr Faber and myself'.[135] Some time earlier, Newman had commented to his old friend, Henry Wilberforce that 'The Cardinal has a thousand good points, but you must never *trust* him'.[136]

In June 1856 Newman wrote from Dublin to his community in Birmingham a lengthy and formal account of the 'painful controversy' which had been taking place with the London Oratory. He ended his letter by admonishing his brethren that in dealing with those of the London Oratory they should 'be kind to them individually; pray for the welfare of their Congregation; but keep clear of them. St Philip is not the Saint of far-spreading associations; but of isolated bodies, working severally in their own spheres'.[137]

Throughout 1856, correspondence flowed between Newman and Faber on the highly sensitive issue of

London's independent application to Rome, which had caused Newman so much concern because of the implications that it seemed to him to have for the Oratorian vocation itself. Perceptions clearly differed considerably regarding the seriousness of the alleged breach of the founding Brief which Newman had drawn up from St Philip Neri's Rule and amended to fit conditions in England. Faber's letters show an almost over-eager willingness to seek forgiveness for anything done to cause so much distress to Newman. But at the same time, Faber seemed to lack – or deliberately avoid – any understanding of the real issue involved.[138] Newman 'professed very great satisfaction' in hearing from Faber again, and regretted to learn of 'his continued indisposition'. Sadly, the gap between them seemed unbridgeable; also, Faber, on his admission, was still far from well.[139]

Further correspondence resulted in apparent frustration on both sides. Newman declared that if it was to go on, he would recognise no one but the Secretary of the Congregation as the person to write to about the matter in question.[140] Yet another letter of deep regret and profuse apology came from London, signed formally by the Provost (Faber) and the Secretary.[141]

In a lengthy and formal reply, Newman reiterated that 'Our Rule is our Vocation… To touch a Rule is to unsettle vocations'. Any attempt to meddle with the Rule 'by some of its members' which is 'unknown to the rest', stirs 'deeply a religious body'. London without consultation, had applied to Rome for 'an interpretation of a Decree' and when he had expostulated, they had put 'aside his expostulation'. He had felt sure that they would now realise they had caused him 'the deepest pain'. He stated that 'the substance of his complaint remains', and so far, 'they had done nothing to remedy matters'.[142]

Newman's concerns about London's unilateral

application to Rome were again expressed in two more letters to Faber.[143] A formal letter from London Oratory indicated that they did not regard their application to Rome in 'the serious light you do'. They trusted that 'no fresh act of their Congregation would ever suggest that they were unmindful of their obligations owed to Newman and his relationship as founder of their House'.[144] The next letter Newman sent to Faber – from Dublin – was a cordial invitation for him to 'take our University Sermon on Sunday, 20th July'. Faber at first accepted this, but then declined.[145]

Newman then sent to Wiseman 'as a melancholy memorial of the past', a detailed account of the correspondence which had passed between the two Houses. In it he referred to 'Three Propositions', the agreed basis on which the London House should be constituted.[146] A copy of this letter was also sent to the London Congregation and it was circulated to the Birmingham Congregation.

Fr Bernard Dalgairns, who had caused Newman considerable annoyance during this troublesome period, had decided to leave the Birmingham Oratory. This was recorded in the Decree Book on 2nd September 1856: 'Fr Bernard Dalgairns, having written to the Father to say that he has not the spirit of the Oratory, and therefore no Vocation for it, and that he asks in consequence to be released from his allegiance to us, is pronounced to be no longer one of our members'.[147] Fr Dalgairns then rejoined the London Oratory.

Gilley reports that feelings between the two Oratories had been further aggravated in 1856 when London requested Rome for a separate Brief and the Pope demanded that Newman should be consulted; but Barnabo, now Cardinal Prefect of Propaganda, stated that Newman himself had suggested separate Briefs for the two Houses and that he had written to Rome in support of London's application.[148]

In Newman's judgement 'the harm done to him by the London Oratory letter to Propaganda was lasting',[149] and his reputation in England was damaged by the unedifying quarrel. Committing his innermost thoughts to paper, he wrote in his journal that 'First in 1853, came my mistake in asking for Dalgairns from the London House; then my going to Ireland, in order to impinge upon Dr Cullen, while Dalgairns intrigued at home in my absence. Then the great plot of him, Faber, etc., – my going to Rome – and the treatment I met at Propaganda. Then the thousand whisperings against me at the London Oratory, which have succeeded in prejudicing the Catholic body to a great extent against me… all sorts of suspicions and calumnies have attended my name'.[150]

On Faber's death in September 1863, Newman assisted at his Requiem at London Oratory. From correspondence it is evident that Newman's memories of the problems he had with Faber and the London Oratory rankled. 'I know no more about them [London Oratory] than you do, nor am likely. They absolutely and intentionally threw me off eight years ago just'.[151]

NOTES

1 *LD* XII. 19-20, 19 January 1847.
2 *LD* XII.114, Mrs J. W. Bowden, 15 September 1847.
3 Ward, 1913, p.199.
4 Dessain, 1980, p.93.
5 *LD* XII.140, 31 December 1847).
6 *LD* XII.143, 2 January 1848.
7 *LD* XII.144, January 1848.
8 *LD* XII.145.
9 *LD* XII.148, 11 January 1848.
10 Trevor, 1996, p.117.

11 *LD* XII.243, 12 July 1848.
12 *LD* XI.105, 1 February 1846.
13 *LD* XII.66, 31 March 1847.
14 *LD* XII.137.
15 *LD* XII.140, 31 December 1847.
16 *LD* XII.197, 2 April 1848.
17 Cf Norman, 1985, p.317.
18 Murray, 1980, p.95.
19 Trevor, 1996, p.120.
20 *LD* XII.162 *footnote*.
21 *LD* XII.162-3, 26 January 1848.
22 *LD* XII.162, 26 January 1848.
23 contract *LD* XII.184-5, 17 March 1848.
24 *LD* XII.169, 11 February 1848.
25 *LD* XII.172, 25 February 1848.
26 *LD* XII.184-5, 17 March 1848.
27 *LD* XII.264 *footnote*.
28 *LD* XII.275 *footnote*.
29 *LD* XII.75, Michaelmas Day 1848.
30 Dessain, 1980, p.92; also see Chapter 3 of the present work, page 56.
31 *LD* XII.278, 4 October 1848.
32 *LD* XII.278 *footnote*.
33 *LD* XII.284-5, 10 October 1848.
34 *LD* XII.297, 14 October 1848.
35 *LD* XII.314, 28 October 1848.
36 *LD* XII.316, 30 October 1848.
37 *LD* XII.302, R. A. Coffin, 22 October 1848.
38 *LD* XII.319, Bishop Ullathorne, 2 November 1848.
39 *LD* XII.320, 3 November 1848.
40 *LD* XII.345, 24 November 1848.
41 *LD* XII.349, Bishop Wiseman, 26 November 1848.
42 *LD* XII.352-3, 29 November 1848.
43 *LD* XII.360, 30 November 1848.
44 *LD* XII.353 *footnote*.
45 *LD* XII.362, 3 December 1849.
46 Newman, 1956, p.256.
47 Ward, 1913, p.205.
48 *LD* XII.198, 6 April 1848.
49 *LD* XII.279-80, Mrs J. W. Bowden, 5 October 1848.
50 *LD* XIII.302, 22 October 1848.
51 *LD* XII.362-3, 3 December 1848.
52 *LD* XII.368 *footnote*, 8 December 1848.
53 *LD* XII.368-70, 9 & 13 December 1848.
54 *LD* XII.369-70, 10 December 1848.
55 *LD* XII.374, Mrs J. W. Bowden, 17 December 1848.
56 *LD* XII.383, 30 December 1848.
57 *LD* XIII.16.
58 *LD* XIII.335, F. W. Faber, 9 December 1949.
59 Ker, 1990, pp.342-3.

60 Ffinch, 1992, p.164.
61 Dessain, 1980, p.94.
62 Norman, 1985, p.317.
63 *LD* XIII.48-49, 15 January 1849.
64 *LD* XIII.44, 13 February 1849.
65 *LD* XIII.29-30, 5 February 1849.
66 *LD* XIII.30, F. W. Faber, 7 February 1949.
67 *LD* XIII.34, F. W. Faber, 9 January 1849.
68 *LD* XIII.44, F.W. Faber, 13 February 1849.
69 *LD* XIII.57 Dessain *footnote*.
70 *LD* XIII.54-7, F.W. Faber, 17 February 1849.
71 Murray, 1980, p.118.
72 *LD* XIII.76 *footnote*.
73 *LD* XIII.76 *footnote*.
74 *LD* XIII.108. Mrs J.W. Bowden, 12 April 1849.
75 Murray, 1980, p.455.
76 Trevor, 1996, p.124.
77 *LD* XIII.124 5, Faber, *footnote*.
78 Norman, 1986, p.234.
79 *LD* XIII.165-7, 31 May 1849.
80 Gilley, 1990, p.260.
81 Decree Book of the Birmingham Oratory, 13 January 1850; Murray, 1980, p.456.
82 *LD* XIII.238, 23 July 1849.
83 Trevor, 1996, p.130.
84 *LD* XIII.390, F.W. Faber, 18 January 1850.
85 *LD* XIII.439, Dessain *footnote*.
86 Ward, 1913, p.231.
87 Chadwick, 1971, p.289.
88 Ward, 1913, pp.232-3.
89 *LD* XIII.470, F.W. Faber, 2 May 1850.
90 Dessain, 1980, p.97.
91 *LD* XIII.453, F.W. Faber, 31 March 1850.
92 *LD* XXVI.115, R.W. Church, 16 June 1872.
93 *LD* XIX.360, 10 June 1860.
94 Preface to *Lectures*, p.x.
95 Chadwick, 1971, p.306.
96 *Present Position of Catholics*, p.329.
97 *LD* XIV.99, 10 October 1850.
98 Dessain, 1980, pp.100-101.
99 *LD* XIV.274, Richard Stanton, 3 May 1851.
100 *LD* XIV.213, J.M. Capes, 18 February 1851.
101 *LD* XIV.216-18, J.M. Capes, 21 February 1851.
102 *LD* XIV.236, J.M. Capes, 12 March 1851.
103 *LD* XIV.250-52, J.M. Capes, 10 April 1851.
104 *LD* XIV.4, Archbishop Cullen, 7 July 1850.
105 Newman, 1956, p.280.
106 *LD* XIV.32, Bishop Ullathorne, 6 August 1850.
107 Norman, 1986, p.313.

108 Ker, 1990, p.360.
109 Newman, 1874, p.137.
110 Gilley, 1996, pp.265-6.
111 *LD* XIV.140, 24 November 1850.
112 *LD* XIV.13, Dessain *footnote*.
113 *LD* XIV.17-21, 22 July 1850.
114 *LD* XIV.21, 27 July 1850.
115 Cf. *LD* XIV.22, Mrs J.W. Bowden, 29 July 1850.
116 *LD* XIV.305, Dessain *footnote*.
117 *LD* XIV.76, F.W. Faber, 22 September 1850.
118 Murray, 1980, p.457.
119 *LD* XIV.102, Dessain *footnote*.
120 Trevor, 1996, p.132.
121 *LD* XVII. xiii, Dessain, *footnote*.
122 Trevor, 1996, p.157.
123 Newman, 1956, p.329.
124 *LD* XVII.440-51, 9 November 1853.
125 *LD* XVII.100, 23 December 1855.
126 *LD* XVII.103, Cardinal Wiseman, 27 December 1855.
127 *LD* XV.xiv, Dessain.
128 *LD* XVII.103 Dessain *footnote*.
129 *LD* XVII.128-30, Edward Caswall, 20 January 1856.
130 *LD* XVII.135-8, Edward Caswall, 25 January 1856.
131 Trevor, 1996, p.160.
132 Murray, 1980, pp. 298-346; Newman's Oratory Papers 24 & 25.
133 Murray, 1980, p.145.
134 *LD* XVII.255, Cardinal Wiseman, 7 June 1856.
135 *LD* XIX.100-101, Robert Monteith, 5 April 1859.
136 *LD* XVIII.49, 27 May 1857.
137 *LD* XVII.266-70, 14 June 1856.
138 *LD* XVII.234, *from* Faber, 8 May 1856.
139 *LD* XIV.235-6, F.W. Faber 1856, 9 May 1856; *LD* XIV.293-40, *from* Faber,
     10 May 1856.
140 *LD* XVII.241, F.W. Faber, 13 May 1856.
141 *LD* XVII.246-7 from F.W. Faber & Richard Stanton, 22 May 1856.
142 *LD* XVII.248-9, Richard Stanton, 27 May 1856.
143 *LD* XVII.250, 31 May 1856; *LD* XVII.252, 3 June 1856.
144 *LD* XVII.254, *from* F.W. Faber & Richard Stanton, 5 June 1856.
145 *LD* XVII.257, *from* Faber, 9 June 1856.
146 *LD* XVII.259, 10 June 1856.
147 Murray, 1980, p.462.
148 Cf Gilley, 1990, p.287.
149 *LD* XVII.135, Dessain *footnote*.
150 Newman, 1956, p.256.
151 *LD* XX.530 Miss M.R. Giberne, St Michael's Day 1863.

5

Newman:
Intellectual Excellence

THE history of the university in Ireland up to the middle of the 19th century has the 'merit of simplicity'. Only one university existed – the University of Dublin with its sole college that of Trinity College (TCD).[1] This ancient institution, founded in 1591 during the closing years of Elizabeth I's reign, had imposed religious tests on students and staff from 1637 – Charles I's reign – which excluded Roman Catholics and Protestant Dissenters from membership of the college. Only practising members of the established Church, who had sworn to uphold its supremacy, and had also taken oaths against fundamental Roman Catholic beliefs such as Transubstantiation, were admitted. This discrimination was theoretically eased by the Catholic Relief Act of 1793, by which Catholics were to have right of entry to any college of the University of Dublin which might be founded thereafter. More practical benefit was given by a Royal Letter of 1794 which partially abolished religious tests at TCD, although Roman Catholics were barred from scholarships or fellowships. 'A mere handful of the vast Catholic majority in the country availed themselves of the partial concession.'[2] However, the general ethos of TCD was 'deemed to be inimical and hostile to the Catholic faith'.[3]

For two and a half centuries, the only university in Ireland had, therefore, been virtually closed to the majority of its inhabitants, although many, admittedly, would not have been academically acceptable and others would have lacked aspirations of this kind. But it was clearly a source of substantial irritation to more liberally-minded politicians and other leaders of society that Roman Catholics and Protestant Dissenters had, for generations, suffered from lack of equality with those of a minority, although established, Church in matters of higher education.

Following a conciliatory policy and to counter O'Connell's political agitation, Sir Robert Peel, in the spring of 1845, increased the grant to Maynooth Seminary and proposed the establishment of a non-sectarian system of higher education in Ireland, based on the Queen's Colleges in Belfast, Cork and Galway for those Roman Catholics and Protestant Dissenters who were unable or unwilling to attend TCD, where some degree of religious intolerance was still apparent. 'No religious tests were to be imposed either at entrance or admission to degrees, no religious instruction was to be given except what might be provided by the various religious bodies at their own expense, no religious topics were to be introduced into the classrooms, and no religious considerations were to weigh in the appointment or dismissal of officials'.[4]

The explicitly secular and non-denominational nature of Peel's university proposals immediately aroused suspicions and downright hostility from the Roman Catholic bishops as well as leading politicians. Sir Robert Inglis, for example, anathematised the system as 'a gigantic scheme of godless education' and the epithet 'Godless Colleges' was popularly applied to the Queen's Colleges where so-called 'mixed education' was to be introduced into Ireland on 31st July 1845. ('Mixed education' referred to the mingling of pupils of various faiths, which was unusual in Ireland at that time.)

In England, non-sectarian higher education had become available in 1835, when London University received its charter. This secular institution, although distasteful to some Roman Catholics, conferred benefits to some Catholic schools and colleges, such as Ushaw, Stonyhurst, Oscott and St Edmunds, who sought affiliation and modified their curricula to make them compatible with the new, non-residential, degree courses. Apart from a few Catholics who had attended Oxford and Cambridge universities in the early part of the 19th century, and a small number who had entered TCD from the 18th century onwards, degree-level education had not generally been available to Roman Catholics.[5] Although the University Tests Act of 1871 opened up Oxford, Cambridge and Durham universities generally to men of any or no religion, Roman Catholic bishops, as a body, refused to permit Catholics to attend, although the prohibition tended to be disregarded by many upper-class Catholics. Catholic bishops – apart from the converts Manning, Coffin and Brownlow, who were Oxbridge graduates – had no direct experience of the ancient universities and so they 'feared what they imagined'. This lack of knowledge was even more pronounced at Propaganda in Rome.[6]

In Ireland the Roman Catholic hierarchy were not of one mind on the radical innovation on 'mixed education'. While some bishops vehemently opposed the concept of the Queen's Colleges, which were opened in 1849 at Belfast, Cork and Galway, a minority led by Archbishop Daniel Murray of Dublin and also the Primate, Dr Crolly, were prepared to give their support and see how the novel system worked out. At least it provided access for Roman Catholics to university education. But the majority, headed by the adamantine Dr MacHale of Tuam, rejected it outright, and urged the Pope 'to take action against the Colleges'.[7] A Papal Rescript in October 1847 instructed the bishops to take no part in the colleges. Although this decision was not regarded as final, a second Rescript, in October 1848, confirmed the ban on co-operation. It is of particular interest to note that in this document 'occurred the first reference to the project of founding a Catholic University in Ireland'.[8] The Papal pronouncements did not, however, inhibit the Government from going ahead with the Queen's Colleges scheme.

In April, 1849, Dr Crolly died and, after rejecting three names submitted by the Irish hierarchy, Rome appointed as his successor Dr Paul Cullen, rector of the Irish College in Rome. As young ecclesiastical students in Rome, Cullen and Wiseman had met, and, some years later, were to be given the responsibility of leading the hierarchy and imposing Ultramontane disciplines respectively in Ireland and in England. Cullen was influential in Rome, where he had lived since the age of 17 years. Newman records that he first knew him at Rome in 1847 'when he was very civil to me, and took the trouble of being the official theological censor of my four Latin dissertations then and there published'.[9] Over the next few years, Newman was to become more deeply involved with this subtle prelate. Cullen was consecrated Archbishop of Armagh in February 1850, and came to Ireland with the added authority of Apostolic Delegate. One of his first tasks was to convoke and preside over the Synod of Thurles – the first national synod in Ireland since 1642. At it the bishops, following the Papal Rescripts, duly condemned the Queen's Colleges. A minority of them petitioned Rome for further discussion of the matter, but Pius IX replied firmly that the question had been settled. Cullen issued a pastoral letter on 9th September 1850; this was adopted by all the hierarchy. Cullen had thus stamped his authoritative leadership on the Irish Church very soon after assuming his new responsibilities, which included setting up a Catholic University Committee of four archbishops and four bishops, to consider how the recommendations of the second Papal Rescript, mentioned earlier, should be made effective.

There was, as Owen Chadwick comments, 'no theoretical absurdity in attempting to create a Roman Catholic university'. Such universities existed in Catholic countries, as at Louvain in Belgium, and they could also exist elsewhere where there was religious toleration. Admittedly, for such institutions to become 'reputable rivals of the ancient universities' adequate funding was vital.[10] But, as will be seen later, the concept of a Catholic university in Ireland, based on the Louvain model, was to be fraught with difficulties at almost every stage of its short life.

Meanwhile, Peel's ambitious – and well-meaning – scheme to open up opportunities of higher education for those who felt that TCD was an inhospitable environment, was severely affected by the decisions of the Holy See and of the Irish hierarchy. Further, the lack of an adequate secondary education system in Ireland meant that comparatively few pupils were able to attain university entry standards. These two factors resulted in a bleak existence for the Queen's Colleges during their first decade.[11] According to Wilfrid Ward, the new 'secularist education' was viewed suspiciously by the Irish hierarchy because of its results in England, as well as the fact that 'in countries like France and Belgium the undenominational universities were avowedly free thinking'. He adds that their fears were shared by 'some of the ablest and most religious men in the Church of England'.[12]

To achieve the foundation of a Catholic University in Ireland, Cullen recognised that it was imperative to have someone of acknowledged intellectual eminence to head it, and for some time he had his eye on Newman. On 15th April 1851, he wrote to Newman telling him that the collection of funds for establishing a Catholic University had been very successful and that the next step would be to 'select a fit and proper superior'. Newman's advice was sought about this appointment and also those of a vice-president and professors. Cullen invited him to attend a meeting of the University Committee in Dublin. Further, if Newman could give 'a few lectures on education', he would be rendering good service to religion in Ireland'.[13]

Newman responded that 'there is nothing at all which I can feel more interest in than the subject of Irish education'– but he excused himself from accepting Cullen's invitation to visit Dublin. He referred to 'one difficulty' in staffing the proposed University: 'that leading men must necessarily be priests... and England... has none to spare'. He suggested, however, that chairs in classics, history, and maths need not be reserved to clerics.[14] About two weeks later he sent Cullen a list of 'persons who at present strike me as fit candidates for Professorships in the New University'.[15] Among the candidates was T.W. Allies to whom he wrote enthusiastically about the prospects of the new University, 'It will be the Catholic University of the English tongue for the whole world'.[16] Here Newman was echoing the Papal Rescript of October 1848, which urged the establishment of a Catholic University for students from the old and new worlds where English was spoken as a mother tongue. This message was also reflected in the appeal in 1851 by the University Committee to the clergy and laity of England, when it was declared that the new University was destined to benefit not merely the Catholics of Ireland but those of the empire as well.

On 8th July 1851, Newman entered in his diary that

'Dr Cullen came, and slept' (at the Birmingham Oratory).[17] No doubt they then discussed the projected new University. On his return from a London meeting, Newman records that Cullen, on 18th July, called again, and that during conversation he proposed that he, Newman, should be President (rector) of the planned University. Newman responded that he felt 'it would be sufficient if I was Prefect of Studies', in view of his Oratorian duties.[18] Newman pursued this point in a later letter to Cullen but had to admit that 'Our Fathers here feel reluctant that I should be any thing but rector'. He desired to do as much as possible for the University but with 'as little absence as possible' from the Oratory. 'This problem being satisfied, I do not care what you are pleased to make me'.[19] (The problem of having responsibilities in two locations and divided loyalties was never resolved; it was to prove the root cause of Newman's eventual severing of his connection with the Catholic University of Ireland.)

Dr Cullen generously, and no doubt diplomatically, sent Newman a donation to the Birmingham Oratory on 22nd July 1851.[20] At a meeting of the University Committee on 12th August 1851, Newman was nominated rector of the Catholic University, and he together with Dr Leahy and Myles W. O'Reilly were requested to draw up a scheme for the organisation of the University.[21] Nevertheless, Newman noted that, 'However, I did not at once pledge myself, either to be rector or Prefect of Studies; but became one of a subcommittee of three... charged with the duty of reporting on the best mode of commencing, on the course of studies, etc., etc.'.[22]

Newman reported to Cullen that although the subcommittee had sent letters of inquiry about university education to members of the consulting committee, no replies had been received. Regarding the Archbishop's proposal for Newman to give a series of lectures, Newman 'most readily' acceded to it but felt that he 'ought to know... the state of public opinion and knowledge in Ireland on the subject of education', and also Cullen's own ideas on what the lectures should be about.[23] The Archbishop's reply reflected his distinctly narrow concept of education: 'What we want in Ireland is to persuade the people that education should be religious. The whole tendency of our new systems is to make it believed that education may be so conducted as to have nothing at all to do with religion'. He added a list of perceived, feasible topics..[24] Shortly before Newman delivered his first lectures in Dublin (which we will look at later) he wrote to one of his old friends: 'My subjects, I suppose, will be advertised next week, and will seem dry – but (in confidence) they were suggested by high authority....[25] As Culler comments, 'Dr Cullen was the "high authority", and if Newman's first few lectures do seem dry to some persons, one can only consider what they would have been if he had followed more closely the suggestions in this [Dr Cullen's] letter. Doubtless he foresaw the difficulty and so replied, rather vaguely, "Thank you for the subjects you mention for Lectures. They are most important ones but will take a long time thinking out."'[26]

Newman sought advice from three old friends, English converts to Catholicism now living in Dublin: Frederick Lucas, Robert Ornsby and Henry Wilberforce. From discussions with them he built up 'a picture of Irish society, whether it was accurate or not, from which he worked in planning the rhetoric of his opening lectures'.[27] He gathered some diverting impressions; for instance, that nothing was more mixed about 'mixed education' than the question itself; that Dr Cullen was for an education that was religious before all, Dr MacHale for an education which was Irish before all, and Dr Murray for an education which could only be provided by a government that was neither Irish nor religious; while at the same time the bishops were alienated from more influential members of the laity.[28]

It dawned on Newman that he was being led by Cullen into highly dangerous territory, both in terms of nationalism and of controversial points of view. 'The Irish were having a quarrel over education, and he, as a distinguished Englishman, was being called in to settle it'.[29] He sensed the delicate situation in which he was being placed, and was decidedly unwilling to be treated like a puppet of the Irish prelate. 'If Dr Cullen had dirty work to do, he ought to do it himself or get an Irishman to do it; and, therefore, as the Archbishop continued to write to him reminding him of the lectures, Newman began to prepare him for not finding in them exactly what he had hoped'.[30] Newman's approach was, therefore, influenced by, but did not blindly follow, Cullen's expectations, as indicated in his letter to Ornsby quoted earlier. Cullen was not entirely satisfied but his criticism was constrained, and he reminded Newman that he should emphasise the need to unite religion with education, especially among those who had been 'educated in Trinity College and other Protestant establishments'.[31]

After a short visit to Ireland to discuss with his associates the development of plans for the new University, Newman wrote a long letter to Cullen in which he stated: 'It strikes me that the only right way of beginning the University is that which your Grace proposes, experimentally – the rector (with a constant subordination of course to a board – say of the Archbishops) should be autocrat'.[32] To Mrs William Froude he confided that 'I suppose in a few days I shall know what is decided on in Ireland about the University. It is a most daring attempt but first it is a religious one, next it has the Pope's blessing on it. Curious it will be if Oxford is imported into Ireland, not in its members only, but in its principles, methods, ways and arguments'.[33] McGrath states that it is undeniable that Newman embodied in the Catholic University of Ireland 'certain features of the great university to which he owed so much', notably college residence and the tutorial system. He was also inspired by the medieval model in which 'the lower faculty of arts led on to the higher faculties of theology, law and medicine, and so covered the whole field of human knowledge'. This model had, in fact, been adopted by the Catholic University of Louvain, which, as noted already, had been projected as an appropriate prototype for the new Catholic University of Ireland.[34]

On 12th November 1851, Newman recorded that the University Committee passed a resolution that, subject to his acceptance, he should 'be named the first President of the Catholic University of Ireland'.[35] Newman's appointment was generally welcomed, although Dr Murray, Archbishop of Dublin, who had shown a liberal attitude towards the concept of the Queen's Colleges, 'was still unenthusiastic, but his opposition was to the University rather than to its rector'.[36] This potential problem dissolved with the death of Dr Murray on 24th February 1852, and Dr Cullen's translation to Dublin meant that prospects for the new University had greatly improved.

Over the preceding few months, Newman had become aware of the threat of a libel action by the notorious ex-friar Achilli, and he duly advised the Archbishop of this impending case, which arose from the fifth lecture in the series, *Lectures on the Present Position of Catholics in England*, given in Birmingham in July 1851 (see Chapter 4). In this lecture, Newman had repeated some of the charges against the former Dominican friar which

Wiseman had made in an article in the Dublin Review. Cullen reassured Newman – who had dedicated the published volume of the lectures to him – and advised him to contact Wiseman 'who had all the police reports on this unsavoury character'. He graciously accepted the dedication of the published collection, and promised Newman assistance in his legal costs[37] (see Chapter 6 below for an extended discussion of this subject).

Newman had been busily preparing the lectures which Cullen had invited him to give in Dublin. They were not written without causing him 'infinite difficulty'.[38] He told Robert Ornsby that, 'My lectures have taken me more trouble than any one could by a stretch of the fancy conceive. I have written almost reams of paper, – finished, set aside – then taken them up again, and plucked them – and so on. The truth is, I have the utmost difficulty of writing to people I do not know, and I have commonly failed when I have addressed strangers'.[39]

On Friday, 7th May 1852, Newman travelled overnight to Dublin and delivered the first University lecture, or 'discourse', in the Exhibition Room of the Rotunda the following Monday. This venue was the scene of all the fashionable gatherings, musical entertainments and public meetings of Dublin in the 18th and 19th centuries..[40] The following day Newman wrote to Ambrose St John that 'The lecture... has been a hit; and now I am beginning to be anxious lest the others should not follow up the blow'. The room 'being very small' – holding about 400 – 'was nearly full... all the intellect, almost, of Dublin was there'.[41] Newman's anxieties seem, however, to have been groundless, for he was to write to H.E. Manning (who was to succeed Wiseman as Cardinal Archbishop of Westminster) at the close of the lectures: 'I have prospered here in my lectures beyond my most sanguine expectations, or rather beyond my most anxious efforts and pains – for I have had anxiety and work beyond belief in writing them, expectations none'.[42] But in his 'Memorandum on the Catholic University', dated 25th November 1870, Newman referred, rather dismissively, to his Dublin lectures – attended by Cullen – as a 'flash in the plan' – and the only public recognition given to him since he had been appointed rector.[43] However, Culler emphasises that Newman's reference to the lectures should be read in context: he did not mean that the lectures were a failure, but that 'their effect, though brilliant at the time, was not lasting'.[44] In this, it might be said, that they shared the fate of oratorical deliveries, although, of course, they were, as published later, to achieve lasting fame and influence. Newman, in fact, arranged for his lectures to be published in Dublin by the official publisher to Archbishop Cullen. Newman continued the series of lectures on the four Monday afternoons following his opening success on 10th May. These five discourses, completed on 7th June, were the only ones which Newman actually delivered. Exactly why he decided to deal with the remainder as 'closet lectures' is undetermined; perhaps pressure of work, disinclination, or because summer would be an inappropriate time for the lectures.[45] Whatever the explanation, he was clearly stressed by producing these remarkable discourses, a task which, on returning to the Birmingham Oratory in early June, had stretched through to almost the end of 1852, and had exhausted him. 'The Discourses, now – thank God – all but finished', had been 'the most painful of all' his written works.[46] As Dessain puts it, the discourses, with 'certain alterations and omissions of ephemeral matter, now form the first part on *The Idea of a University*. All his Oxford life Newman had fought for the place of religion in education, so that in a certain sense he had a congenial theme'.[47]

There are two separate, and skilfully blended, themes in *The Idea of a University*: 1) the need to include religious teaching in any scheme of studies; and, 2) the fact that 'the cultivation of the mind, rather than immediate preparation for professional occupations, is the primary end of a university'. The first theme was the focus of attention at the time Newman delivered his discourses; the second theme, as McGrath points out, 'receives almost exclusive attention from writers on education today'.[48]

In the preface to *The Idea of a University*, dated 21st November 1852, Newman stated that the view taken in the discourses is that a university is a place of *teaching* universal knowledge; its object is, on the one hand, intellectual, not moral, and, on the other, it is concerned with the diffusion and extension of knowledge rather than with its advancement. While a university of such a type is essentially free and independent of the Church, it cannot fulfil its role and responsibilities – as discussed in the *Idea* – without assistance from the Church: in theological terms, the Church is necessary for its integrity. 'Such are the main principles the Discourses will follow'.[49] Newman profoundly believed that religion should have a recognised place in a university, and that without this it could not rightfully claim this academic eminence. He also thought that religious teaching in a university should be controlled by the Church, as had been the practice for generations at Oxford and Cambridge. At Dublin, he argued, the Roman Catholic Church should fulfil this function. But this did not mean that some form of censorship or repression of knowledge should be exercised in the name of religion; he always insisted that a university was not a convent or a seminary – it was a place to fit a man for the world.[50]

In 'broad outline' the Discourses are as follows: 'In

the first four and in part of the fifth, all knowledge is declared to be one, each division of which can only be studied adequately in relation to others'. Hence the omission of theology from any curriculum 'falsifies the content of the other subjects contained in it'. The fifth to eighth Discourses enquire closely into the nature of knowledge which university studies are aimed to give. Pursuit of such knowledge may be for intellectual cultivation or for 'some immediate utilitarian purpose'. The former – culture of the mind – is 'a good in itself and is the primary end of university education'. Subjects of study may be broadly divided according to their relative powers of cultivating the mind, so a university concerns itself primarily with those subjects which tend to contribute most to intellectual culture. At the same time – and secondarily – it provides for professional studies both directly and mental cultivation – which is the best preparation for them. The last two Discourses discuss in general terms the relationships between mental culture and religion.[51]

Newman attempted to reconcile three factors in higher education in his lectures: 1) the autonomy required by the intellect so that it can develop freely, without 'arbitrary and external constraint; 2) the rights and functions of theology 'within the economy' of a university; and, 3) how far the Church has a right to exercise a pastoral authority within the university. His approach is that the branches of knowledge form one whole (the principle of unity is discussed more fully later), but he also invokes the principle of limitation – which he calls *abstraction*, in the sense that the mind cannot grasp an entire set of knowledge at once but in a kind of sequential progression, *abstracts* parts and eventually achieves a state of more comprehensive knowledge. The limits within each of the three factors specified by him may legitimately be exercised, and need to be defined, so that an equilibrium of functions is achieved which enables students to pursue their higher education. Further, this desirable equilibrium should be applicable to the university itself.[52]

Newman stressed the qualities of liberal education which 'makes not the Christian, not the Catholic, but the gentleman. It is well to be a gentleman; it is well to have a cultivated intellect, a delicate taste, a candid, equitable dispassionate mind, a noble and courteous bearing in the conduct of life:- these are the connatural qualities of a large knowledge; they are the objects of a University'.[53] In another passage – from which the title of this chapter is taken – Newman says that 'liberal education viewed in itself, is simply the cultivation of the intellect, as such, and its object is nothing more or less than intellectual excellence'.[54]

Newman's preoccupation with the relationship between liberal education and the fostering of gentlemanly qualities has prompted a modern biographer and critic to comment that he wanted the new University to be for gentlemen, and that in *Discourse VIII: Knowledge viewed in relation to religion*, 'he came very near to saying that gentlemanliness was next to godliness'.[55] This observation has the hallmarks of a politician's *bon mot*: it is a diverting but not necessarily reliable opinion.

Vargish points out that in his spirited response, some years earlier to Peel's Tamworth Reading Room speech, Newman showed his deep concern for the moral principles which should underlie the education of the masses, who could not afford to buy books for private study, whereas in the Dublin *Discourses* he focused specifically on 'the education of gentlemen'. He excluded from his theory of university education the teaching of 'practical secular knowledge, or utilitarian training', and concentrated on the intellectual ideals which should animate the education of professional men, who were badly needed at that time in Ireland. As noted already, Roman Catholics had largely been excluded from higher education in Ireland, and so the professions were closed to them. However, Newman's preoccupation with this level of intellectual development attracted sharp criticism on the grounds that he wanted an education exclusively to produce gentlemen but for which 'money was collected from the peasants in order to pay for it'. In defence, however, it has been said that Newman was asked to help to found a university, not a technical college to train skilled workers who could alleviate the distressing poverty of Ireland. It should be remembered that the bitter toll of the famine years of the 1840s was still evident, particularly in the west of Ireland.[56] The charge of educational elitism against Newman seems, therefore, hardly fair in the circumstances. Certainly, he was dedicated to scholarship and to the pursuit of academic excellence, but he had also experienced at first hand the pressing need for educational opportunities for the poor. In the first Birmingham Oratory in the slum district of Alcester Street, Newman had organised an evening school for the children of the needy families (see Chapter 4). Also, in his Anglican years at Littlemore he had organised an elementary school for the children of the village and he had visited regularly. Newman had a fine intellect and was a renowned scholar, but he also took a very practical role in the provision of education for children, particularly for those who otherwise would be likely to lack it. As his activities in Birmingham and Littlemore show, Newman viewed education as an intrinsic and inseparable part of pastoral care. Although his educational efforts in Dublin were primarily committed to the foundation of the Catholic University, he also organised evening classes open to the general public.

The projected university was not intended by the Holy See to be purely an Irish institution – although subsequent events suggest that the Irish hierarchy failed to appreciate this in their dealings with Newman. As Culler puts it, 'Properly considered, the university was not the Catholic University of Ireland but the Catholic University in Ireland, although Ireland, Newman believed, was the proper soil to produce it and Dublin was its natural seat'.[57] Some years after the founding of the CUI, Newman wrote that he had responded to Cullen's invitation because 'the Holy See had decided that Dublin was to be the place for Catholic education of the upper classes in these Islands'.[58] It is interesting also to note that McGrath – who is widely accepted as an authoritative source of information on Newman's Dublin activities – has suggested that 'the concept of the University as one for English-speaking Catholics originated in the mind of Cullen, and was not improbably suggested to him by his conviction that Newman was the only man existing who could make the scheme a success'.[59] It was, in fact, the concept definitely put forward in all the public documents issued by the University Committee. The Papal documents of 1852 and 1854 could at least be reconciled with it, and a good case could be made that they formally enunciated it. Since Cullen was influential in Rome, he doubtless persuaded Propaganda in this direction when the Rescript was being drafted.

Newman confessed that before becoming involved with the concept of a Roman Catholic university, he knew little of Ireland: 'I was a poor innocent as regards the actual state of things in Ireland when I went there, and did not care to think about, for I relied on the word of the Pope, but from the event I am led to think it is not rash to say that I knew as much about Ireland as he did'.[60] While he was to become aware of the volatile nature of Irish nationalism, he avoided association with any political activists. He wrote, for example, to Bishop Grant, 'What is Ireland to me, except the University here is a University for England, as well as for Ireland? I wish to do good, of course, to all Catholics if I can, but to English Catholics, as is my duty. I have left England for a while, for what I conceive to be a great English interest'.[61]

It seems, therefore, that Newman saw his educational 'mission' as a supra-national one in essence: Dublin was the arena – temporary as it turned out – for his involvement in higher education, but the philosophical base on which he built the Catholic University of Ireland was in no way restricted to that particular foundation. The Dublin *Discourses* were not parochial in content or chauvinistic in their orientation. From them, as has been seen, came *The Idea of a University* which, according to McGrath, is 'considered by many to be Newman's greatest [work], is almost universally acknowledged as an English classic, and is remarkable that it is the only standard treatise on university education in that tongue. The ideas which it formulates had been germinating in Newman's mind during his thirty years at Oxford, but their final form was determined by events connected with ... Dublin [Catholic] University'.[62] In Chadwick's opinion, Newman's 'noble book' has remained the historic statement of an 'ideal of higher education which influenced Britain and through Britain the educational systems of many other countries'.[63]

The universality of Newman's treatise has influenced – and continues to influence – educationalists the world over. Unlike the Catholic University itself, his educational philosophies have survived and guided those who seek inspiration in developing their own educational efforts. In Nicholas Lash's opinion, Newman's *Discourses* 'still speak freshly to our so different situation [and] this is in no small measure due to the way in which, again and again, the values and assumptions of the standard accounts of the nature and purposes of liberal education are bounded, corrected, checked, set in tension with the requirements of a very different vision'.[64] Newman himself observed to one of his friends: 'My two most perfect works, artistically, are my two last – the former of them [*The Present Position of Catholics in England*] put me to less trouble than any I ever wrote – the latter [*Discourses on University Education*] to the greatest of all'.[65]

Vargish has stated that Newman's mind, like Bacon's, was impelled towards the concept of wholeness or the idea of unity, and that when he used the word *idea* in *The Idea of a University* he wished it 'to denote a vast often apparently heterogeneous complex'. Liberal education would provide the student with a key to unlock the treasure chest of knowledge contained in the various sciences, so that his mind 'begins to reflect the unity of creation. He gains some insight into the architecture of the universe, social and spiritual as well as physical'.[66] Newman promoted the prime importance of the 'enlargement of the mind' which would be the fruit of a liberal system of higher education, such as he advocated in the Dublin *Discourses*, and which he believed to be vitally necessary for the development of an educated laity. Each specialised branch of knowledge – the circle of sciences – in his theory of higher education, 'provide an approach to the ultimate unity of existence, enabling the mind to perceive truth in the only way it can, through various aspects of the whole'.[67]

In the preface to *The Idea of a University*, Newman dismissed any notion that his treatise was concerned with 'the true mode of educating': rather, the *Discourses* were 'directed simply to the consideration of the *aims and principles* of Education'.[68] Culler takes up this point when he declares that *The Idea of a University* deliberately omits any consideration of means and concentrates exclusively upon ends and that from this viewpoint it 'is not an educational work at all'. But this qualified opinion is somewhat diluted when it is acknowledged that – as Newman's own words have shown – the purpose of his work was 'concerned with constructing an intellectual and cultural ideal'.[69] Essentially, Newman had no ambitions to write a manual of teaching practice. Instead, he sought to show what should be at the heart of higher education – a philosophical concept of learning that had roots in Aquinas and Aristotle and which, in McGrath's judgement, he presented with eloquence and erudition.[70] His occasional forays into flamboyant rhetoric have sometimes attracted critical comment; but he was writing at a time when such phraseology was more acceptable than today, and was to be found in literature, political speeches, sermons, and the like. Newman wrote with fervour – even vehemence – as well as with scholarly zeal, and the language he used reflected his own intellectual dedication.

After delivering these historic *Discourses* in Dublin – which attracted partisan criticism as well as general acclaim – Newman returned to the Oratory in Birmingham where he completed his writings on theories of higher education, and waited anxiously for Cullen to indicate what further progress had been made by the University Committee. Newman was not a member of this exclusively prelatic group, which Cullen, as Apostolic Delegate as well as Archbishop of Dublin, increasingly dominated.

In his memorandum, Newman deliberated: 'Universities are not brought into existence every day'; they tend to grow organically and without deliberate origination, whereas in Dublin 'private men' seek to 'dispense with time and circumstance, and to create in a day' and, apparently, without regard to the many problems and complications surrounding such a decision.[71] Newman listed the many, and mostly fruitless, negotiations about professorial appointments that had occurred and about suitable sites for the University. He says that this correspondence with Dr Cullen is 'illustrative of the fog through which I had to find my way... [and] of the bearing which Dr Cullen, while really wishing to keep me, had thought most suitable to adopt in his dealings with me'. Newman did not know 'whom to trust and whom to choose'. As noted earlier, he had 'no seat on the University Committee which was composed of men of whom I knew nothing... I was of no party myself, and did not wish to be advised by party men, nor did I consider ecclesiastics were the best advisers in a great lay undertaking'.[72] In Newman's view, the purpose of the University was to provide the Catholic laity with an opportunity for higher education, so he sought the support of prominent laypeople, as well as bishops and clergy, and encouraged them to become 'associates' of the University. In time, he hoped that such close links would lead to laypeople being able to assume specific responsibilities in the development and administration of the institution. This new approach was, however, not acceptable to the hierarchy, and the University was to suffer from the lack of a strongly committed body of laypeople who could have contributed significantly to its formation and development. Clearly, Cullen did not share Newman's views; he regarded clerical control of such a novel educational venture to be unquestionable. The Catholic University had been ordered to be established by the Pope; it was not a lay initiative.

While Cullen had listened to Newman's *Discourses*, he did not fully share some of the philosophical aspects of higher education which had been presented. Like

177

Wiseman, he was an Ultramontanist, steeped in Roman conventions – these often appeared to include deferment of decisions for unconscionable periods of time. Newman confided in his fellow Oratorian and close friend Ambrose St John, 'Why Dr Cullen should make such a mystery of his plans, and not talk with me like a friend, I cannot make out. I suppose he wishes to throw all responsibility on me, not to commit himself, and make me ask every point as it comes, as a favour from him'.[73] He thus found himself in 'a quagmire of Irish civil and ecclesiastical politics' from which he endeavoured to emerge and survive to pursue the development of the CUI. How well he actually understood the complexities of the situation is, however, open to some doubt.[74]

After a protracted delay, Newman received a letter, dated 21st October 1853, from Dr James Taylor, secretary of the University Committee, summoning him to Dublin as soon as possible. Newman welcomed this news but, adding that he could not come until January, stated that 'I have no scruples in this delay, since for many months I sacrificed all engagements to the prospect of being called over'.[75] He then discovered that only two prelates had been present at the University Committee meeting, and that Cullen was absent in Rome. Feeling dissatisfied, he wrote to Cullen in December: 'Should I not be publicly admitted or recognised as rector of the University, as soon as possible now?'.[76] Through Dr Taylor he received a reply that 'nothing public could be done at present: that the Bishops were to be gained over first'.[77] This rebuff was followed by a letter postponing any immediate action, which led Newman to ask Hope-Scott for his advice on whether he should resign forthwith.[78] He was advised not to do so. It was not until 4th January 1854 that Cullen wrote, in rather oblique terms, and from this letter Newman deduced that he could

178

now expect to receive some formal recognition of his role in Dublin.[79]

Two days earlier, Newman had written to Wiseman about the problems he was experiencing in dealing with the Irish hierarchy. He conceded that 'Dr Cullen from first to last has given me the *most generous support* but he cannot do every thing he wishes at his mere will'.[80] This letter was translated and shown to the Pope by Wiseman during a private audience and acting in his role as a Cardinal, who is 'bound to assist the Holy See... on any matters proposed ... by it, without reference to country'.[81] At a private audience, the Holy Father agreed at once to a proposal that Newman should be created a Bishop *in partibus*. This would give 'the right to sit with the Bishops in all consultations'.[82] To Newman this news was stimulating: 'I really did think the Cardinal had hit the right nail on the head, and effected what would be a real remedy against the difficulties which lay in my way'.[83] Wiseman had told Newman to treat the news of his impending bishopric discreetly but Ullathorne, Newman's bishop in Birmingham, had got to hear the news and announced it at a public banquet. It soon became public knowledge, and congratulations and gifts began to pour in. Newman now felt free to advise his friends of the Papal decision.[84]

As the weeks went by and the honour failed to be confirmed, Newman suspected that something or someone, had blocked his advancement. Exactly what had caused it was not readily discernible. Various speculations were rife, among which were the following: there was a certain degree of confusion about the Pope's actual intentions; Dr MacHale and other Irish bishops had placed some pressure on Cullen to oppose the proposed promotion; there were suspicions that the English hierarchy were seeking control of the new University, and so on.

Perhaps, as McGrath suggests, it is possible, as so often occurs in human events, that no one cause was the determining one.[85] Certainly, Cullen wrote to Rome on two occasions (23rd January 1854 and 2nd February 1854) urging that it would be better to defer for a while making Newman a bishop: 'It is better not to begin with too much fuss... In Belgium the Rector Magnificus is not a bishop'. He even went so far as to suggest that jealousy would be aroused if the English Cardinal Wiseman were known to have intervened in the matter.[86] In his private journal Newman wrote resignedly that, 'The Cardinal never wrote to me a single word, or sent any sort of message to me, in explanation of the change of intention about me, till the day of his death... Nor did Dr Cullen, nor Dr Grant, nor Dr Ullathorne, nor any one else, ever again say one single word on the subject; nor did they make any chance remark by which I have been able to form any idea why that elevation which was thought by Pope, Cardinal, and Archbishop so expedient for the University, or at least so settled a point, which was so publicly announced, was suddenly and silently reversed'.[87]

In early 1854 Newman started a series of visits to the Irish bishops and priests to seek support for the new University. He wrote that 'I am received everywhere... with the greatest cordiality and affection'.[88] Among those on whom he called was Dr Charles Russell of Maynooth who, some years earlier, had influenced his conversion to Catholicism (see Chapter 3) and who was not sanguine about prospects for the new University.[89] His views were shared by others; some suspected that the new University was part of a sinister Anglicisation, a perception which may have been fostered by forceful clerics such as the Archbishop of Tuam. According to McGrath, Dr MacHale's support for the University became 'more and more grudging and his attitude towards Newman more and more discourteous, whilst Dr Cullen, seeing the differences growing greater as the University took shape, kept exasperating Newman by his policy of silent procrastination'.[90] Between the two prelates antipathy became so strong that the work of the University Committee was virtually halted; eventually, Dr MacHale withdrew from taking any active part in the proceedings.

Newman also discovered that the prospect of a new University failed to stir those who had suffered, and were still suffering, from the effects of the devastating famine years. Looking back on his activities at this time. Newman later wrote that, 'from what he had gathered about clerical and lay opinions of the prospective University, the Pope had been poorly served by his counsellors and he might well have taken a different approach to the Queen's Colleges or at least not decreed that a Catholic University should be set up in Ireland'.[91] However, the Papal Brief establishing the Catholic University of Ireland was issued on 20th March 1854. This was the fourth formal act on this topic taken by the Holy See. It is noted that two years had elapsed since the previous brief yet so far the bishops had taken no steps to advance the foundation of the University. They were thus ordered to hold a synod, under the presidency of Dr Cullen, with a view of opening the new institution without delay.[92] The Brief also confirmed Newman as rector of the University 'in the most flattering terms'.[93] Newman then wrote to Cullen, offering to 'come to Dublin as soon as convenient after Easter'.[94]

The Synod opened in Dublin on 18th May, the statutes of the University were approved and Newman was formally appointed as rector, with Dr Leahy as Subrector. Just before the meeting Newman had asked Cullen to consider putting before the Synod a proposal that he should be given the rank of vicar general, as he believed was the custom at Louvain, as this would be helpful in the 'most arduous' task of developing the new University and assisting in his negotiations with the bishops.[95] Nothing resulted from Newman's request[96] and, like the 'rumours' of a bishopric, the matter was never again raised by Newman. He achieved, however, some satisfaction from the Synod's endorsement of the *Memorandum* that he had submitted and which was to be the academic blueprint of the University. There were to be five faculties: theology, law, medicine, philosophy and letters, and science.[97]

Over the next few months, Newman was busily engaged in the University building in Harcourt Street, Dublin, recruiting academic staff and students. He stressed that the reputation of the professors would be of paramount importance in the successful development of the Catholic University of Ireland, and he told Cullen that, if possible, he would prefer the majority of the professors to be Irishmen, provided they were up to his expectations.[98] Cullen, however, insisted on personally approving any such appointments and submitted Newman's list of candidates to the University Committee. This resulted in friction with the Archbishop of Tuam, Dr MacHale, who stated that 'with few exceptions' he was unable 'to express approval or disapprobation', and that he intended to raise the matter at the next meeting of the University Committee.[99] As McGrath points out, 'This letter was another manifestation… of the obstructive attitude Dr MacHale was to maintain all through'. It seemed that the Archbishop could only give 'grudging' support because the University was so closely identified by him with Cullen.[100] Newman replied vigorously yet with traditional courtesy, that while the bishops had the power of veto over professional appointments, unless they exercised their powers with discretion, the commencement of the University would be at risk.[101] Newman sent copies of the correspondence to Cullen in Rome, and he proceeded to publish the list of professors and lecturers in the *University Gazette* of 19th October. 'The Lion of the West' – a popular soubriquet of the Archbishop of Tuam – had 'roared at me, and I have roared again', Newman commented to Ambrose St John.[102] The unfortunate tendency of Dr MacHale to frustrate matters related to the University then became apparent in Rome, when he attempted to prevent confirmation of the University regulations. The Pope ignored his protests and ordered that the regulations should be approved for an initial period of five or six years. Cullen told Newman that MacHale had declared that 'he would have nothing to do with the University – so much the better – but I fear that he will excite a storm against it'.[103]

In between his new duties as rector, Newman made several visits to England to fulfil his responsibilities at the Birmingham Oratory. On returning to Dublin, he was – at long last – formally installed as rector on Whit Sunday, 4th June 1854, as he informed several of his close friends and acquaintances.[104] One of Newman's 'sidelines' was the publication of a University Gazette. This appeared weekly and contained official University information and also papers by Newman on aspects of academic life. It survived, as a monthly, until the end of 1856. Another of Newman's ventures – mentioned earlier – was the introduction of evening classes for young Dublin men who were working full-time. 'The Catholic University was a pioneer in University Extension Lectures, which were not begun in England until 1873.'[105]

On 3rd November 1854, the Catholic University of Ireland formally opened its doors: Newman wrote to Henry Wilberforce that, 'We number more than sixty –

but not in residence or lecture; which is a good beginning. Those actually in lecture at once are, of course, much fewer'.[106] From Rome, Cullen sent his congratulations and assured Newman that the Pope and Cardinals were much interested in the progress of the University.

In early December 1854, Newman asked Cullen permission to build a church in Dublin, and this was granted.[107] Both hoped that an Oratory could be established in Dublin in due course, but an Oratorian foundation in that city never materialised. Newman was to allocate a 'sizeable surplus' from a national appeal for funds towards the costs of the Achilli trial to building the University church in Dublin (see Chapter 6). After considerable searching for a suitable site, Newman succeeded in acquiring a site next to the main university premises in St Stephen's Green. The University Church formed an essential part of Newman's overall scheme of a Roman Catholic ethos in higher education.

Newman's views on ecclesiastical architecture had been developing for some time. On his way to Rome in 1846, Newman and Ambrose St John visited Paris and Milan, and in the latter city they went to the church of St Fidelis. This was once a Jesuit church before the suppression of the order, and was 'Grecian' or 'Palladian' in style. Newman acknowledged that 'however my reason may go Gothic, my heart has ever gone with Grecian. I loved Trinity Chapel at Oxford more than any other building. There is in the Italian style such a simplicity, purity, elegance, beauty, brightness, which I suppose the word classical implies, that it seems to befit the notion of an Angel or Saint. The Gothic style does not seem to me to typify the sanctity innocence of the Blessed Virgin, or St Gabriel, or the lightness, grace and sweet cheerfulness of the elect as the Grecian does'.[108]

In Discourse IV of *The Idea of a University*, Newman

conceded that the Gothic style 'is endowed with a profound and commanding beauty, such as no other style possesses'. But he argued that the revival of the Gothic style 'which is at present taking place' may lead to the same kind of 'excesses' that followed the Renaissance in literature and art. He admitted that Pugin was 'a man of genius' and that Catholics owed him a great debt, but he 'is intolerant' of any other school of Christian art. 'Gothic is now like an old dress, which fitted a man well twenty years back but must be altered to fit him now'. Newman summed up by saying that for Oratorians, whose roots go back to the 16th century, 'to assume the architecture simply and unconditionally of the 13th, would be as absurd as their putting on them the cowl of the Dominicans or adopting the tonsure of the Carthusians... I, for one, believe that Gothic can be adapted' to meet the needs of an Oratory.[109]

Newman secured the services of a talented architect, John Hungerford Pollen who, at Newman's invitation, had become honorary professor of fine arts in the CUI towards the end of 1854. In accordance with Newman's distinct preferences, the basic design of the University Church was later described by the architect as 'a plain brick hall with an apsidal end, timber ceiling, etc., somewhat in the manner of the earlier Roman basilicas'. He added that Newman 'felt a strong attachment to those ancient churches with rude exteriors, but solemn and impressive within, recalling the early history of the Church, as it gradually felt its way in the converted Empire, and took possession'.[110]

Newman involved himself closely with the design, decoration and furnishings of the church, and he minutely checked the resulting costs. As an Oratorian, he took special interest in its suitability for music and preaching, and also for use as a lecture theatre and graduation hall.

Building commenced in May 1855 and was completed in time for a ceremonial opening on Ascension Thursday, 1st May 1856. The day before, Newman had sent a cheque to Pollen, asking 'the kindness not to present it for some little while' because he was 'so hard up just now, having overdrawn both my private and the church accounts'.[111] Eventually, Newman arranged for the outstanding debt on the church to be cleared by a loan from the Birmingham Oratory.

The launch of a medical faculty was to be the next step in expansion of the CUI. Newman had assessed the medical training facilities in Dublin and had found that 'Catholics were very inadequately represented in the existing schools of medicine'.[112] It was intolerable, Culler observes, that 'a profession whose duties were so intimately involved with religion, should be dominated by Protestants in the various hospitals and medical schools'.[113] As part of the medical faculty, Newman was determined to establish a first-rate Roman Catholic school of medicine, whose graduates would be both Roman Catholic and professional. Through an intermediary, he was able to acquire the fully equipped and privately-owned Cecilia Street Medical School. This School was recognised by the Royal College of Surgeons. It was up for sale because of the departure of two of its leading professors. To Mrs Bowden, Newman reported that, 'We are getting on with the University as well as we possibly can. It is swimming against the tide to move at all; still we are in action. The great thing is to set up things. That we are doing. The Medical School will begin in October; the church is building; and an institution for Physical Science in course of formation. It will be years before the system takes root, but my work will be ended when I have made a beginning'.[114] The acquisition of Cecilia Street Medical School enabled Newman to develop a flourishing medical faculty which was to outlive the other faculties and become, in time, part of the National University.

Newman continued doggedly to put into practice the theoretical ideas which he had so persuasively presented in his *Disclosures*. At the same time, he began increasingly to feel the tide of events was against him; he was suspected by Cullen of nationalist sympathies, of being too lax with his students, and failing to keep adequate checks on expenditure. These irritating misconceptions were resented and added to the considerable anxieties which Newman endured concerning the recruitment of students and trying, desperately, to keep the University viable. From August 1854 to July 1855, Cullen was in Rome, taking part in the solemn definition of the dogma of the Immaculate Conception of the Blessed Virgin Mary. He was also 'defending his pro-government policy against Irish nationalists like Archbishop MacHale', and Cullen wrote to Newman to warn him to keep the University free of Young Irelandism. Newman's response was limited to an assurance that he had intended to exclude politics, but it fell short of a promise not to appoint Young Irelanders to the staff. As a result his further letters were left unanswered and he had no further contact with Cullen till the latter's return to Dublin.[115] Newman felt that his task was becoming intolerable because of Cullen's prolonged absence in Rome as well as because of his continued procrastination and secretiveness. This type of behaviour had become so habitual that no effective communication now existed between them, and Newman felt that he was labouring in vain. In April 1856, he mentioned to Cullen that he wished to leave the University in July 1857 and, as he told Ambrose St John, although the Archbishop was 'at first startled or rather surprised, he quite acquiesced – and I consider I have gained a step'.[116]

In June, Newman was summoned to appear before a synod of the Irish bishops; before attending, he circulated a long and detailed statement of the objectives and related expenditure plans of the University. A copy was sent to Cullen for distribution to the bishops.[117] Newman's document received overall approval, and he was reappointed for a period of three years. He noted, however, that while he was committed for three years, 'it ensured my getting away at the end of it'.[118]

In a letter to J.H. Pollen, the architect of the University Church, Newman alluded to the possibility of the Birmingham Oratorians opening a boys' school: 'a certain number of persons who are interested in a Catholic Eton should form themselves into a quasi-trust with a certain sum of money at their disposal'.[119] (This early reference to what was to become the Oratory School will be discussed later.)

Meanwhile, Newman was experiencing the inevitable stresses arising from trying to work in two places at the same time, and in two decidedly different institutions. His partial residence in Dublin had irritated Cullen who thought that he should relinquish his other duties. When the Birmingham Oratory Congregation indicated their unwillingness to approve Newman's continued stay in Dublin, Newman devised a 'middle plan', which would involve residence for a few weeks of each term; the proposal was agreed, but it was not really an effective solution. At the beginning of April, 1857, Newman wrote to the Irish bishops, individually, stating his intention of resigning the rectorship in November; he felt that he could no longer leave his own Congregation without his regular guiding presence. As he commented in a letter to Ambrose St John, 'it seems to me that really I may be *wanted* in England, and that there may be a providential reason, over and above the compulsion of the Fathers at

Birmingham, for me to return'.[120] On 6th May 1857, the Birmingham Congregation had made a 'formal recall of the Father Superior from Dublin',[121] to which Newman had to conform. He returned to Birmingham in November 1857, but agreed to remain in office as rector of the CUI until his successor and also a Vice-rector had been appointed. The following November he left Dublin, never to return.

Newman was a distinguished man; he had taken on an almost unsupportable burden. Now he was fatigued, disillusioned and frustrated by his Irish experiences. Also he felt let down by the English who 'had failed to rise to his vision of a University for the English-speaking world'.[122] He told Henry Wilberforce that 'We are at great disadvantage, abused in Ireland for being English, and neglected in England for being Irish'.[123] In his private journal, he elaborates on this theme: 'It was (also) the fact, which by this time had become so plain, that English Catholics felt no interest at all in the University scheme and had no intention to make use of it, should it get into shape. I had gone to Ireland on the express understanding that it was an English as well as an Irish University, and the Irish had done all in their power to make it an Irish University and nothing else. And further, I say, the English Catholics had given up. It had begun a very little time, when Dr Ullathorne told me, as if a matter in which he acquiesced, that "the English gentlemen would never send their sons to it"'.[124]

After Newman had relinquished his formal association with the University, he continued to display an interest in its activities. Fairly quickly, his feelings about his experiences in Ireland appeared to have mellowed. This is seen, for instance, in a letter to his friend Robert Ornsby in which he stated, 'Don't fancy I feel annoyance at my plans being put aside… The great thing is to *set up*, and then leave the direction of things to the currents which would determine it... I could not have begun without a plan. I could not have begun with any other... When I am gone, something may come of what I have done at Dublin. And since I hope I did what I did, not for the sake of men, not for the sake of the Irish University, not even for the Pope's praise, but for the sake of God's Church and God's glory, I have nothing to regret and nothing to desire, different from what it is.'[125]

Dr Woodlock was appointed the next rector of the CUI in 1859. His conception of the University was that it was a definitely Irish institution. Of 986 students registered during his rectorship, only 37 came from outside Ireland.[126] By 1873, the University had few students or professors, limited finance and was still seeking legal recognition for its degrees.

Woodlock put forward a restructuring scheme but, despite his strenuous efforts, the institution's terminal decline seemed inevitable. In 1879 legislation resulted in the Royal University of Ireland being set up. This was purely an examining body, which also provided a number of Fellowships, evenly divided between Roman Catholics and Protestants. Although this step was generally regarded as academically regressive, it relieved the financial burdens of the CUI. In 1882, Newman's University House – St Patrick's – in St Stephen's Green, became, officially, University College. The hierarchy passed it over to the Jesuit Order for management. According to McGrath, 'This date may be said to mark the end of the Catholic University as a living educational institution, though it continued to exist juridically in the group of institutions which had been named its constituent colleges'.[127]

Historians and others have deliberated at length about whether Newman's University should be judged as a success or a failure. Clearly, the criteria used influence the opinions expressed. Was it more than a brave academic experiment that was before its time (in the sense that, for instance, it was founded when the Roman Catholic Church in Ireland exerted a powerful influence over the lives of its members)? Or was it not merely an academic venture but one which was part of a crusade for recognition of the rights of the majority of the Irish population, i.e. Roman Catholics, to have access to higher education? Was it doomed to die after a short, painful existence because political, academic and religious motivations were inextricably mixed and conflict was inevitable after a while?

There were certainly several identifiable factors which contributed to the fate of the Catholic University of Ireland; together, these were a potent and destructive mix which Sencourt, with acknowledgements to McGrath, lists as: 1) the lack of a charter resulting in an inability to confer degrees (except in the medical faculty which was recognised by the Royal College of Surgeons as successor to the Cecilia St Medical School); 2) inadequate financial resources (the CUI had no endowments and the Irish poor had to contribute to support it); 3) the lack of support from the Catholic laity – some preferred TCD or Queen's, or had no interest at all in higher education; 4) The Holy See. Both Cullen and Newman were mistaken in believing that support from the English Catholic community would be forthcoming, because the CUI had originally been projected for the English-speaking world (see page 162); 5) the fact that the ideals of Cullen and Newman were in virtually continuous conflict.[128] Of these multiple factors, the last was probably the one which had the most serious effects, as has been shown by observations already made. These two eminent clerics had distinctly different perceptions about the essential nature of higher education, and also about the role of the laity in developing and managing such an innovative institution as a Catholic University in Ireland. Personality factors added to the complexities and difficulties of communication between Cullen and Newman: both were determined, driven men whose conflicting temperaments and perceptions tended to cause both of them endless frustration. Cullen suffered also from regular outbreaks of deliberate harassment by senior ecclesiastics, such as the fiery Archbishop of Tuam.

Although Newman's foundation itself may be judged by some to have been a failure, he left a rich legacy of thought about higher education which, as we saw above on page 174, has endured to this day. He once remarked that to write effectively he needed a spur: Ireland was the stimulus which brought to fruition 'the noble ideas which he sketched in immortal prose'.[129] Perhaps on that count alone, Newman's Irish higher educational venture should be judged successful. Coulson asserts that the validity of Newman's *Idea* 'is that of a university so organised, socially as well as academically, as to make possible a way of teaching by which the student is enabled to develop his powers of judgement and, thereby, to enlarge his mind'.[130]

After Ireland, Newman's next commitment to educational excellence was with the proposal to found an Oratory School for the sons of middle and upper-class Catholic families. This was to prove a more lasting enterprise than the Catholic University of Ireland. As Culler puts it, 'Newman's ambition was to provide an education that would be no less English. for being Catholic... He saw himself as raising up an educated elite, who would be the Catholic leadership of the coming generation'.[131]

In 1852, in the preface to *The Idea of a University*, Newman had stated that for centuries the 'Catholics of

192

these Islands' had not been able to secure the type of education needed for the 'man of the world, the statesman, the landholder, or the opulent gentleman'. The time had come, he declared, when 'this moral disability must be removed'.[132] He was, of course, directly referring to the disabilities related to the lack of higher education suffered by Catholics in particular, although he became increasingly concerned about the poor standard of Catholic education in general, which impeded the progress of Catholics in the world at large. His anxieties were shared by several notable converts, who had approached him, seeking to attract his interest in their discussions on how to remedy the acknowledged inadequate provision for the education of their sons.

Wilfrid Ward alludes to 'the touch of mutual contempt occasionally visible' between 'old Catholics' (see Chapter 1) and recent converts, many of whom were influenced by Newman or were his friends of longstanding. The converts regarded the typical 'old Catholics' 'as not having quite the education befitting a gentleman', while the 'old Catholics' tended to be 'slow to admit the newcomers to the intimacy which had for generations existed among the historical families belonging to the old faith' – among which, it may be added, a marked degree of inter-marriage took place.[133]

Dessain has commented that Newman had spent his early years as a Catholic founding first the English Oratory and then the Irish University at the request of the Pope. Now he would try 'to remedy some of the "miserable deficiencies" on the practical and apologetic level which were hindering the cause of the Church in her preaching of Revealed Religion in England'.[134] Among these 'deficiencies', appropriate education for middle and upper-class Catholic families was urgently needed.

Newman had already discerned the need for Catholics

to be well-educated at all levels, and he welcomed the opportunity to associate himself and the Oratory with those who were seeking to find a means of providing a typical English public-school education with a Catholic ethos. According to Ker, he 'was ideally suited… because, unlike some other converts… he had not rejected his English past on becoming a Catholic'.[135]

In April 1857 Newman wrote to Sir John Simeon that 'having set the University off, which is all I proposed to do – I could be instrumental also, in setting up another great Catholic desideratum, a public school'. He thought that 'ultimately' a school of this nature should be in the country, but that while it was small, the neighbourhood of the Oratory – 'airy, high and covered with trees and gardens… would not be inappropriate'.[136] Sir John replied that he had not yet seen a single 'old Catholic', priest or layman, whom he considered to be a 'well educated man'. It was his firm opinion that unless the education of 'our boys' improved, it would be 'impossible for the Catholic body in England to elevate themselves in intellectual equality with their fellow citizens'.[137]

Newman heard, in November 1857, from another of his upper-class Catholic friends, Serjeant Bellasis. This prominent lawyer told him that Hope-Scott and he were delighted that he was making a start with the concept of an Oratory School – of which Newman had sent a draft prospectus for their professional evaluation.[138] With legalistic precision, they had amended this document and returned it to Newman who noted that 'I am amused at your and Hope-Scott's lawyer-like caution, in cutting off every unnecessary word from my manifesto'.[139] He had written that the school was for 'the education of boys not for the ecclesiastical state' and not over 12 years of age on admission. 'He takes this step at the urgent instance of friends, and with the concurrence and countenance of a number of Catholic gentlemen whose names have been transmitted to him'.[140]

Newman's school project was progressing; in January 1858, he consulted Ullathorne, who encouraged the idea of a 'separation of Catholic schools from seminaries'.[141] Among the prominent Catholic laymen becoming involved in this educational move was Sir John Acton (later, Lord Acton), a Shropshire landowner and historian.

But, as usual, Newman was to encounter problems as he busied himself with developing his school plans and, at the same time, maintaining his commitments to the Catholic University in Dublin. He told J.S. Flanagan that 'The Cardinal has washed his hands of the school plan and has pointedly told our bishop that he will have the whole responsibility. Our Bishop (post propter, I know not) has advised us strongly against it because it is sure to be a failure, yet, when he gives reasons, they are so unintelligible, as to show they are not his real difficulty, whatever it is…' Newman added that Bellasis and Acton had attempted to get the Bishop to clarify his views, but that they seemed to be experiencing considerable difficulties. However, the original plan would be reinstated and, 'as a trial, a house will be rented for two or three years to accommodate boys under 12 years of age'.[142]

On 21st April 1858, Fr Nicholas Darnell was 'appointed Father Superior's representative to act as Prefect in undertaking the establishment of a Public School'.[143] Fr Darnell, ambitious and keen to rival the public schools, 'never asked Newman for advice and ignored his suggestions'.[144] Newman was being deliberately isolated from the development of the school, and he was also subject to persistent rumours that he was no longer fit for responsibility. He was also concerned to hear criticism that the boys were not receiving religious instruction and that punishments were too severe. Added to these problems, according to Trevor, was an upheaval in the school caused by misunderstandings between the headmaster and the matron which resulted in her leaving the school.[145] Newman felt that he had ultimate responsibility for the school, and so he put to the Congregation of the Oratory the problem and requested their decision as to whether Darnell or he had this responsibility. The Congregation endorsed Newman's authority, and Darnell left precipitously, followed by most of the staff, whose resignations Newman had accepted.[146] By a Decree of 1st April 1861, the Congregation assumed the liabilities of the school,[147] and on 18th July 1852, Fr Darnell's request for release from the Congregation of the Birmingham Oratory was granted.[148] Fr Ambrose St John became headmaster, a post he filled zealously until his death in 1876; Thomas Arnold, son of Dr Arnold of Rugby, was appointed senior master. The latter had been Professor of Literature at the Catholic University in Dublin but poor pay and prospects had forced him to look elsewhere for a suitable post. Newman himself undertook some teaching in the school and adapted Latin comedies for the boys to play in.

Newman scorned the idea that 'if a lot of knowledge is packed into young heads in schools', adult society would become more virtuous. As Chadwick puts it, 'The error lies in the belief that excellence comes from without, whereas it comes only from within. It cannot come if a child sits passive and receiving. It comes only through personal struggle and suffering. No one can be taught, no one can be interested, no one can be amused, into morality'.[149] Education, therefore, involves a moral mission; it was this responsibility which was recognised by Newman, and it was at the heart of his strenuous efforts to found the Oratory School. During his lifetime the school remained small but successful. Dessain holds that 'its example and competition raised the standard of the other Catholic schools'.[150] In these ways Newman made distinguished contributions to the concept of education at both university and school levels.

Between 1864 and 1871, Newman was once again involved in the matter of higher education for Catholics, this time in England, and arising from plans to open an Oratory in Oxford. In August 1864, Newman had bought for £8,000 a 5-acre site behind St Giles', and later in the month Ullathorne authorised him to develop an Oxford Mission. Newman started to raise funding from his wealthy friends, several of whom were keen that their sons should be able to study at Oxford, particularly if Newman founded a Catholic hall associated with the Oratory. He realised that to make the project viable in the long term – because there were only about 100 middle-class Catholic residents in Oxford – the Oratory's role would only be relevant if Catholic undergraduates were at Oxford.[151]

In November 1864, Newman called on Wiseman to explain his Oxford plans, but found him decidedly unwell. He listened 'half querulously' to Newman's scheme.[152] More positive opposition came from Manning which resulted in 'the Oxford scheme being thwarted for the present – for me probably for good... Bellasis told me that, from what he saw at Rome, he felt that Manning was more set against my going to Oxford, than merely against Catholic youths going there'.[153] Meanwhile, Manning had written to Propaganda stating that Wiseman had 'declared himself entirely opposed to any contact between the faithful in England and the heretical culture of the country'.[154] Newman, hearing of the hierarchy's entirely negative attitude, reflected: 'The same dreadful jealousy of the laity, which has ruined things in Dublin, is now at the bottom of this unwillingness to let our youths go to Oxford... Propaganda and our leading Bishops fear the natural influence of the laity'.[155]

Newman accepted an offer from the University for the site he had bought, and advised Ullathorne: 'I believe your Lordship considers the arrangement for the Oratory to take the Oxford Mission as at an end. I certainly so consider it myself'.[156]

In August 1865, Ullathorne again approached Newman about an Oxford Mission, and although Newman had, once more, bought some land, seemingly with an eye to the future, he firmly rejected the bishop's proposal. This new site was, in fact, opposite Christ Church – which displeased Ullathorne as being too close to the University – but this did not prevent him from putting the matter to Newman, again, in the following year. This time Newman accepted, subject to obtaining certain clarifications and assurances.[157] In acknowledging Newman's acceptance, Ullathorne referred to the earlier decision of the Bishops regarding the education of Catholics at the University: 'they hold it their duty to discourage Protestant university education for Catholics'. This decision was approved by the Holy See; what future steps might be taken he could not say, but the whole matter might have to be reconsidered if 'the practice of sending Catholics to the University' became more prevalent.[158]

Manning's reaction was, however, adamantine – he warned Talbot of the likely outcome: 'The English national spirit is spreading among Catholics, and we shall have dangers'.[159]

Propaganda's approval was sought for the establishment of an Oratory under the supervision of Birmingham, and by the end of 1866 permission had been given. At last, with Ullathorne's backing Newman issued a formal circular asking for contributions to set up the Oxford Oratory. All seemed to be going well until hopes were shattered by a letter which Ullathorne received from Propaganda containing a 'secret instruction' that he should 'blandly and suavely' (*blande suaviterque*) recall Newman if he showed signs of intending to reside in Oxford. Newman was devastated, and wrote bitterly to Wilberforce[160] and to Coleridge,[161] and drafted a memorandum,[162] in which he itemised the 'correspondence and conversations' relating to the Oxford scheme.

Only a few days earlier, Newman had been presented with an 'Address' signed by about 200 prominent English laymen supporting him, probably with expectations of an Oxford education for their sons.[163] It is said that this initiative 'caused Manning some alarm in case it might influence Propaganda's decision on the Oxford question, and 'he wrote to Mgr Talbot with the object of stiffening its back'.[164]

In August 1867, Newman reported Ullathorne's conversation with him 'on the subject of the Oxford matter… He said abruptly and with a grave face, looking straight at me, "I find at Rome they consider the Oxford question at an end"'.[165] This position was confirmed when Propaganda instructed the English hierarchy 'to issue pastorals explaining that those who frequented the non-Catholic universities incurred most grievous danger to faith and morals and that it was well nigh impossible to envisage circumstances in which Catholics could attend without sin'.[166] On Hope-Scott's advice, Newman circularised subscribers to the projected Oxford Oratory offering to refund their contributions, and emphasising that the 'sole ground' of the restriction barring him from taking up residence in Oxford was the 'apprehension' that this would attract Catholics youths there.[167]

Three days later, Newman requested permission from Ullathorne 'to withdraw from my engagement to undertake the Mission of Oxford'.[168] Ullathorne replied that he 'was not at all surprised' at Newman's decision. 'Were I in the same position I should do the same'. He added that it was his 'complete conviction that you have been shamefully misrepresented at Rome, and that by countrymen of our own'.[169] So, for the time being, ended the opportunity of founding an Oxford Oratory and of giving Catholics access to higher education. Newman was to refer later to this unhappy period as only one of various instances 'of what may be called Nihilism in the Catholic Body, and in its rulers. They forbid, but they do not direct or create'.[170] His profound dillusionment is evident in a letter to his friend Fr Henry Coleridge in which he mentioned, that 'after so many rebuffs' he felt no call to go on with the Oxford undertaking. He would wait to be asked by Propaganda before becoming involved in any other schemes[171] (see Chapter 7 for further discussion).

NOTES

1 McGrath, 1951, p.1.
2 McGrath, 1951, p.5.
3 Meenan, 1987, p.2.
4 McGrath, 1951, p.43.
5 Norman, 1985, pp.292-3.
6 Chadwick, 1972, p.455.
7 McGrath, 1951.p.63.
8 McGrath, 1951, p.64.
9 Newman, 1956, p.280.
10 Owen Chadwick, 1972, pp.453-4.
11 Cf McGrath, 1951, pp.80-82.
12 Ward, 1913, p.309.
13 *LD* XIV.257, *footnote*.
14 *LD* XIV.257, Archbishop Cullen, 16th April 1851.
15 *LD* XIV.267, Archbishop Cullen, 28 April 1851.
16 *LD* XIV.262, 20 April 1851.
17 *LD* XIV.305.
18 Newman, 1956, p.282; *LD* XIV.313 *footnote*.
19 *LD* XIV.315, 23 July 1851.

20 *LD* XIV.320 *footnote*.
21 *LD* XIV.331, footnote.
22 Newman, 1956, p.281.
23 *LD* XIV.357, Dr Cullen, 16 September 1851.
24 *LD* XIV.364, *footnote*, from Dr Cullen, 20 September 1851.
25 *LD* XV.71, Robert Ornsby, 18 April, 1 1852.
26 Culler, 1965, p.137; *LD* XIV.364-5, Archbishop Cullen, 22 September 1851.
27 Culler, 1965, p.138.
28 Cf Culler, 1965, p.139.
29 Culler, 1965, p.139.
30 Culler, 1965, p.140.
31 *LD* XV.29, *footnote*, *from* Dr Cullen, 8 February 1852.
32 *LD* XIV.382, 11 October 1851.
33 *LD* XIV.389, 14 October 1851.
34 McGrath, 1951, p.107.
35 Newman, 1956, p.283; *LD* XIV.393.
36 McGrath, 1951, p.123.
37 *LD* XIV.343 *footnote*.
38 Culler, 1965, p.142.
39 *LD* XV.66-7, 14 April 1852.
40 Cf MrGrath, 1951, p.153 *footnote*.
41 *LD* XV.83, 11 May 1852.
42 *LD* XV.98, 8 June 1852.
43 Newman, 1956, p.304.
44 Culler, 1965, p.154.
45 Cf Culler, 1965, p.154.
46 *LD* XV.182, Sister Mary Poole, 22 October 1852.
47 Dessain, 1980, p.102.
48 McGrath, 1951, p.135.
49 Newman, 1987, p.3.
50 Cf Chadwick, 1990, p.57.
51 Cf McGrath, 1951, pp.163-4.
52 Cf Coulson, 1970, p.87.
53 Newman, 1987, *Discourse V*, p.137.
54 Newman, 1987, *Discourse V*, p.138.
55 Roy Jenkins, 1990, p.147.
56 Cf Vargish, 1970, pp.129-31.
57 Culler, 1965, p.168.
58 *LD* XVII.179, Bishop Thomas Grant, 7 March 1856.
59 McGrath, 1951, p.186.
60 Newman, 1956, p.320.
61 *LD* XVII.178, 7 March 1856.
62 McGrath, 1951, p.viii.
63 Chadwick, 1990, p.52.
64 Lash, 1990, p.195.
65 *LD* XV.225, Henry Wilberforce, 20 December 1852.
66 Vargish, 1970, pp.148-9.
67 Vargish, 1970, p.154.
68 Newman, 1987, p.12.

69 Culler, 1965, p.189.
70 McGrath, 1951, p.275.
71 Newman, 1956, p.285.
72 Newman, 1956, p.290.
73 *LD* XVII.411, 9 November 1856.
74 Redmond, 1990, p.83.
75 *LD* XV.471, Dr Taylor, 23 October 1853.
76 *LD* XV.507, 24 December 1853.
77 Newman, 1956, p.305.
78 *LD* XV.514, 28 December 1853.
79 Newman, 1956, p.312.
80 *LD* XVI.6, 2 January 1854.
81 Newman, 1956, p.315.
82 *LD* XVI.31, *from* Cardinal Wiseman, 20 January 1854; Newman, 1956, p.315.
83 Newman, 1956, p.316.
84 *LD* XVI.44, R. Stanton, 14 February 1854; XVI.55, James Hope-Scott, 24 February 1854; XVI.66, Mrs Wm. Froude, 2 March 1854; XVI.73, The Earl of Shrewsbury, 8 March 1854.
85 Cf McGrath, p.250.
86 *LD* XVI.99-100, Dessain *footnote*.
87 Newman, 1956, p.319.
88 *LD* XVI.76, J.L. Paterson, 9 March 1854.
89 Newman, 1956, p.323.
90 McGrath, 1951, p.200.
91 Newman, 1956, p.320.
92 Newman, 1956, p.322.
93 *LD* XVI.99, James Hope-Scott, 7 April 1854.
94 *LD* XVI.112 *footnote*.
95 *LD* XVI.126, Archbishop Cullen, 11 May 1854.
96 *LD* XVI.127 *footnote*.
97 *LD* XVI.557-61, Appendix 2, 29 April 1854.
98 *LD* XVI.166-7, 18 June 1854.
99 *LD* XVI.273, 6 October 1854.
100 McGrath, 1951, p.325.
101 *LD* XVI.273-4, Archbishop of Tuam, 8 October 1854.
102 *LD* XVI.275, 8 October 1854.
103 *LD* XVI.339, *from* Archbishop Cullen, 20 December 1854.
104 Wiseman, *LD* XVI.146, 5 June 1854; Ullathorne, *LD* XVI.146, 5 June 1854; et seq.
105 *LD* XVIII.xv Dessain.
106 *LD* XVI.286, 3 November 1854.
107 *LD* XVI.321 Archbishop Cullen, 8 December 1854.
108 *LD* XI.252 Henry Wilberforce, 24 September 1846.
109 *LD* XII.221 Ambrose Phillipps de Lisle, 15 June 1848.
110 *LD* XVI.477 *footnote*.
111 *LD* XVII.229, J.H. Pollen, 30 April 1856.
112 Meenan, 1987, p.5.
113 Culler, 1965, p.159.

114 *LD* XVI.535, 31 August 1855.
115 Cf Ker, 1990, p.417.
116 *LD* XVII.216, 14 April 1856.
117 *LD* XVII.286, 20 June 1856; *LD* XVII.280-5, *Memorandum*, 19 June 1856.
118 *LD* XVII.301, J.S. Flanagan, 29 June 1856.
119 *LD* XVII.510-11, 28 January 1857.
120 *LD* XVIII.30, 7 May 1857.
121 Murray, 1980, p.456, 'Decree Book, Appendix 6.
122 Gilley, 1990, p.291.
123 *LD* XVIII.228, 12 January 1858.
124 Newman, 1956, pp.392-30.
125 *LD* XIX.253, 15 December 1859.
126 Rigney, 1995, pp.325-6.
127 McGrath, 1951, p.494.
128 Cf Sencourt, 1948, p.160.
129 McGrath, 1951, p.508.
130 Coulson, 1978, p.235.
131 Culler, 1965, p.298.
132 Newman, 1987, preface p.9.
133 Ward, 1913, p.452.
134 Dessain, 1980, p.110.
135 Ker, 1990, p.464.
136 *LD* XVIII.16-17, 17 April 1857.
137 *LD* XVIII.17 *footnote*, 30 April 1857.
138 *LD* XVIII.527 *footnote*, 29 November 1858.
139 *LD* XVIII.527, 4 December 1858.
140 *LD* XVIII.527 *footnote*.
141 Ker, 1990, p.468.
142 *LD* XVIII.312, 5 April 1858.
143 Murray, 1980, Decree Book, p.462.
144 Trevor, 1996, p.188.
145 Cf Trevor, 1996, pp.188-9.
146 Trevor, 1996, p.190.
147 Murray, 1980, Decree Book, p.464.
148 Murray, 1980, Decree Book, p.465.
149 Chadwick, 1990, p.50.
150 Dessain, 1980, p.110.
151 *LD* XXI.332 memorandum, 21 September 1864.
152 *LD* XXI.286, Ambrose St John, 5 November 1864.
153 Newman, 1956, p.261.
154 *LD* XXI.308, 8 October 1864.
155 *LD* XXI.327, T.W. Allies, 30 November 1864.
156 *LD* XXI.412-13, 10 February 1865.
157 *LD* XXII.21-24, Bishop Ullathorne, 23 April 1866.
158 *LD* XXII. 224 *footnote*.
159 Butler, 1926, 2, p.14.
160 *LD* XXIII.164-5, 16 April 1867.
161 *LD* XXIII.190, 26 April 1867.
162 *LD* XXIII.192-3, 26 April 1867.

163 *LD* XXIII.145, 12 April 1867.
164 Ward, 1913, II, pp.144-45.
165 *LD* XXIII.281, James Hope-Scott, 2 August 1867.
166 *LD* XXIII.xv.
167 *LD* XXIII.298-99, 15 August 1867.
168 *LD* XXIII.312, 18 August 1867.
169 *LD* XXIII.312 *footnote*.
170 *LD* XXX.143 Lord Braye, 2 November 1882.
171 *LD* XXIII.326, 30 August 1867.

6

Newman:
Challenges and Controversies

NEWMAN relished argument; his polemical skills were honed at Oriel College where 'he learned much through academic duels and more by intellectual osmosis'.[1] The challenge of controversy fired his intellect and emotions, and he set about it with enthusiasm. In his writing and publishing he needed a stimulus, without which, he confessed, he could write 'neither with spirit nor with point'.[2] Through most of his adult life, Newman was engaged in controversial issues. As Butler puts it, 'for all his gentle and retiring nature, Newman was fated to be the storm centre'.[3]

In the face of the 'storm of obloquy' that resulted from *Tract 90*, Newman had stood his ground; and, according to McGrath, his 'resolute bearing' in later controversial encounters revealed a 'steely courage that is all the more remarkable in an avowedly sensitive nature'.[4] Newman was fully aware that his polemical skills were highly developed and largely influenced what he chose to write about. He told W.G. Ward, who had enquired whether, as rumoured, he was writing a book on the doctrine of papal infallibility: 'I am a controversialist, not a theologian'.[5]

Involvement in controversy often brought Newman

great personal distress, as with the Achilli case, but he bore this suffering with patience, especially when his reputation was assailed on all sides. Only his private correspondence and his journal reveal the depth of his feelings and disappointments. While, however, this 'remotely intellectual and almost introspective' figure may to some 'have seemed altogether too subtle and refined, even old-maidish' for the tough job of 'militant apologetics',[6] any such assessments of Newman were soon shown to be superficial. He entered the arena and achieved a reputation for his devastating satirical wit and rhetorical skills. As Chadwick observed: as an Anglican Newman had 'slaughtered the Roman Catholic Church with scorn and satire. As a new Roman Catholic he slaughtered the Church of England with scorn and satire, he whipped Achilli and trampled upon... Kingsley'.[7]

In his Anglican days, Newman had been a prime influence in the Oxford Movement (see Chapter 2), and had challenged the Church of England to wake up to the perils which, in his view, threatened her very existence. His intellectual leadership through the Tracts that he wrote and others that he arranged to have written, and also by his other writings, marked him out as a gifted communicator and controversialist. It was in those years that Newman had become involved in a controversy provoked by Sir Robert Peel's speech at the opening, in 1841, of a new library and reading room at Tamworth, near to where he lived. Peel had emphasised the utilitarian aspects of education (see Chapter 2). He declared that if people used the new reading facilities now available, 'they would gain knowledge and become more virtuous'.[8] McGrath states that Peel's speech was infused with 'the new religion of secular enlightenment which was to supplant the traditional creeds'.[9] It was this that fired Newman to make what Vargish describes as 'a brilliant and cruelly unqualified attack on liberal hopes for the moral and social effects of education'[10] (see Chapter 5 for discussion of Newman's philosophy of education).

In February 1841, Newman wrote a series of seven letters to *The Times*. These had been commissioned by the editor at the instigation of his son, who had just come down from Oxford and was full of enthusiasm about Newman. In his letters Newman subjected Peel's utterances to blistering satire. He condemned the Benthamite principles which underlay them and attacked 'the notion that education makes people morally better'.[11]

Richard Church – who was to became a disciple of Newman – alerted Frederic Rogers (later Newman's intimate friend and a legal adviser) that *The Times* had been letting in letters signed by 'Catholicus' against Sir R. Peel' and even 'puffed them in its leading article'. These letters were 'thought to smack strongly of Puseyism, and brought out furious attacks on the Puseyites'.[12] The identity of 'Catholicus' was never revealed, although suspicions about the origin of the letters were obviously aroused. Some time later, the letters appeared in a collection entitled: 'The Tamworth Reading Room'.

Gilley's summary of the debate is apt: 'Poor Peel: he had helplessly strayed into a rather simple-minded refutation of Newman's whole philosophy, in its assumption that reason or rational knowledge alone is the highway to Christian truth. Newman's refutation is one of his finest bursts of rhetoric'.[13] Apart from the interest and antagonism that these letters aroused in political and ecclesiastical circles, they are valuable in indicating the direction in which Newman was to develop his theories of education in the Dublin *Discourses* and the resultant *The Idea of a University* (see Chapter 5).

With the agitation caused by the 'Catholicus' letters still active, Newman was, once again, embroiled in controversy when, on 27th February 1841, *Tract 90* appeared, anonymously, although its authorship, as noted in Chapter 2, was an open secret. The consequences for Newman resulted in a fundamental redirection of his life. He retired to Littlemore and, four years later, became a Roman Catholic. Eventually he left Oxford in 1846.

An historic occasion for the resurgent Roman Catholic Church in England occurred when the first Provincial Synod of Westminster was held in July 1852, at Oscott. At the opening of the second session, Newman delivered a sermon which was later published as *The Second Spring*. This sermon celebrated the re-establishment of the Roman Catholic hierarchy and the growth of the Roman Catholic Church with what Ker describes as 'an exuberant, even (to modern ears) embarrassing triumphalism'.[14] Some other writers have been less inhibited in their praise of Newman's rhetoric. Gwynn said that the sermon 'expressed most vividly the feelings of all those present, in one of the most memorable discourses ever written... The eloquence and music of his style rose superbly as he described the ending of that winter and the return of spring' for English Roman Catholics.[15] For Norman, some of Newman's *Second Spring* was 'rhetorical embellishment, the justifiable exultation of those who had crossed to Rome, and landed more safely upon her shores than they could have expected; it was the relief of ancient families whose recusancy was at last no longer the whispered tradition of the rural English catacombs'.[16]

Chadwick says that while *Second Spring* expressed 'the euphoria which was felt in all the Churches', it was Newman's 'most eloquent (though far from his best) sermon'.[17] Gilley, however, has serious reservations. While Newman's 'evocation of the present perfectly captured the mood of the moment among the Oscott Fathers', Gilley describes the sermon as 'the bane of

English Catholic historiography in its dim and dismal view of the vigorous if hidden Catholic life in England in the previous three centuries'.[18] This irritation is understandable, for Newman's rhetoric tended at times to lose touch with historical facts. For example, he alluded mournfully to the days when Roman Catholicism 'was not a body... but a mere handful of individuals, who might be counted like the pebbles and detritus of the great deluge... a set of poor Irishmen, coming and going at harvest time, or a colony of them lodged in a miserable quarter of the vast metropolis. There, perhaps, an elderly person, seen walking in the streets, grave and solitary, and strange, though noble in bearing, and said to be of good family, and a "Roman Catholic"'.[19] Newman appeared to have overlooked – or even ignored for the sake of his rhetoric – that Roman Catholics in the early 19th century, as noted in Chapter 1, were a coherent body of some size whose members practised their faith in a 'quiet style... in order to respect Protestant sensibilities'. Unfortunately, as Norman suggests, this secretive behaviour had 'something of a reverse effect' and led to suspicions of Roman Catholicism.[20] The heightened emotional atmosphere generated by Newman's oratory overpowered both the preacher and his audience: 'When he came out from the Synod, they crowded upon him, giving full flow to the ardent outpourings of their gratitude'.[21]

Newman had preached this sermon shortly after he had been notified of the adverse verdict in the Achilli trial, because he had not been able, in the time available, to collect all the evidence necessary to prove his charges as we will later discuss. On hearing of the verdict, Wiseman had expressed 'amazement' and invited Newman to preach at the Synod. At the close of the Synod, Newman wrote to Henry Wilberforce: 'We ended the

Synod yesterday in great triumph, joy and charity'.[22] The only other references in his *Letters and Diaries* to the Synod and to his sermon are three one-line diary notes recording his attendance and 'preached before the Synod'.[23]

In Birmingham, during 1951, Newman had delivered 'a set of lectures in which I made charges against Dr Achilli, a Dominican friar, who had become a convert to the Protestant faith, which involved me in an action for libel'.[24] These lectures, as we saw in Chapter 4, were published as *Lectures on the Present Position of Catholics in England*. As he later told R.W. Church, he had 'ever considered' it as his 'best written book'.[25] Newman had heard that Achilli was to visit Birmingham during a lecture tour organised by the 'respectable but fanatical' Evangelical Alliance.[26] This 'former Dominican friar had become a popular hero in London by exposing the scandals of the Roman Inquisition. He himself had already been exposed by Cardinal Wiseman in the *Dublin Review* as a person notorious in his own country for the crimes of rape and adultery'.[27] This article, which appeared in July 1850, was reprinted as a pamphlet. In the fifth lecture of his series, *The Logical Inconsistency of the Protestant View*, Newman inserted a denunciation of Achilli, in the belief that 'Wiseman had all the Italian documents necessary to prove what the Dublin Review asserted'.[28] Thus he declared with confidence that Achilli was 'not to be believed', as his behaviour over a period of twenty years clearly showed.[29]

Unfortunately for Newman, a rumour circulated that Achilli, supported by the Evangelical Alliance was going to 'prosecute me for what I said of him in Lecture 5, though I only repeated the Cardinal's words, which he let pass'.[30]

Three days later Newman sent a Memorandum of the

Achilli case to Edward Badeley: 'From the enclosed, I fear I shall be proceeded against. It will take the Catholic body utterly by surprise, and I trust I shall have their whole energy to get me evidence'.[31] Newman also asked Mgr Talbot in Rome for documents and other assistance in this 'most anxious matter'.[32] He was assured of help by these correspondents.[33] On 27th October 1851, Newman recorded in his diary, 'legal notice served on me by Achilli's lawyers'.[34] He approached Talbot again, asking him to send at once an attested copy of Achilli's confession, which he had mentioned in conversation.[35] He also requested Wiseman to provide the documents on which he had based his accusations in the *Dublin Review* of July 1850. The Cardinal promised to do so. Fathers John Gordon and Nicholas Darnell were sent to Italy to seek information about Achilli but their search was unsuccessful because they had not been given adequate instructions and introductions by the Cardinal. 'He has been in a daydream, now he is awakened, and everyone is horribly frightened and very earnest and busy, when two good months or rather three have been lost'.[36] Wiseman was, of course, immersed in church affairs and 'overwhelmed with public activities of every kind since the hierarchy was announced',[37] so it is not surprising that Newman's demands failed to have his exclusive attention. The vital documents had been mislaid and were discovered too late, as was the evidence from Rome, to be of effective use. 'Newman was crippled because he could not yet produce evidence to counter Achilli'.[38] He told James Hope that 'Our great difficulty is this, that *at present we have no one good piece of evidence in our hands* – we cannot get any thing, people are so dilatory. I believe there is good evidence, but I have nothing to show the lawyers'.[39] Sister Maria Giberne, who was a sister-in-law of the Rev Walter Mayers, Newman's old schoolmaster and friend and who became a Roman Catholic in 1845, undertook, at Newman's request, a search for Italian witnesses of Achilli's scandalous behaviour. Eventually she located some and brought them to England and, as McGrath puts it, 'shepherded them during the trial'.[40] Many, however, 'could not be traced or would not come'.[41] Newman pleaded for time to collect evidence but his plea was rejected and the trial fixed for February 1852,[42] on the serious charge of criminal libel. Meanwhile, a national appeal had been opened by Wiseman to meet the costs of the trial. Donations flooded in to such an extent (nearly £13,000) that after disbursements, a sizeable surplus resulted, which Newman was to apply in building the University Church in Dublin.

After a 'series of portentous court hearings before the very anti-Catholic Chief Justice, Lord Campbell... on the 24th June a verdict was given against Newman'.[43] Newman's lawyers sought a re-trial but this was refused, and on 31st January 1853, he was sentenced by Judge Sir John Coleridge to a fine of £100 and imprisonment until paid. Furthermore, he had to endure the public humiliation of a 'misjudged lecture' from Coleridge to the effect 'that he had deteriorated in character since he became a Roman Catholic'.[44] As Norman notes, 'Even *The Times* judged the court hearings prejudicial... Newman had to endure a terrible sequence of events [from Achilli's continued lies] and his reputation sank to its lowest level in Protestant society'.[45] But despite his experiences, Newman felt able to reassure his friends: 'Of course the said fine was paid there and then and we walked off in triumph amid the hurrahs of 200 paddies'.[46] He told Mrs William Froude that Coleridge 'had committed a great mistake and impertinence in what he said... his speech was full of mistakes and inconsistencies... But I really think he was performing a duty'.[47] The Evangelical

Alliance withdrew their sponsorship of Achilli, and he went to New York and joined the Swedenborgian Church. So ended this sordid episode, but until the later years of the 19th century, 'the lectures of ex-priests or allegedly ex-priests were apparently a fashionable past-time for the Victorians, for as many as twenty such persons were plying their trade throughout England'.[48]

Shortly after the Oratory School was founded, Newman was entailed in another controversy. This arose from an article that he had written in the July, 1859 issue of the *Rambler*. This Roman Catholic journal had been launched by John Moores Capes, a Balliol convert, in 1848. Its contributors, for the most part, were well-educated lay converts who tended to have outspoken views across a wide rang of topics, including freedom to criticise the acts of the English Roman Catholic bishops.[49] This independent editorial policy became even more pronounced when an Oriel convert, Richard Simpson, was appointed assistant editor in 1854. The *Rambler's* 'latitudinarian spirit manifested by Simpson' caused Ullathorne to write to Newman in 1856 expressing his concern.[50] In 1858, Sir John Acton – 'Dollinger's brilliant pupil'[51] became part-proprietor of the *Rambler*, and Simpson was made editor. The journal continued its policy of free discussion of fields, including theology, to the increasing annoyance of the Roman Catholic hierarchy. According to Ward, the readers of the *Rambler* included 'English country gentry and clergy... descendants of the persecuted Roman Catholics long excluded from the Universities and from public life, or High-Church convert clergymen, few of whom were sensitive to intellectual interests' and who 'in their piety and religious instincts were startled at the manner adopted by the *Rambler*'.[52] Although the journal's circulation was only about 800, 'its influence was out of all proportion'.[53]

Matters came to a head when the January and February 1859 issues of the journal contained criticisms of the hostile attitude taken by the Roman Catholic hierarchy to a Royal Commission on elementary education. It was suspected by the bishops that co-operation with the government would lead to interference with the methods of religious teaching in Roman Catholic schools.[54] This unfavourable comment on the Roman Catholic hierarchy's reaction was anonymous. It had, however, been contributed by one of the Roman Catholic Inspectors of Schools who was the leading lay authority on Roman Catholic education, Scott Nasmyth Stokes.[55]

Ullathorne, on behalf of Wiseman and the other bishops, told Newman that it was their unanimous opinion that 'something must be done' about the *Rambler*, and that nothing short of Mr Simpson's retiring from the editorship will satisfy'.[56] Newman's intervention resulted in Simpson's immediate retirement, and, after much soul-searching, Newman accepted, although reluctantly, Acton's invitation 'to be editor... for a while'.[57] This decision was approved by Wiseman and Ullathorne. Newman issued an 'Advertisement' with the May issue of the *Rambler* stating that its editorial aims were 'to combine devotion to the [Roman Catholic] Church with discrimination and candour in the treatment of her opponents; for the refinement, enlargement and elevation of the intellect of the educated classes, etc.' Coverage would be 'a manly investigation of public interest under a deep sense of the prerogatives of ecclesiastical authority'.[58] Publication would be bi-monthly to allow extended discussion of topics. In Coulson's words, 'His short term policy was to take it out of the front line of controversy'.[59]

Newman's editorship was to be brief and turbulent, for in his very first issue he offended Wiseman and the rest of the Roman Catholic hierarchy by defending Stokes, whose article on education had already annoyed them. While apologising for the earlier criticisms of the bishops, Newman suggested that 'their Lordships really desire to know the opinions of the laity on subjects in which the laity are especially concerned'.[60] This opinion further incensed the bishops; Ullathorne called on Newman and 'expressed a wish that I should give up the *Rambler* after the July number'.[61] As Dessain remarks, the result was that Newman stopped the Tracts for the Times at 'a word from his Anglican bishop. He resigned the *Rambler* at Ullathorne's wish'.[62] Newman's Memorandum regarding Ullathorne's visit gives insight into the bishop's views: 'Our Laity were a peaceful set, the Church was *peace*. They had a deep faith they did not like to hear that any one doubted'. Newman responded that he saw one side only, the bishop another – 'that the bishop, etc., did not see the state of the laity (etc) in Ireland – how unsettled, yet how docile'. To which Ullathorne 'said something like, "Who are the Laity?" I answered that the Church would look foolish without them – *not* those words'.[63] Some years earlier, Newman had referred to Ullathorne's 'horror of laymen' and remarked that he himself was 'sure that they may be in this day the strength of the Church'.[64] In Ullathorne's opinion, according to Gilley, 'the Church teaching, the *ecclesia docens*, meant the clergy; and this *ecclesia docens* was not the laity, who were merely the passive *ecclesia docta*, the Church taught'.[65]

Newman reflected sadly to Wilberforce: 'All through my life I have been plucked… it made me feel that my occupation was gone when the Bishop [Ullathorne] put his extinguisher on the *Rambler*.[66]

Newman's final edition of the *Rambler*, in July 1859, added coals to the fire that he had already set alight when he developed the theme of asking the opinions of the laity in an essay entitled *On Consulting the Faithful in Matters of Doctrine*. In this essay he stressed the significance of the united testimony of the faithful, the *consensus fidelium* – which involves both clergy and laity. 'This had been very fully done in the case of the definition of the Immaculate Conception, 1854'.[67] Dessain comments that 'Newman laid great stress on the consent of the faithful... [which] was more than a witness to the truth... The Church was a Communion, with a common conscience, that of all its members, and was not to be looked on as a mere juridical entity, ruled by officers. Bishops, priests and laity formed one body, and there must be consultation and trust, for the laity was an essential part of the Church'. Dessain states that this teaching was to be incorporated in the Conciliar Decree on the Church at the Second Vatican Council. Although Newman's original declaration was resented by English Catholic theologians and authorities, 'no-one was in a position to dispute Newman's facts'.[68]

Some misunderstanding arose, however, over Newman's use of the term 'consulting'. Objections were raised, for example, by Dr John Gillow of Ushaw Seminary, to whom Newman explained, 'Doubtless had the passage been in Latin and formally dogmatic, "consult" was not the word to have used. But in popular English it seems to me neither inaccurate nor dangerous. To the unlearned reader, the idea conveyed by "consulting" is not necessarily that of asking an opinion. For instance, we speak of consulting a barometer about the weather. The barometer does not give us its opinion, but ascertains for us a fact... I had not a dream of understanding the word, as used in the Rambler, in the sense of *asking an opinion*'.[69] Gillow accepted Newman's explanation, 'It is most gratifying that there is not a shadow of difference between us on any point of principle'.[70] However, the matter was not to rest with this exchange of personal letters. On 3rd October 1859, Bishop Brown of Newport complained to the Congregation of Propaganda at Rome about a 'most unfortunate essay published in July last in the *Rambler*'.[71] In his delation to Propaganda, the bishop wrote disapprovingly of 'a great portion of the converted clergy' who 'join in considerable numbers the Oratory of Dr Newman in Birmingham, or that of Dr Faber in London, neither of which have I believe more than one of the original Catholics among them, so that there is a great danger of certain Protestant motives and feelings being fostered'.[72] This 'very grave matter[73] was referred to Cardinal Barnabo, Prefect of Propaganda, who asked Ullathorne – who was on a visit to Rome – for an explanation of Newman's article. On his return to England, Ullathorne saw Newman and sought an explanation. Newman was prepared to give this and drafted a letter to Wiseman, asking for specific details of the passages on which Propaganda sought elucidation. This letter was shown to Ullathorne and then sent to Rome via Wiseman.[74] A schedule of the statements in the *Rambler* requiring explanation was presented to Wiseman by Propaganda, but this was never sent on to Newman. This omission resulted in serious misunderstanding in Rome about Newman's behaviour and, as Dessain says, 'it was concluded and thought for years that Newman had refused to comply'.[75] As Trevor puts it, 'At Propaganda Newman continued to be regarded as a writer of heretical articles who did not trouble to defend himself and who was responsible for all the views printed in the *Rambler*'.[76] Since Newman had kept silence and had heard nothing more from Rome he thought 'the whole matter was hushed up', as he told one of his trusted friends, Miss E. Bowles.[77] It was not until 1867, when Ambrose St John showed Barnabo a copy of Newman's letter to Wiseman that this unfortunate matter was cleared up and Newman's reputation was restored.[78]

The passages in the *Rambler* article requiring elucidation were later pointed out to Newman and, according to Butler, 'he wrote a theological explanation which was accepted as satisfactory'.[79] Speculations about the reasons why this lamentable misconception arose have been various. For Butler, 'The thing was but a piece of unfortunate bungling, for which Wiseman must take the principal blame, but neither Manning nor Talbot can be acquitted of a share in the responsibility'.[80] 'Wiseman's negligence' is explained by Gilley on the grounds that 'he was suffering from the onset of diabetes, and was preoccupied with the Errington affair' – a controversy over his likely successor at Westminster – 'as well as by his legendary inefficiency'. But neither could Manning be absolved. He was said to be 'open to the charge of finding it convenient to leave' Newman under suspicion.[81]

After July, 1859, when Newman had relinquished the editorship of the *Rambler*, Acton and Simpson resumed editorial responsibilities. They tended to ignore his advice to 'keep off theology proper and to avoid conflicts with the ecclesiastical authorities and all irritation of average Catholic opinion'.[82] Eventually, complaints from Rome in May 1862, led to the English bishops condemning the journal. Ullathorne wrote to all his clergy censuring the *Rambler* and its successor *Home and Foreign Review*, a quarterly which had just been launched. Newman expressed his gratitude to his bishop for the 'clear and direct way' he had stated his objections and with which he 'concurred with all his heart'.[83] Ullathorne acknowledged Newman's support very affably, and sent a copy of his letter to Wiseman. This was shown to Manning who 'read it with great thankfulness: not that I doubted what he [Newman] would say, but I feared that he would not say it. He has a sort of sensitiveness about standing by his friends even when in the wrong which is very honourable to his generosity'.[84] The *Home and Foreign Review* ceased publication after only eight issues.

Newman recorded in his journal that the reason why he had not written from 1859 to 1864 was his 'failure with the *Rambler*'. He thought that he had 'got into a scrape, and it became one to be silent. So they thought in Rome, if Mgr Talbot is to be their spokesman'.[85] Newman's silence was broken by an unexpected controversy with Charles Kingsley, Regius Professor of Modern History at Cambridge, the rector of Eversley, and a popular novelist. Kingsley's unprovoked attack was unpleasant, and in Chadwick's view it attempted to capitalise on 'Newman's low reputation. For part of public opinion Newman was one, who had been a secret Roman Catholic while he was an Anglican priest and therefore was associated with underhand behaviour'.[86]

The conflict arose from a review in the January 1864 issue of *Macmillan's Magazine* of some volumes of a history of England by James Anthony Froude, a younger brother of Hurrell, and known for his anti-(Roman) Catholic feelings.[87] A copy of the review, which appeared under the initials 'CK', was sent, anonymously, to Newman (the sender was later identified as William Pope when he wrote to Newman),[88] who protested to the publishers that he had been accused of teaching that truth for its own sake need not, and on the whole ought not to be, a virtue with the Roman clergy. This serious allegation was unsupported by any evidence from his writings. Newman emphasised that he was not seeking reparation, but merely wished to draw the attention of the publishers to a 'grave and gratuitous slander'.[89] To Newman's amazement, Kingsley wrote acknowledging authorship of the review, and stating that his 'words were just' and 'expressly referred to one of Newman's sermons on "Subjects of the Day", published in 1844'. He offered to retract publicly his accusation if he had misunderstood Newman's meaning.[90] Newman responded that the sermon in question was given, and published, when he was an Anglican and Vicar of St Mary's, Oxford, and no statement, such as that made in the review, occurred in that sermon.[91]

In a pleasant exchange of letters with Macmillans, Newman conceded that if he 'were in active controversy with the Anglican body, or any portion of it', as he 'had been before now', 'he should consider untrue assertions about me to be in a certain rule of the game, as times go, though God forbid that I should indulge in them in the case of another. I have never been very sensitive of such attacks; rarely taken notice of them'. But sometimes he was sent examples of such attacks and 'sometimes they are such as I am bound to answer'.[92] Thereupon, Kingsley sent Newman a draft of the apology he had submitted to his publishers, adding that this was 'the only course fit for a gentleman'.[93] Newman referred the 'apology' to his lawyer friend, Edward Badeley, who considered it 'totally inadequate'.[94] It contained the words: 'no man knows the use of words better than Dr Newman. No man, therefore, has a better right to define what he does, or does not, mean by them'.[95] In a letter to Kingsley, Newman declared that the main fault of the proposed apology was that it 'would lead the general reader' to believe that he 'had been confronted with definite extracts from his works' to support the allegations made in Kingsley's criticism of him.[96] Newman also wrote again to Macmillans about the review,.'which I considered a great affront to myself, and a worse insult to the Catholic priesthood'. He pointed out that as Kingsley's draft apology ignored his principal objection, he had no hesitation in rejecting it.[97]

As he had earlier intimated to the publishers, Newman then arranged to publish the correspondence, preceded by a long extract from Kingsley's review and with the addition of *Reflections* which, with devastating satire, commented on Kingsley's letters.[98] This pamphlet, *Mr Kingsley and Dr Newman: A Correspondence on the Question whether Dr Newman teaches that Truth is not Virtue*, appeared on 12th February 1864.[99] It caused a sensation and aroused much previously latent sympathy for Newman among English Roman Catholics, including many of the clergy as well as laity. Among well-known journalists who supported Newman was Richard Holt Hutton, editor of the *Spectator* and a former Unitarian who had become an Anglican. He wrote an article, *Father Newman's Sarcasm* (20th February 1864), in which he referred to Newman as 'not only one of the greatest of English writers, but, perhaps, the very greatest master of delicate and polished sarcasm in the English language... Mr Kingsley is a choice though, perhaps too helpless a victim for the full exercise of Father Newman's powers'.[100]

Kingsley was stung by this and 'proceeded to make his case a great deal worse'[101] by publishing, on 20th March, *What then does Dr Newman mean?*. This 'proved to be both violent and unscientific in its numerous charges'[102] and according to Maisie Ward was a 'complicated tissue woven out of half truths and entire falsehoods'.[103] Oddie's view is that Kingsley's accusation was not a 'careless mistake' but, on the contrary, 'the result of a long and deeply-felt distaste for the Catholic religion and for Newman personally'.[104]

Newman had been reflecting on the grave but unsubstantiated charges made by a prominent public figure against him and the Catholic priesthood, and he began to recognise the need to develop a well-argued defence of his life and activities. A decade or so later, he wrote that Kingsley had been 'accidentally the instrument in the good Providence of God, by whom I had an opportunity given me which otherwise I should not have had, of vindicating my character and conduct in my Apologia'.[105] At the time he had confided to Church that 'it had always been on my mind that some day I should be called on to defend my honesty while in the Church of England'. He had been publicly challenged by Kingsley – 'a furious fellow' – so he must speak, 'unless I speak strongly, men won't believe me in earnest'.[106] He told Copeland, 'I am writing my answer to Kingsley's pamphlet, and this is what I think. The whole strength of what he says, *as directed rhetorically* to the popular mind, lies in the antecedent prejudice that I *was a Papist while I was an Anglican*. Mr K. *implies this*. The only way in which I can destroy this, is to give my history, and the history of my mind, from 1822 or earlier, down to 1845'.[107]

After Easter, Newman started to assemble some of his relevant papers, and he also asked his old Anglican friends, such as Church, Keble, Rogers, and Copeland, and also his sister Jemima, to lend him letters, which they gladly did. Chadwick notes that 'Without intending to write this book, he prepared to write it for three or four years… when his entire life was challenged, he hardly needed to think what to say. Almost all the material lay at his fingertips'.[108] This was also the view of an earlier writer on Newman, who said that 'there already lay in Newman's mind a series of long-standing, though dormant, unrelated, thoughts and attitudes which were capable potentially of combining for action, let the right stimulus occur'.[109]

Newman thanked Richard Hutton for an article in the Spectator, 26th March, *Roman Casuistry and Protestant Prejudice*, in which Kingsley's pamphlet, *What, then, does Dr Newman mean?,* was dismissed as 'aggravating the original injustice a hundredfold'. He assured Hutton that 'it is impossible not to feel that you have uttered on the whole what I should say of myself, and to see that you have done me a great service in doing so, as bearing external testimony'.[110]

Newman got down quickly to writing the *Apologia pro Vita Sua.* Sencourt says that 'He wrote with a concentration of effort, passion and genius kindred to that with which he had written at Littlemore nineteen and twenty years before'.[111] He worked long hours, 'sometimes at my work for 16 hours running'.[112] He informed Sir John Acton that 'I am writing from morning till night, and against time, which is not pleasant'.[113] By mid-June the *Apologia* was written and, as he told Canon J. Walker, an old friend, 'At length I am a free man... I have had a terrible time of it, not only from the extreme stress of my work, but from my great anxiety, and also for the special trial it has been to my feelings'.[114]

The *Apologia* first appeared in weekly parts on the seven Thursdays from 21st April to 2nd June, 1864, with the title: *Apologia pro Vita Sua being a reply to a pamphlet entitled 'What then does Dr Newman mean?'.*[115] In May 1865, Newman brought out a second definitive edition of the *Apologia* which omitted the first two polemical sections against Kingsley.[116] Maisie Ward describes the omitted passages as 'journalism, and out of place when the book had taken its permanent form',[117] and Chadwick judges that 'some epigrams against Kingsley were more cheap than worthy'.[118] Newman also inserted a short preface and re-titled the volume simply as *History of my Religious Opinions.* In 1873, the original title was restored with an additional subtitle, *Being a History of Religious Opinions.* As Chadwick points out, the contents of the *Apologia* were 'somewhat changed in successive editions with a view to meeting important critics'.[119] Certain Roman Catholic critics, for example, had regarded some of Newman's remarks about the Church of England offensive, and he modified them.[120] But he told another ecclesiastical critic, 'I have altered only with the purpose of expressing my own meaning more exactly'.[121]

Kingsley was in France while the *Apologia* was appearing and on returning he sent Macmillans an 'ultimatum on the Newman question which could be shown, privately, to any and every one you like'. It was an unrepentant endorsement of what he had written earlier, remarkable only for its bitter animosity and invective. He declared that, 'I cannot be weak enough to put myself a second time, by any fresh act of courtesy, into the power of one who, like a treacherous ape, lifts up to you meek and suppliant eyes, till he thinks he has you within his reach, and then springs, gibbering and biting, at your face'.[122] But when, just over ten years later, Newman heard of Kingsley's 'so premature death', he wrote that he was 'shocked' and added that 'I never from the first felt any anger towards him. As I said in the first pages of the *Apologia*, it is very difficult to be angry with a man one has not seen'.[123]

In his journal Newman noted that 1864 had been 'marvellously blest, for which I have regained, or rather gained, the favour of Protestants, I have received the approbation, in formal addresses, of a good part of the English (Roman Catholic) clerical body... Then again it has pleased Protestants, and of all parties, as much or more'.[124] In Chadwick's judgement, Newman's *Apologia* did more than clear himself of the charge that he did not care for truth; it 'persuaded Protestants that the Roman Catholic Church cared for truth'.[125] Once more, Newman became a well-known and respected figure to whom 'men and women of all religions and none turned to for guidance'.[126] Non-Catholics appreciated the fairness and historical accuracy with which Newman discussed his Anglican days, and his obvious respect and warm feelings for the Church of England were reflected in the *Apologia*. Coulson states that the work made clear that Newman's move to Rome 'did not imply a wholesale repudiation of the tradition in which he had been formed, but rather its affirmation in what Newman came to regard as its legitimate setting'.[127] This fits in with what he had written to Canon E. Estcourt a few years earlier when he had declared that 'Catholics did not make us Catholics; Oxford made us Catholics'.[128] His generous references to the Church of his early life warmed Anglican hearts; they had not expected a Roman convert to acknowledge publicly and with affection the influence of the Church of England in his spiritual odyssey.[129] As Norman points out, Manning and fellow ultramontanes bristled at Newman's references to Anglicanism as 'capable of authentic spirituality'[130] and Newman himself was aware that, for some years, he was regarded with suspicion by the Roman authorities as well as by sections of the Roman Catholic community in England.[131] While Ullathorne voiced the general approbation of Roman Catholics, Butler notes that these feelings were not shared by 'the Manning group, whose antagonism to Newman had by this date become definite and pronounced'. They were 'little pleased' by the prestige which the *Apologia* brought to him.[132] In a letter to Hope-Scott, Newman revealed his awareness of certain hostile attitudes towards him: 'As to my writing more, speaking in confidence I do not know how to do it. One cannot speak ten words without ten objections being made to each... I never can be sure that great lies may not be told about me at Rome'. There had indeed been some rumours that he had been about to leave the Church

Mgr Talbot 'put it about that I had subscribed to Garibaldi'. He 'knew well enough how the movement against me in Rome began, in 1855', and he alluded to the correspondence between London Oratory and Propaganda against him (see Chapter 4).[133]

The *Apologia* is not readily classifiable. Griffin describes it as 'in part a chronicle of Newman's own perplexities'.[134] It has also been popularly referred to as Newman's spiritual autobiography, although he did not describe it so himself.[135] It is, as Oddie states, 'notably deficient in the usual biographical details' to qualify as an autobiography, but in Ker's opinion, it is essentially an autobiography, 'an austerely intellectual work', as its subtitle indicates. He agrees that it is often called a 'spiritual' autobiography, but points out that 'in the strictly narrow sense of the word it is very far from being a spiritual work like St Augustine's Confessions, with which it is often compared'.[136] Earlier, the same writer described the *Apologia* as 'an intellectual – rather, theological – autobiography'.[137] In a preface to an edition of the *Apologia*, Ker states that it 'stands clearly within a recognisable genre' and was influenced by the English Protestant autobiographical traditions of conversion originated by Bunyan and followed by the Evangelical Thomas Scott'.[138] Gilley, however, considers a central portion of the *Apologia* (parts III-VI) 'hardly critical autobiography'; rather, it is the 'spiritual romance of a soul in its loves and hates, and though the facts as Newman reported them were coloured and occasionally distorted by his imagination, the work convinced not so much by its truthfulness as by its obvious allegiance to the spirit of truth, a burning sincerity'.[139]

Chadwick expresses a similar view when he writes that Newman 'must convince the public of his sincerity because it was his sincerity which was challenged, and the book is manifestly true'.[140] This evaluation seems to uphold the comment of an earlier writer, namely that although the title *Apologia* suggests 'consciously intended distortion', after 'examination of his private letters and diaries, and his published works, and the comments of contemporary friends and enemies, we come away convinced that the picture is substantially true. Of course it is shaded a little... The admirable thing is that under the circumstances Newman deviated so little from the truth'.[141] A modern writer, A.N. Wilson, in a reflective view of Newman's text, states that, 'As a religious treatise, the *Apologia* must be one of the most paradoxical documents in the history of the world... It describes how Newman came to an unequivocal faith in the Roman Catholic religion... Yet as every page in the *Apologia* makes clear, Newman was guided by something more mysterious than argument'.[142] Newman himself said that the *Apologia* was not a history of the Oxford Movement but of himself: 'it is an egotistical matter from beginning to end. It is to prove that I did not act *dishonourably*'.[143]

While immersed in the Kingsley controversy, Newman had been seized with 'a very vivid apprehension of immediately impending death, apparently derived from a medical opinion'.[144] After the *Apologia* had been published, and on a sudden inspiration, he started writing, on 17th January 1865, what was to be his longest and most successful poem: *The Dream of Gerontius*, which was completed the following month. As he told a close friend: 'I wrote on till it was finished, on small bits of paper. And I could no more write with any thing else by willing it, than I could fly'.[145] Apparently, when Newman had completed the poem, he put it to one side and it was only when he was asked to contribute to the journal *Month*, founded by Fanny Margaret Taylor in 1864 for 'educated readers', that he unearthed it and sent for publication.

After a year the journal was taken over by the Jesuits and edited by Newman's friend Fr Henry Coleridge, and *The Dream of Gerontius* appeared under his editorship during April and May 1865.

With poetic intensity and religious fervour, *The Dream of Gerontius* described the passage of the faithful Christian soul from this world to its eternal destiny. 'It pierces, indeed, beyond the veil, but in strict accordance or analogy with what every Catholic holds to be there... [it is] at once an allegory and an act of faith'.[146]

The 'other-worldliness' of *The Dream* attracted immediate attention. Newman had once belonged to a study group in Oxford, which was set up in 1829 in line with the popular vogue for prophetical speculation about millennial expectations.[147] It was read by all classes; in 1868, *Hymns Ancient and Modern* included the anthem 'Praise to the Holiest in the height' from the 'Fifth Choir of Angelicals' in *The Dream*. Added appeal was acquired when, allegedly, the ill-fated General Gordon was reported to have an annotated copy with him at Khartoum in the 1880s.[148] But it was not until Elgar set Newman's poem to music in his Oratorio, first performed in 1900, that it achieved national recognition. Gilley has commented that to modern sensibilities the 'frank Christian eschatology' of the words of the oratorio 'must sound even more odd than most sacred music to secular sensibilities'.[149]

In September 1865, Pusey sent Newman a copy of a book that he had written whose extended title suggested a peace-offering: *The Church of England a Portion of Christ's One Holy Catholic Church and a Means of Restoring Visible Unity, an Eirenicon, in a letter addressed to the author of the Christian Year'*. It was thus ostensibly addressed to John Keble. This publication resulted from a controversy between Manning and Pusey.

The former had published the *Workings of the Holy Spirit in the Church of England, a Letter to the Rev. E.B. Pusey* at the end of 1864. In friendly terms it acknowledges the 'great religious wave and outpouring of grace' being experienced by individual members of the Christian community, irrespective of their affiliations, but nevertheless maintains, as Butler puts it, that 'the Church of England is in no part of the Church Catholic, and in the strictest sense no Church at all'.[150] Pusey had attacked what he alleged were extravagances in the Roman Catholic doctrine and devotion relating to the Blessed Virgin Mary, and also to the infallibility of the Pope (even though the doctrine of papal infallibility was not defined as such until 1870). Pusey's plea for peace and unity between the Churches was, however, curiously designed, for, as Chadwick notes, he 'spent most of the time telling the world what were the main obstacles to unity, which were the errors of the Church of Rome, and therefore his olive branch looked, as Newman said, as though it were 'discharged from a catapult'.[151]

Newman was reluctant to become involved in this controversy, and told Pusey that he felt he had no 'imperative duty to remark on anything you said in your book. I dare say there is a great deal on which I should agree'.[152] This detached view was soon to be discarded for a rigorous response, presumably provoked by reading the book in detail. Newman then wrote that, 'It is true, too true, that your book disappointed me. It does seem to me that Irenicon [sic] is a misnomer; and that it is calculated to make most (Roman) Catholics very angry – and that is because they will consider it rhetorical and unfair… An Irenicon smoothes difficulties; I am sure people will think that you increase them'. People were saying that his book was an *attack* on Rome, as the *Guardian* had observed, in his references to 'the cultus of the BVM'.[153]

In reply, Pusey avowed that he had 'no intention of attacking anything'. He wished 'the official teaching of the Church [of England] alone to be of obligation and the popular manifestations of devotion to the BVM to be disowned'.[154] Newman commented on this that 'If I am led to publish any thing (of which I have no present intention) I should treat the book simply as an Irenicon [sic], as you wish'.[155] Over the next few weeks several letters were exchanged, culminating in one in which Newman told Pusey that he intended to 'publish a Letter on your Irenicon. I wish to accept it as such and shall write in that spirit'. He wished to correct any misapprehensions that may have arisen about Pusey's book.[156] Newman also advised Keble of his intention, adding that Pusey's book 'has made people very angry'.[157] Pusey responded at once 'As you said of me, "I am safe in your hands."'[158]

Despite illness Newman completed *A Letter to the Rev. E.B. Pusey DD on his recent Eirenicon* on 8th December 1865, the feast of the Immaculate Conception of the BVM, and it was published on 31st January 1866. It sold 2,000 copies in a fortnight. Newman limited discussion to Roman Catholic 'belief and devotion to our Lady, and appealed to the witness of the primitive Church'. He also insisted that the 'undeniable devotional extravagances cited by Pusey should be disowned by Roman Catholics'.[159] Keble and Pusey welcomed the *Letter*, and *The Times* gave it a one-page sympathetic review, written by R.W. Church, later Dean of St Paul's. Various 'old' Roman Catholic clergymen gave it their approval but the ultramontanes were 'fiercely indignant'.[160] Manning was warned by Talbot 'to stand firm as the advocate of Roman views in England against Newman and the Old Catholics who rally round him in opposition to you and Rome... To be Roman is to an Englishman an effort. Dr Newman is more English than the English. His spirit must be crushed'. Manning, now Archbishop-elect after the death of Wiseman in February, 1865, assured Talbot that his views of Newman were correct, and that there was 'much danger of an English Catholicism of which Newman was the highest type. It is the old Anglican, patristic, literary, Oxford tone transplanted into the Church... In one word, it is worldly Catholicism, and it will have the worldly on its side, and will deceive many'.[161]

Thomas Allies wrote to Newman complaining of Pusey's 'untruthfulness' which he found 'so revolting'. Newman responded charitably that, 'As to Pusey, it is harsh to call any mistakes of his untruthfulness. I think they arise from the same slovenly habit which some people would recognise in his dress, his beard, etc. He never answers letters, I believe, which do not lie in the line of the direct work which he has on hand. And so, in composing a book, he takes uncommon pains about some points... but he will combine with this extreme carelessness in respect to other statements... He goes into print with the same heedless readiness and decisiveness with which he would say words in conversation'.[162] In similar vein Newman wrote to a Jesuit priest, Fr H.J. Coleridge that 'It must be recollected that your object is to convince those who respect and love Dr Pusey, that he has written hastily and rashly and gone beyond measure'.[163]

On 12th February, Ullathorne wrote thanking Newman for his 'most beautiful Reply to Dr Pusey's *Irenicon*, but added that 'some priests were uneasy about Newman's exposition of original sin'.[164] Newman immediately replied, 'corrections are being sent to the printers by tonight's post'.[165] Ullathorne sent a copy of this letter to Manning to reassure him of Newman's orthodoxy and wish to clarify what he had written. In general, according to Butler, 'theological opinion among the English Catholics ran with Newman, the counter-current being limited to the group of Manning's inner circle. At Rome, too, the sympathy seems to have been with him'.[166]

Newman's own assessment of the reception given by Roman Catholics to his *Letter to Pusey* is contained in a personal letter in which he thanked Pusey for his 'sympathy about the attacks he had suffered'. He assured Pusey that *The Times*' review was very satisfying, and that 'my own bishop, Dr Clifford and most of the other bishops are with me'. He had received letters from the 'most important centres of theology and of education through the country, taking part with me'.[167]

In view of the opposition he had encountered, mostly from the ultramontanes, Newman decided not to write on other matters, namely, 'the development of Revelation and papal infallibility',[168] which Pusey had raised in his *Eirenicon*. He refuted a press report alleging that he had been 'prevented by superior authority from publishing a second letter to Dr Pusey on the subject of Papal Infallibility, or on any other subject whatever'.[169]

Newman had been aware of the furore aroused in the 1860s by the publication of *Essays and Reviews*. This controversial collection of essays by six prominent Anglican clerics and a notable layman (the *Septem contra Christum*) represented Broad Church or liberal views in Victorian Anglicanism. Natural rather than miraculous or supernatural explanations of long-held beliefs were promoted. Biblical narratives should be subject to rigorous historical and critical evaluation, bearing in mind, for example, scientific discoveries. Such radical opinions were condemned by the Anglican bishops and by almost 11,000 clergy, although Dean Arthur Stanley suggested that the Church should be prepared to discuss the Scriptures in relation to the field of modern knowledge.

At that particular time, Newman argued that the issues raised by the Essayists were less critical for Catholics than for other Christians, because 'Catholics had a sufficient base of faith in an infallible Church and did not depend on Scripture alone'.[170] He amplified this point in a letter to a High Church clergyman: 'The religion of England depends, humanly speaking, on belief in "the Bible and the Whole Bible"... Now the plenary inspiration of Scripture is peculiarly a Protestant question; not a Catholic. We indeed devoutly receive the whole Bible as the Word of God, but we receive it on the authority of the Church and the Church has defined very little as to the aspects under which it comes from God, and the limits of the inspiration'.[171]

It was not until the First Vatican Council's closer definition of the notion of inspiration that Newman considered that a belief in biblical inspiration was likely to cause Catholics any particular difficulties.[172] That he was aware of the problems of biblical criticism may be seen from one of his later letters: 'It is clear that we shall have to discuss the question whether certain passages of the Old Testament are or are not mythical. It is one of the gravest of questions, and we cannot spend too much time in preparing for it'.[173] Newman recognised the highly sensitive nature of the task he had taken on, and so he consulted Archbishop Errington and Bishop Clifford during the time he was writing his article. However, despite his careful approach a Maynooth professor of theology attacked what he had written, but there was no long-standing disagreement. While engrossed in writing the article, Newman commented that he wished that Scripture should be read 'as a book given us by God, inspired, a guide – and a comfort'.[174] His approach to biblical studies was to influence the deliberations of the Second Vatican Council.

In the elections of July 1874, Gladstone's government suffered defeat. Gladstone attributed it largely to the Irish hierarchy's opposition led by Cullen, now a Cardinal, to his Irish University Bill. This proposed integrating the Catholic University in Ireland into an undenominational system of higher education. The concept of 'mixed education' had already been rejected by the Irish bishops, as was discussed earlier in Chapter 5. As a result of losing the election, Gladstone was forced to resign and, freed from prime-ministerial responsibilities and leadership of the Liberal Party, and without the need to cultivate the Irish vote, he felt free to comment publicly and adversely on the influence of Roman Catholicism on political life.

In an article, *Ritualism*, in the 1874 issue of the *Contemporary Review*, Gladstone commented on the Public Worship Regulation Bill, which aimed to suppress the growth of ritualism in the Church of England, and declared that attempts to 'Romanise' the Church of England were 'utterly hopeless' for several reasons. Among these was that any one becoming a Roman Catholic renounced his moral and mental freedom and 'placed his civil loyalty and duty at the mercy of another'.[175] As Chadwick puts it, the decree that defined the doctrine of papal infallibility having been issued in 1870, had been misunderstood and misrepresented by many, including Gladstone, as meaning that a Roman Catholic 'would not be likely to be a loyal citizen of Great Britain'.[176] Gladstone also made several misleading references to the *Syllabus of Errors*, issued in Rome on 8th December 1864, as an appendix to the encyclical *Quanta Cura*. In a pamphlet, *The Vatican Decrees in their bearing on Civil Allegiance: a Political Expostulation*, which was published on 5th November 1874, and sold almost 150,000 copies within a few weeks, Gladstone made what

Norman describes as an 'extraordinary outburst' which was a 'classic of antiCatholicism'.[177] According to Sencourt, not only was his 'language intemperate' but 'his ideas were inexact'.[178] He confused, for instance, the hostility of the Irish bishops towards the Irish University Bill and the definition of papal infallibility and its powers. Griffin says, however, that Gladstone's *Expostulation* represents 'the last major complaint of English Protestants against Roman Catholics – that they were subject to a foreign power and therefore suspect in their loyalty to the English nation'.[179] Such public distortions attracted vigorous responses from several prominent Roman Catholics, including Manning and, most notably, Newman, who was pressed by his friends, including the Duke of Norfolk, to respond.[180]

Newman confided to R.W. Church that 'I never thought I should be writing against Gladstone... but he is unfair and untrue as he is cruel'.[181] Initially he experienced problems in tackling Gladstone's 'parenthetic, sweeping declamation'[182] but on receiving a copy of Gladstone's pamphlet from Ambrose Phillipps de Lisle, he was able to tell Lord Emly, 'Today I have begun on a new arrangement of matter'.[183] He obtained the agreement of the Duke of Norfolk that, in order to avoid addressing Gladstone directly, his reply should take the form of a Letter.[184] As Newman told Mrs Henry Wilberforce, 'I could not help answering Mr Gladstone: so many friends and strangers asked me – and I felt something was due to my own character – for *could* I allow that I was instrumental in bringing a number of persons into a Church in which they lost their mental and moral freedom and were bad subjects of the State?'.[185]

In a diary note for 21st December 1874, Newman recorded, 'finishing the pamphlet by this day, making altogether 4 weeks'.[186] He wrote to Lord Emly advising him that the *Letter* was completed and remarked that 'I am very bold – and cannot be surprised if I make some people very angry. But, if I am to write, I will say my say'.[187]

The *Letter to the Duke of Norfolk* was published on 14th January 1875, and Gladstone wrote at once, thanking Newman for the 'genial and gentle manner' in which he had treated him.[188] In thanking Gladstone for his 'forbearing and generous letter', Newman assured him that it had been 'a great grief to have to write against one' whose career he had always followed with 'loyal interest and admiration'.[189] Among Roman Catholics, the *Letter* received immediate acclaim. Newman told Lord Blachford, 'I certainly had my reward... from the old Catholics, from bishops, Jesuits, Dominicans, and various clergy, who have with one voice concurred in what I have written'.[190] In a pastoral letter, on 14th October 1875, Cardinal Cullen had referred to Gladstone's *Expostulation* which had been 'admirably answered by the venerable Dr Newman, for many years the great and pious rector of the Catholic University, whom Ireland will ever revere'.[191] Such widespread public support was reassuring to Newman because some complaints had been made about certain passages in the *Letter*, over which Ullathorne had been asked to remonstrate with Newman. He refused to do so, and Manning's support for Newman is also evident from his correspondence with Rome.[192] The doctrinal soundness of Newman's pamphlet was finally agreed by Rome. As Fr Henry Tristram observes, 'it was Newman who, of all that distinguished statesman's (Gladstone's) Catholic opponents, made by far the most effective defence of the encyclical *Quanta Cura*, the *Syllabus*, and the Vatican definition (of papal infallibility) in his *Letter to the Duke of Norfolk*'.[193]

About six years after the controversy which brought

about the *Letter*, Newman received from Gladstone – who was again prime minister – a letter with documents alleging that some Irish Roman Catholic priests were giving sermons that, if they were laymen, might well be considered seditious. Gladstone asked Newman to make representations to Rome so that the Pope should direct these priests 'to fulfil the elementary duties of citizenship'.[194] Newman replied, 'I think you overrate the Pope's power in political and social matters. It is absolute in questions of theology, but not so in practical matters... local power and influence is often more than a match for Roman right'.[195]

The last public controversy in which Newman took part occurred in 1885, when he was in his 85th year. This arose from an article in the *Contemporary Review* of May 1885 written by A.M. Fairbairn, Principal elect of the Airedale (Congregationalist) Theological College, Bradford, in which Newman was accused of 'philosophical scepticism in removing the proofs of religion from the sphere of reason into that of conscience and imagination'.[196] This assertion mirrored an earlier one made by James Fitzjames Stephen who, in *St James Gazette*, had declared that Newman had said that Catholicism was the only possible alternative to atheism. Newman declined to write a rejoinder: 'My brain works too slowly and hand too feebly to allow of my interfering'. Earlier he had discussed Stephen's arguments and told him: 'It is no good our disputing, it is like a battle between a dog and a fish – we are in different elements'.[197]

In Fairbairn's case, Newman felt that he should rebut the serious charge made against him. He set to work on an article, *The Development of Religious Error*, which was published in the October issue of the *Contemporary Review*. 'It was his last explanation of the relations between reason and faith, and the final clarification of his teaching'.[198] Fairbairn responded with another article, to which Newman drafted a reply, on which he sought Lord Blachford's opinion.[199] On Blachford's advice, Newman decided that it was not becoming to continue the controversy, but he circulated his reply privately (sending a copy to Fairbairn, who courteously acknowledged it), so that any misunderstanding of his views – which might give rise to scandal among Catholics – would be avoided.

In the postscript to a letter to Pusey in September 1869, Newman wrote: 'The *one* question which is occupying people's minds is "Will the Pope's Infallibility be determined?" All questions sink before that'.[200]

Two years earlier, Newman had written to Wilberforce deploring the extreme views expressed by some Ultramontane laymen like W.G. Ward. He added that he 'had never taken any great interest in the question of the limits and seat of infallibility'. He had become a Catholic because he recognised that the Church in 'substantial likeness or in actual descent', could rightly claim apostolic descent. The 'great principle' of *securus judicat orbis terrarum* had guided his faith (see Chapter 2). 'I see arguments here, arguments there – I incline one way today, another tomorrow – on the whole I more than incline in one direction – but I do not dogmatise – and I detest any dogmatism when the Church has not clearly spoken'.[201]

To Peter Le Page Renouf, a renowned oriental scholar and theologian, Newman wrote, about a year later: 'I hold the Pope's Infallibility, not as a dogma, but as a theological opinion; that is, not as a certainty, but as a probability... To my mind the balance of probabilities is still in favour of it. There are vast difficulties, taking facts as they are, ii the way of denying it... Anyhow, the doctrine of Papal Infallibility must be fenced round and limited by conditions'.[202] Newman's concerns about the dangers of misunderstandings about papal infallibility arising from extravagant claims being made by some over-enthusiastic promoters are also reflected in a letter to Mrs William Froude: 'I have ever held the Pope's Infallibility as an opinion, I am not therefore likely to feel any personal anxiety as to the result of this Council'. He was still, however, 'strongly opposed to its definition' because there seemed no necessity for it: 'there is no heresy to put down', and it is 'dangerous to go beyond the rule of tradition in such a matter... I am against this definition, because it opens up a long controversy'.[203]

Newman relieved his anxious feelings to Ullathorne – who was at Rome in what he was to describe as 'one of the most passionate and confidential letters that I ever wrote'. In it he referred to 'an insolent and aggressive faction' – some Ultramontanists – who were propagating what seemed to be an extreme view of papal infalli-bility.[204] Although Newman's explosive letter was re-garded by him as confidential it was shown to several bishops in Rome; copies were taken and distributed. Newspapers featured extracts including Newman's reference to an 'aggressive insolent faction'. Ullathorne wrote reassuringly to Newman that 'whatever mischief is doing outside by our own newspapers... moderation will be the upshot of the Council'.[205] Now that his letter was virtually public property and to avoid inaccurate ver-sions of it appearing, Newman sent a copy of it to the *Standard*, where it was published and widely repro-duced..[206] Meanwhile, Newman informed Coleridge that 'the great charge which I bring against the immediate authors of this movement, is that they have not given us time. [The last part of this sentence was written in capital letters]. The beginning and end of my thoughts about this Council is "You are going too fast"'.[207] Newman had written a similar letter to Fr Robert Whitty SJ the day before.

On 18th July 1870, at the last public session of Vatican I, the definition of Papal Infallibility was solemnly declared. Voting was not, however, unanimous; two bishops voted against it, and more than eighty 'had already departed after a compromise was refused by the Pope himself... the definition restricted infallibility to faith and morals, and could not even be held to infallibilise the Syllabus of Errors'.[208]

The actual text of the decree allayed Newman's fears: 'I am pleased at its moderation... the terms used are vague and comprehensive; and personally I have no difficulty in admitting it'.[209] To Ambrose St John, he wrote: 'I have ever since a Catholic held the Pope's Infallibility as a matter of opinion, at least I see nothing in the definition which necessarily contradicts Scripture, Tradition or History'.[210] Earlier, Newman had told James Hope-Scott that he thought that Manning had thrown his lot in with the middle party holding the Pope 'to be inerrable in matters *de fide*', which was '*very far short*' of what his own extreme position had been. W.G. Ward had also modified his earlier theory of infallibility and had admitted that in his original writings 'he had extended it too far'.[211] As Ker puts it: 'The Ultramontanes had not achieved all that they wanted at the Council. But their victory was fairly complete throughout the Church and the repercussions were various'.[212]

Obedience to authority had, as Dessain observes, always marked Newman's life both as an Anglican and a Roman Catholic: 'He stopped the *Tracts* at a word from his Anglican bishop. He resigned the *Rambler* at Ullathorne's wish... he twice dropped the plan of founding an Oratory at Oxford... at the request of higher authority'.[213] Wilfrid Ward notes that Newman 'very soon treated the dogma Infallibility as of obligation, and urged on all his friends the duty of submission'.[214]

In this chapter Newman can be seen to have entered fully, if sometimes reluctantly, into controversial debate over issues which he deemed important for the good name of Roman Catholics and of Catholicism itself during the Victorian era. As he told one of his friends, Edward Bellasis, 'I think best when I write. I cannot in the same way think while I speak. Some men are brilliant in conversation, others in public speaking – others find their minds act best, when they have a pen in their hands.[215] Newman's sword was his pen, which he used with expert effectiveness.

NOTES

1 Chadwick, 1990, p.14.
2 Newman, 1956, p.273.
3 Butler, 1926, p.307.
4 McGrath, 1951, p.219.
5 *LD* XXII.157, 18 February 1866.
6 Nicholls and Ker, 1991, pp.4-5.
7 Chadwick, 1990, p.63.
8 Chadwick, 1990, p.51.
9 McGrath, 1951, p.77.
10 Vargish, 1970, p.124.
11 Trevor, 1996, p.72.
12 Mozley, 14 March 1841, p.327.
13 Gilley, 1990, p.196.
14 Ker, 1990, p.382.
15 Gwynn, 1946, pp.240-41.
16 Norman, 1985, p.10.
17 Chadwick, 1990, p.2.
18 Gilley, 1990, p.272.
19 Newman, 1874, pp.172-73.
20 Norman, 1985, p.10.
21 Butler, 1926, p.197.
22 *LD* XV.128, 18 July 1852.
23 *LD* XV.126.
24 Newman, 1956, p.13.
25 *LD* XXVI.115, 16 June 1872.
26 Trevor, 1996, p.134.

27 Culler, 1965, p.135.
28 Chadwick, 1971, p.307.
29 Newman, 1851, p.209.
30 *LD* XIV.338 J.S. Northcote, 28 August 1851.
31 *LD* XIV.340, 31 August 1851.
32 *LD* XIV.344, 1 September 1851.
33 *LD* XIV.345; 352, 8 September 1851.
34 *LD* XIV.408.
35 *LD* XIV.408, 27 October 1851.
36 *LD* XIV.428, J.J. Gordon, 19 November 1851.
37 Gwynn, 1946, p.237.
38 *LD* XIV.430, Dessain *footnote*.
39 *LD* XIV.434, 25 November 1851.
40 McGrath, 1951, p.208.
41 McGrath, 1951, p.236.
42 *LD* XIV.iv.
43 Jenkins, 1990, p.146.
44 Chadwick, 1971 p.308.
45 Norman, 1985, p.328.
46 *LD* XV.278, F.S. Bowles, 31 January 1853.
47 *LD* XV.308, 23 February 1853.
48 Griffin, 1993, p.63.
49 Butler, 1926, p.309.
50 Butler, 1926, p.310.
51 Dessain, 1980, p.111.
52 Ward, 1913, p.475.
53 Coulson, 1970, p.102.
54 Cf Dessain, 1980, p.111.
55 *LD* XIX.xiii Dessain, 1969.
56 *LD* XIX.41, 16 February 1859.
57 *LD* XIX.85, James Burns, 21 March 18S9.
58 *LD* XIX.88-89, Lady Day 1859.
59 Coulson, 1970, p.104.
60 *LD* XIX.xiv Dessain.
61 *LD* XIX.142, Robert Ornsby, 24 May 1859.
62 Dessain, 1980, p.119.
63 *LD* XIX.140-41, 22 May 1859.
64 *LD* XIV.252, J.M. Capes, 10 April 1851.
65 Gilley, 1990, p.303.
66 *LD* XIX.181, 20 July 1859.
67 Butler, 1926, p.315.
68 Dessain, 1980, pp.115-16.
69 *LD* XIX.134-35, 16 May 1859.
70 *LD* XIX.144, *from* Dr John Gillow, 18 May 1859.
71 *LD* XIX.175, Dessain, *footnote*.
72 *LD* XIX.240, *from* Bishop Brown, 3 October 1859.
73 *LD* XIX.241, Dessain *footnote*.
74 *LD* XIX.289-90, 19 January 1860.
75 *LD* XIX.xiv, Dessain, 1969.

76 Trevor, 1996, p.183.
77 *LD* XX.446, 19 May 1863.
78 XIX.290, *footnote*.
79 Butler, 1926, p.321.
80 Butler, p.321.
81 Gilley, 1990, p.307.
82 Butler, 1926, p.473; *LD* XIX, 24 October 1859.
83 *LD* XX.324, 24 October 1862.
84 *LD* XX.325.
85 Newman, 1956, p.272.
86 Chadwick, 1996, p.163.
87 Barry, 1905, p.125.
88 *LD* XXI.62, 27 February 1864.
89 *LD* XX.571-72, 30 December 1863.
90 *LD* XXI.10, *from* Charles Kingsley, 6 January 1864.
91 *LD* XXI.11, 7 January 1864.
92 *LD* XXI.12-16, 8 January 1864.
93 *LD* XXI.19, *from* Charles Kingsley, 14 January 1864.
94 *LD* XXI.19, Dessain *footnote*.
95 *LD* XXI.18.
96 *LD* XXI.20, 17 January 1864.
97 *LD* XXI.26, 22 January 1864.
98 *LD* XXI.37-39, Edward Badeley, 5 February 1964.
99 *LD* XXI.47, diary note.
100 *LD* XXI.1 Dessain, *footnote*.
101 Maisie Ward, 1991, p.viii.
102 *LD* XXi.xiii, Dessain, *footnote*.
103 Maisie Ward, 1991, p.viii.
104 Oddie, 1993, p.xix.
105 *LD* XXVII.219, 13 February 1875.
106 *LD* XXI.100, 23 April 1864.
107 *LD* XXI.90-91, 31 March 1864.
108 Chadwick, 1990, p.61.
109 Houghton, 1945, p.7.
110 *LD* XXI.89 90, 27 March 1864.
111 Sencourt, 1948, p.189.
112 *LD* XXI.109, Diary, 9 May 1864.
113 *LD* XXI.94, 15 April 1864.
114 *LD* XXI.116, 16 June 1864.
115 *LD* XXI.95.
116 *LD* XXI.468, W.J. Copeland, 16 May 1865: *LD* XXI.xiv Dessain.
117 Ward, 1976, p.ix.
118 Chadwick, 1972, p.415.
119 Chadwick, 1972, p.415.
120 *LD* XXI.221-22, Bishop D. Moriarty, 8 September 1864.
121 *LD* XXI.447-48, Dr Charles Russell, 19 April 1865.
122 *LD* XXI.120 *footnote*.
123 *LD* XXVII.219, Sir W. Cope, 13 February 1875.
124 Newman, 1956, p.260.

125 Chadwick, 1972, p.416.
126 Dessain, 1980, p.163.
127 Coulson, 1970, p.55.
128 *LD* XIX.352, 2 June 1860.
129 Chadwick, 1972, p.414.
130 Norman, 1986, p.100.
131 Chadwick, 1996, p.163.
132 Butler, 1926, p.332.
133 *LD* XXI.144-45, 6 July 1864.
134 Griffin, 1993, p.103.
135 Griffin, 1993, p.97.
136 Ker, 1996, p.186.
137 Ker, 1988, p.548.
138 Ker, 1994, p.xxv.
139 Gilley, 1990, p.330.
140 Chadwick, 1972, p.413.
141 Houghton, 1945, pp.96-97.
142 Wilson, 1990, p.137.
143 *LD* XXI.97, W.J. Copeland, 19 April 1864.
144 Ward, 1913, II, p.76.
145 *LD* XXII.72, T.W. Allies, 11 October 1865.
146 Barry, 1905, pp.210-11.
147 Jay, 1991, p.220.
148 Ward, 1913, II, p.76.
149 Gilley, 1990, p.341.
150 Butler, 1926, p.354.
151 Chadwick, 1990, p.62.
152 *LD* XXII.44, 5 September 1865.
153 *LD* XXII.89-91, 31 October 1865.
154 *LD* XXII.93 Dessain *footnote*.
155 *LD* XXIII.93, 3 November 1865.
156 *LD* XXII.119, 8 December 1865.
157 *LD* XXII.118, 8 December 1865.
158 *LD* XXII.119, Dessain *footnote*.
159 *LD* XXII.xxiv.
160 Trevor, 1996, p.210.
161 Butler, 1926, p.358-59.
162 *LD* XXII.158, 19 February 1866.
163 *LD* XXII.211, 13 April 1866.
164 *LD* XXII.154, Dessain *footnote*.
165 *LD* XXII.154, 13 February 1866.
166 Butler, 1926, p.368.
167 *LD* XXII.201, 2 April 1866.
168 *LD* XXII.xiv Dessain.
169 *LD* XXII.186, Editor of *The Guardian*, 23 March 1866.
170 Holmes, 1979, p.VII.
171 *LD* XIX.488, Malcolm Maccoll, 24 March 1861.
172 Cf Holmes, 1979, p.VII.
173 *LD* XXVI.66, Canon H.P. Liddon, 18 April 1872.

174 *LD* XXX.201, Lord Emly, 9 April 1883.
175 *LD* XXVII.xiii.
176 Chadwick, 1990, p.62.
177 Norman, 1985, p.310.
178 Sencourt, 1948, p.233.
179 Griffin, 1993, p.163.
180 *LD* XXVII.158, 15 November 1874.
181 *LD* XXVII.170, 10 December 1874.
182 *LD* XXVII.153, Lord Emly, 7 November 1874.
183 *LD* XXVII.159, 23 November 1874.
184 *LD* XXVII.177, 19 December 1874.
185 *LD* XXVII.186, 9 January 1875.
186 *LD* XXVII.177.
187 *LD* XXVII.188, 31 December 1874.
188 *LD* XXVII.192 *from* W.E. Gladstone, 15 June 1875.
189 *LD* XXVII.193, 16 January 1875.
190 *LD* XXVII.211-13, 5 February 1875.
191 *LD* XXVII.220 Dessain, *footnote.*
192 *LD* XXVII.Appendix I, pp.401-10.
193 Newman, 1956, p.16.
194 *LD* XXX.36, 17 December 1881.
195 *LD* XXX.36-37, 23 December 1881.
196 Ker, 1990, p.742.
197 *LD* XXIX.337, W.S. Lilly, 17 February 1881.
198 *LD* XXXI.xiii *Introductory Note.*
199 *LD* XXXI.113, 4 February 1886; 114, 6 February 1886; 116-17, 16 February
     1886.
200 *LD* XXIV.332, 12 September 1869.
201 *LD* XXIII.275, Henry Wilberforce, 21 July 1867.
202 *LD* XXIV.91/2, 21 June 1868.
203 *LD* XXIV.377, 21 November 1869.
204 *LD* XXV.19, 28th January 1870.
205 *LD* XXV.27, 4 February 1870.
206 XXV.xvi.
207 *LD* XXV.98-9, 13 April 1870.
208 Gilley, 1990, p.369.
209 *LD* XXV.164, Ambrose Phillipps de Lisle, 24 July 1870.
210 *LD* XXV.168, 27 July 1870.
211 *LD* XXV.9, 16 January 1870; Ward, 1913, II, p.235.
212 Ker, 1990, p.662.
213 Dessain, 1980, p.118.
214 Ward, 1913, II, p.373.
215 *LD* XXV.300, 12 March 1871.

7

Newman:
Resonances and Reflections

ACCORDING to Chadwick, in the first half of his life Newman 'wound up the Church of England to its Catholic heritage. In the second half of his life he wound down the Church of Rome – that is, he sought to persuade its leaders not to push their Catholicity into fanaticism, or superstition, or irrationality, or rigid hierarchy; and therefore to keep their minds open to the old principle of primitive Catholic faith, and from that broader base to listen to the discoveries of the age'.[1] Chadwick's model provides a valuable approach to summing up Newman's life and activities, specific aspects of which we have been discussing in this book.

To 'wind up' has, of course, several connotations; Chadwick seems to use this phrase to draw attention to Newman's belief that, in his Anglican days, he had the mission of saving the Church of England from the perils which he perceived to be threatening it.[2] This sense of personal responsibility led to the foundation of the Oxford Movement, and to the first of the 'Tracts for the Times', *The Ministerial Commission* (1833). This publication, as discussed in Chapter 2, was a vigorous call to the clergy of the Church of England to recognise that their spiritual authority was based on their apostolic descent. Newman openly challenged the clergy, who were diversified in their observances, ranging from High Church to Low Church and Evangelicals, to realise that they had a Catholic heritage. In this self-imposed task of 'winding up' the Church of England Newman worked closely with several of his Oxford contemporaries, especially Pusey, Froude and Keble, whose joint efforts produced what became known as the Oxford Movement. Newman's influence was considerable and pervasive. He wrote most of the Tracts, and gave a series of lectures and sermons by means of which he acquired a reputation for stirring up discussion on religion in the University.[3] But even in the midst of his many activities, Newman experienced doubts about the essential nature of the Church of England. To an intimate friend he confided as early as 1836 that 'my heart is with Rome'.[4] His anxieties persisted, as can be seen in his correspondence.[5] Eventually these led to his secession from the Church of England, as discussed in Chapter 3. In the process of 'winding up' the Church of England, Newman had argued that a form of Catholicism existed that was not Roman. This view resulted in the Anglo-Catholic revival in the Church of England.[6] After Newman had become a Roman Catholic, the Oxford Movement entered a second phase of its existence in parochial activities in the industrial cities and towns, as was noted in Chapter 3. Anglo-Catholics 'adopted the language and ritual practices of Roman Catholicism without the structure of doctrinal authority'.[7]

In the matter of 'winding down' the Church of Rome, Newman also made significant contributions (as preceding chapters have shown), and these will be summarised under the topics of his persistent emphasis on the need for an educated, well-instructed laity; the cultivation of an identifiable type of English Roman Catholicism in harmony with the traditions of the 'old'

Catholics; the importance of intellectual excellence in higher education in which spiritual values were recognised; the foundation of a distinctive English style of Oratorianism; and his remarkable capacity for combining spiritual and intellectual stimulation through his sermons and treatises and by his contributions to controversial issues.

Chadwick relates his assertion that Newman 'wound down the Church of Rome', to Newman's influence on the emergence of the Roman Catholic Church from relative obscurity in English national life to a respected place in society. As Dessain states, 'He wanted Roman Catholics to come out of the ghetto and take their place in the world, to adapt themselves, to enlarge their minds in the confidence that truth could never contradict truth, and to be guided like responsible men by their enlightened consciences'.[8]

Although Newman left the Church of England and became a Roman Catholic, he always had an affectionate regard for the Church in which he had spent the first half of his life. He viewed the established Church as 'a great power in English society for good – for religion and against the growth of infidelity'. He declared that 'to weaken the Establishment was to damage a bulwark of religion, while Roman Catholics had as yet no adequate force to supply in its place'.[9] These attitudes are reflected in his correspondence with J.M. Capes 'Who at *this moment* would any how not adopt Roman Catholicism, but go the other way were the Establishment destroyed?'.[10] In a further letter to Capes, Newman emphasised, 'I don't look on the Church of England as important, in contrast to *Dissent*, but as a bulwark against Infidelity, which Dissent cannot be. Were the Church of E. to fall, Methodism might remain a while – I can't tell, for I don't know – but, surely, on the whole, the various denominations exist under the shadow of the Establishment, out of which they sprung, and, did it go, would go too... Infidelity would take possession of the bulk of the men and women'.[11]

Towards the end of his life, Newman told another correspondent that as a boy he had 'learned those great and burning truths' from evangelical teaching. 'The Holy Roman Church has added to the simple evangelicism [sic] of my first teachers, but it has obscured, enfeebled, nothing of it'.[12] Accordingly, as Gilley puts it, Newman 'died as he had lived, a Catholic but an Evangelical as well'.[13] He never repudiated the fifteen University sermons he preached as an Anglican. In 1853 he wrote, 'I stand by my [Oxford] University Discourses... and am almost a zealot for their substantial truth',[14] and in 1872 he issued a third edition of these sermons. Newman thus claimed that a convert like himself 'had the advantage of both knowing Catholic doctrine and having Protestant experience'. But he admitted that this meant that he was 'too often looked at with suspicion by the Protestant because he had become a Catholic and by the Catholic because he had been a Protestant'.[15]

Newman disliked ostentation and public display. He wished Roman Catholicism in England to grow quietly, avoiding devotional excesses, and preferring 'English habits of belief and devotion'.[16] Newman himself told Mrs Froude that, 'There is a marked contrast in Catholicity between the views presented to us by doctrine and devotion respectively. Doctrines never change, devotions vary with each individual. Catholics allow each other, accordingly, the greatest licence, and are, if I may so speak, other *liberals*, as regards devotions, whereas they are most sensitive about doctrine'.[17] A few years later he revealed to another correspondent that, 'As an Englishman I do not like a Romaic religion – and I have much to say, not, God forbid, against the Roman Catholic, but against the Romaic Catholic Church. I have no great sympathy with Italian religion, as such – but I do not account myself the worse Catholic for this'.[18] Although he found Faber's Italianate-style devotions and writings personally unappealing, Newman was prepared to tolerate them. He wrote to one correspondent that, 'As to Fr Faber's book [*Growth in Holiness*], I suppose it is a perfect magazine of valuable thoughts – but it must not make you scrupulous. What suits one person, does not another'.[19] Soon after meeting Faber, Newman noted in his diary that 'he is much more poetical in the largest sense of the word than the Oratorians'.[20]

Like the 'old' Catholics, Newman disliked the exaggerated pious practices and emotionalism associated with Ultramontanism (see Chapter 4). His journal shows clearly that he was not devoid of emotion, but it also discloses that he felt uneasy about excessive dependence on emotional appeals and satisfactions in religion. He counselled Faber, 'The *end* of the Oratory of Brothers is doubtless to *save the soul*. If any one or any Oratory can arrive at this end by no means or by any other means (allowable), let him do it. One can't prescribe one's own means to others. If you can attain the end directly and immediately, by all means do it and use no means.'[21]

Maisie Ward states that 'Newman's genius found its scope in a unique vocation – at once spiritual and intellectual – of drawing the world nearer to God not by prayer but by thought... he lived and moved more among the early Fathers than among his living friends close as they were to him'.[22] This blending of the spiritual and intellectual was developed by Newman in *The Idea of a University*. He saw the need for religion to have a recognised place in a university, without which it could not rightfully claim academic eminence. Hence, spiritual growth and intellectual excellence were essential constituents of higher education (see Chapter 5 for extended discussion).

Closely associated with his stimulating views on higher education, was Newman's persistent advocacy of the role of the laity in the Catholic Church. He wanted Catholics to be better educated so that they could become accepted into English political and social life. At the same time, he urged that the distinctive role of the laity should be readily acknowledged by the clergy. In a series of lectures in Birmingham during 1851, which were published as *The Present Position of Catholics in England*, Newman not only attempted to dismiss popular myths about Catholicism, but also stressed that the laity should accept their responsibilities to become better informed about their faith, so that they could give enquirers reliable knowledge about its beliefs and practices. He told his listeners, 'I want a laity, not arrogant, not rash in speech, not disputatious, but men who know their religion... I want an intelligent, well-informed laity... I wish to enlarge your knowledge, to cultivate your reason, to get an insight into the relation of truth to truth, to learn to view things as they are, to understand how faith and reason stand to each other'.[23]

Newman developed the concept of the *consensus fidelium* – 'the consensus of the faithful, the common mind of ordinary worshippers'.[24] He wanted an end to the submissive passivity of the laity, such as he had discovered during his stressful years in Ireland. There the laity 'were treated like good little boys – were told to shut their eyes and open their mouths, and take what we give them – and this they do not relish'.[25] He held that the opinions of the laity on matters of special concern to them should be listened to by the English Catholic hierarchy (see Chapter 6 the discussion on the *Rambler*). On this issue, Newman was forthright in his correspondence:

'As far as I can see, there are ecclesiastics all over Europe, whose policy is to keep the laity at arms-length; and hence the laity have become disgusted and become infidel, and two parties exist, both ultras in opposite directions'. He had left Ireland 'with the distressing fear' that, as time passed, there would develop 'an antagonism between the hierarchy and the educated classes'.[26]

In England, Manning was planning a Catholic University College at Kensington, which would be under strict clerical control. When, however, Newman was invited to serve on the Senate, he told Manning, 'I feel an insurmountable difficulty… I could not without a great inconsistency take part in an Institution, which formally and "especially" recognises the London University, a body which has been the beginning, and source, and symbol of all the Liberalism existing in the educated classes for the last 40 years'.[27]

Some months earlier, Newman had warned one of his close friends, a member of the subcommittee set up by the Catholic hierarchy to consider the state of Catholic higher education, that, 'The Archbishop [Manning] is not contemplating a real University education for young Catholics; but wishes to do just as much as will stop the present clamour, and take off the edge of the evident injustice of forbidding Oxford and substituting nothing for it'. Newman did not favour the establishment of a Catholic University or College at Oxford, because his experiences in Ireland in 1851-8, and in England over 1864-7 (see Chapter 5), had caused him to lose faith in Church authorities. He 'dreaded a minute and jealous supervision on the part of authority which will hamper every act of the heads of the University'.[28] In a further letter, Newman advised that, 'On the whole, perhaps delay is the best thing for us – though we may suffer through it for a whole generation. We may do a bad thing now;

we may do a good thing years hence. Great changes are taking place at Rome… The is no reason why both [clergy and laity] should not be well educated for their respective duties in life'. But he confessed that he was 'inclined to think that the Archbishop considers only an ignorant laity to be manageable'.[29]

Manning's concept of a university was that of an institution providing technical and scientific training. This was far removed from Newman's idea of a university. The Kensington venture only lasted about eight years, due to lack of support and problems with the rectorship.

In the early 1880s, some influential English Catholics had, with the agreement of the hierarchy, reopened the proposal that Catholics should be able to finish their education at Oxford. Because of advanced age and infirmity, Newman could not travel to Rome but he willingly authorised Lord Braye and others to represent his supporting views in an audience with Pope Leo XIII. These representations were doubtless influential in the withdrawal, some ten years later, of the ban by the Holy See on Catholics attending the national universities.[30]

Before the second Vatican Council (1962-65), a clear distinction existed between the teaching Church – the *ecclesia docens* (i.e. the clergy) and the taught Church – the *ecclesia docta* (i.e. the laity) (see Chapter 6). As Coulson points out, however, Newman's concept of theology 'implies an active and educated laity'.[31] An educated laity would be able to make a valuable contribution to the 'healthy functioning of the Church'.[32] In his essay, *On Consulting the Faithful in Matters of Doctrine*, Newman emphasised the significance of the combined testimony of clergy and laity, namely, of the *consensus fidelium* (see Chapter 6). As Sullivan points out, 'Far from wishing to divide the Roman Catholic Church between its official teachers and the rest of the Church, Newman was concerned to show that the infallible teaching of the Church resides in the whole community of faith and not exclusively with its official teachers. He is not saying that the infallible party in the Church consults the fallible part in order to reach an infallible decision'.[33] As noted in Chapter 6, Newman's use of the term 'consult' in this matter gave rise to misunderstanding until he clarified precisely what he meant by it.

On 25th April 1867, Talbot, an inverate critic of Newman over many years, wrote to Manning warning him that the laity, influenced by Newman's article in the *Rambler*, 'are beginning to show the cloven hoof... Newman is the most dangerous man in England'. Talbot then added his own idiosyncratic definition of the role of the laity as, 'To hunt, to shoot, to entertain. These matters they understood, but to meddle with ecclesiastical matters they have no right at all'.[34] Manning was annoyed, but treated Talbot's intemperate comments with distinct reserve for he had no wish to cause open conflict among the bishops on the issue in question.[35]

Newman himself was intent on fostering intellectual life within the Catholic Church but, as he told Henry Wilberforce, he deplored the extreme views of (Ultramontane) laymen like W.G. Ward which 'unsettle the minds of I can't tell how many Catholics. He is free to have his own opinion, but when he makes it part of the faith' he is 'making a Church within a Church, or an Evangelical preacher, deciding that the Gospel is preached here, and is not preached there... such behaviour destroys our very argument with the Anglicans', by striking at the heart of doctrinal uniformity.[36] Newman feared that the Catholic Church was in danger of some kind of Novationism – a 3rd century schism in the Roman Christian Church which was characterised by narrow exclusiveness. At the same time, he states that he 'detested any dogmatism when the

Church *has* not clearly spoken. And if I am told "The Church has spoken, then I ask where? and if, instead of having any plain thing shown me, I am put off with a string of arguments, or some strong words of the Pope himself, I consider this a sophistical evasion'. He comforts himself 'with the principle that: *Lex dubia non obligat* – What is not taught universally, what is not believed universally, has no claim on me and, if it be true after all and divine my faith in it is included in the *implicita fides* I have in the Church'.[37] In correspondence with W.G. Ward, Newman said that he considered theological differences between them as unimportant in themselves, whereas Ward made 'great moment' of them. They both shared the same faith, and he, Newman, remained in the 'same temper of forbearance and sobriety which I have wished to cultivate'.[38] A few days earlier, Newman had told Ward, 'now that my own time is drawing to an end, the new generation will not forget the spirit of the old maxim, in which I have ever wished to speak and act myself: *In necessariis unitas, in dubiis, libertas, in omnibus charitas* [sic] [Freely translated as: *Unity in matters that are vital, freedom where there is doubt, and in all things let there be charity (love)*].[39] Gilley says that Newman's impact on Roman Catholic theology has been enormous: he was the 'Church of England's great gift to Catholic theology, his Catholic theology being the development and fulfilment of his theological work as an Anglican. His insistence on the continuities of his own life declares that a convert is someone who discovers he is wrong, but also in some profound sense that he is already right'.[40] Dessain has observed that 'Since the new era in Newman studies it has been recognised that he was no abstract thinker or solitary, but always a pastor. From the time of his Anglican ordination, all his activity had some apostolic purpose. Doctrine was there not for speculation but to be lived'.[41]

Newman was accustomed to being misrepresented and misunderstood. As he informed one of his correspondents, 'Some Catholic papers delight in putting in gossip about me. It is a great thing to set up a puppet in order to knock it down. There is just as much truth in saying that I ever dreamed of writing on Faith or Rationalism, as in saying that any person in authority ever dreamed of hindering me; and that is, no truth at all'.[42] As Chadwick notes, 'While he [Newman] was a Protestant, tutors and heads and bishops poured over his words to decide whether they were unfitting for a loyal English clergyman. While he was a Roman Catholic censors at Rome poured over his words to decide whether they were heretical, or offensive to pious ears, or impudent, or merely unfitting for a loyal priest. His mental processes were all his own, and he did not care if he startled.[43]

Among achievements which were to have lasting effect on English Catholicism was Newman's introduction into England of Oratorian values and a lifestyle based on a specially modified version of the Rule of St Philip Neri (see Chapter 4). The Oratory appealed to him mainly because of its suitability for himself and the group of Oxford converts who had gathered about him; 'it was adapted to the habits of educated men, and seemed most likely to allow of a free development of their combined talents in their priestly work for Roman Catholicism in England'.[44] Community life was closely modelled on that of an Oxford college; unlike a religious, order, no vows were taken and very few rules were imposed. Behaviour was influenced, however, by acceptance of the need to build a common bond of *carita* [sic] or supernatural charity. This was the vocation which Newman chose in 1847, and to which he remained faithful until his death in 1890. In his journal, Newman recorded that despite 'great trials... incidental to a new foundation', the Birmingham

Oratory and, later, the London Oratory 'were successful'.[45] The Oratorian way of life enabled Newman and his associates to apply themselves as missioners and preachers in industrial Birmingham and also in the fashionable district of Brompton in London. Roman Catholicism was made more acceptable by these well-educated Englishmen to whom the Pope had given the specific task of serving the spiritual needs of the educated upper classes in England. They did not, however, confine themselves to this stratum of society, as Chapter 4 shows.

From his *nidulo* or nest – an Oratorian's private room – Newman conducted a remarkable correspondence with prelates, politicians, old Anglican friends, and many others. Dessain says that Newman's letters bring us into touch with him more than any of his works: 'It becomes possible to know him also like a living friend, and in spite of his reserve, they reveal his natural, energetic, humorous and practical character'.[46] He regarded the writing of letters as an important part of his pastoral duties. It was, as Ward observes, 'a means of exerting personal influence on the large numbers who sought his advice and judgement... he devoted immense labour to his letters'.[47] Newman's writing style won the admiration of *The Times* (10 April 1869) which classed him, with De Quincey and Macaulay, as 'the three greatest masters of English style in the generation which is just closing'. In acknowledging this graceful tribute, Newman said that he had to take great pains with everything he wrote and that Cicero, because of 'his clearness', was the 'only master of style' who had influenced him.[48] He frequently rewrote chapters of books and re-drafted letters; all this, he says, 'took me a great deal of time and tried me very much'.[49]

Newman would present the same ideas differently to different correspondents, as is apparent from his *Letters and Diaries.* To intimate friends he frequently displayed a quiet sense of humour; on occasion, his satiric wit enlivened exchanges on controversial issues. From his vast correspondence 'it has become possible to know him almost like a living friend, and in spite of his reserve, they reveal his natural, energetic, humorous and poetic character'.[50]

In thanking Bishop Ilsley for remembering his 80th birthday, Newman responded in typical style: 'A long life is like a long ladder, which sways and jumps dangerously under the feet of the man who mounts, the higher he goes, and, if there is any one who needs prayers for perseverance, it is a man of 80'.[51] Among Newman's many correspondents was Fr Gerard Manley Hopkins, the Jesuit priest and poet, who had been received into the Church by Newman in 1866. He had proposed writing a commentary on the *Grammar of Assent*, but Newman adamantly refused him permission, stating, 'I could not but consider it at once onerous and unnecessary. The book has succeeded in twelve years far more than I expected... Of course those who only read so much of it as they can while cutting open the leaves, will make great mistakes about it'.[52] To a London journalist who asked his views on the Affirmation Bill (which had been rejected in the House of Commons, by only three votes, on 30th May 1883) Newman replied: 'I neither approve nor disapprove. I express no opinion upon it; and that first because I do not commonly enter upon political questions, and next, because, looking at the Bill on its own merits, I think nothing is lost to Religion by its passing and nothing is gained by its being rejected'.[53] Responding to a law student who feared a tide of atheism would result from the passing of the Affirmation Bill, Newman reassured him that he 'had ever anticipated a great battle between good and evil', but over the centuries the Church had survived. 'So I think it will be now. We shall have a bad time of it, but "be still and see the salvation of God"'.[54]

Even as late as his 85th year, Newman had to state firmly his reasons for becoming a Catholic. A letter[55] to Margaret Ellen James reads: 'Cardinal Newman is sure that Miss James's letter did not reach him, or that he has answered it. The notion that he became a Catholic in order to get rid of doubts is utterly unfounded. He became a Catholic because Our Lord set up a Church in the beginning as the Ark of Salvation and the Oracle of Truth. And the Roman was it. So he has said in all he has written. Look to his *Apologia*, his *Sermons to Mixed Congregations*, the postscript to his *Letter to the Duke of Norfolk*, or to his *Development of Christian Doctrine*. He has never had a doubt since he became a Catholic. He became a Catholic because he was certain the Catholic was the true faith. Miss James must excuse his bad writing but he writes with an effort and with difficulty'.

To a Free Church minister, Newman reflected: 'What a mystery it is that in this day that there should be so much which draws religious minds together, and so much which separates them from each other'. While members of the various Christian communities felt 'such tenderness for each other', the differences which divided them were never greater or stronger'.[56]

An earnest enquirer after salvation was told by Newman that the 'only reason for becoming a Catholic, is that the Roman Communion is the only true Church, the Ark of Salvation. This does not mean that no one is saved who is not within the Church, but that there is no other Communion or Polity which has the promises, and that those who are saved, though not in the One Church, are saved, not by virtue of "the Law or Sect which they profess", as the 39 *Articles* say, but because they do not know better, and earnestly desire to know the truth'.[57]

On 15th November 1872, Newman wrote a 'Memorandum on Future Biography'[58] in which he specified how he wanted his papers dealt with. These large collections, which Newman hoped to 'put into shape and chronological order' should be used 'only in defence, i.e. if enemies make misstatements or imply motives... I don't wish my life written... In the *Apologia* I have virtually written my life up to 1845 – and there is little of nothing to say since'.

A few years later, Newman issued another instruction regarding his papers.[59] 'I don't want a panegyric written of me, which would be sickening, but a real fair downright account of me according to the best ability and judgement of the writer'. Such a memoir should be in two parts dealing specifically with his Anglican years and then his life as a, Catholic. In an additional note, dated 22nd October 1876, Newman expressed a wish that 'all statements which reflect on others to be withheld from publication, unless and until reflections are published in any quarter against me... But such publication is not to be determined on hastily, or without real necessity'.

Some 40 years after their original publication, Newman edited his two-volumed *Via Media*. The first volume, *Lectures on the Prophetical Office of the Church,* was first published in 1837 (see Chapter 2). In a letter to the publishers, Newman intimated that the edited first volume – which included an extended new Preface – was 'now nearly ready – the second part not yet begun'.[60] However, the second volume was occupying Newman's attention, and he told an old friend, the architect of the University Church in Dublin, 'I am full of business, racing with time, not knowing how long will be or at least having no confidence how long I can do the head work'.[61] Both volumes were published during the second half of 1877 and were well received among Catholics.

On the death of Pius IX in February 1878, Leo XIII

was elected Pope. According to Ker, 'As nuncio in Brussels he had been familiar with the Oxford Movement, and he had met Dominic Barberi... immediately after Barberi had received Newman into the Church. After being elected Pope, he is supposed to have said that the policy of his pontificate would be revealed by the name of the first Cardinal he created'.[62] Dessain comments on this that, 'At any rate the idea was taken up by the Duke of Norfolk and some of the English laity, who approached Leo XIII. Newman was made a Cardinal, but only after what, now the correspondence has come to light, seems definitely to have been a last-minute manoeuvre of Manning's to prevent it'.[63] Gilley believes that, 'Manning stands convicted of an extraordinarily clumsy misreading of confidential documents in order to deprive Newman of his honour'.[64] Newman himself, however, emphatically or, perhaps, diplomatically, contradicted 'any ideas that may be afloat as to my dissatisfaction with any step taken by Cardinal Manning'.[65] In 1879 he merely added a note at the end of his journal, 'Since writing the above I have been made a Cardinal!'.[66]

The motto chosen by Newman when he received the cardinal's hat in 1879 was: *Cor ad cor loquitur* ('Heart speaketh unto heart'). Harrold reflects: 'All of John Henry Newman's work was addressed to his readers' *hearts*'.[67]

Newman wrote to his old friend Dean Church, 'All the stories which have gone on about me being half a Catholic, a liberal Catholic, under a cloud, not to be trusted, are now at an end'.[68] In January 1888, Lord Selborne gave the Pope a message from Newman, and on hearing of him, His Holiness's face lit up, as he said, 'My Cardinal! it was not easy, it was not easy. They said he was too liberal, but I had determined to honour the Church in honouring Newman. I always had a cult for him. I am proud that I was able to honour such a man'.[69]

Chadwick says that the Pope had overcome opposition in the curia and the reluctance of Manning to make Newman a Cardinal and that 'Educated Protestant England was glad and accepted it as an honour justly conferred upon a great Englishman. This was no small tribute to the change of attitude wrought by Newman. He was the first Englishman to win non-Catholic applause for becoming a cardinal'.[70]

Among the many who sent Newman congratulations on his elevation to the Sacred College was Cardinal Manning on behalf of the English hierarchy. In this letter he recorded that Newman's 'name had been bound up with the Catholic Church in England for the last thirty years, and we have regarded you with so true a friendship and veneration for your many virtues, your sacerdotal example, and your signal services to the Catholic Faith'.[71] Manning preceded this formal note with a personal letter proposing that the 'Catholic laity' should be invited to a reception in London in Newman's honour.[72] Newman, writing from Rome, thanked Manning for his congratulations but regretted that he was not well enough to travel to London at the present time.[73] Manning's formal letter of congratulations was acknowledged by Newman, on his way back from Rome, in a letter written from Leghorn. He asked to be excused the delay in replying formally, due to illness, and expressed his gratitude for the message from Cardinal Manning and the episcopate. It was, he wrote, 'a great satisfaction to be told in so formal an address, that even when there was not such a bias in my favour, equally as when there was, I have through so many years, and under such varying circumstances, and by such men, been so tenderly and considerately regarded'.[74]

Throughout the many celebratory occasions, including a series of receptions in London, as guest of the Duke of Norfolk, a reception by 200 clergy, Vespers and

Benediction at the London Oratory, and a ceremonial visit to Trinity College, Oxford, Newman tried to complete a revision of the *Select Treatises of St Athanasius in controversy with the Arians*. He confided to his intimate friend, R.W. Church, Dean of St Paul's: 'I wonder when I shall get a little quiet; or at least a little leisure to finish my revision of the *Athanasius*. This Cardinalate, I grieve to say, has spoiled the revision, and I shall not live for another... of all my volumes I wished *Athanasius* to be least imperfect, and it will be most so'.[75] His disappointment with the edition, which was published in 1881, is apparent from a letter to Frederic Rogers who was created Lord Blachford in 1871.[76]

During the latter part of 1886, despite growing physical frailty and failing eyesight but with his mind alert and interested in keeping in touch with his wide – but sadly diminished – circle of friends, Newman had increasingly resorted to dictating his correspondence. In one of his last letters of any length which he wrote entirely by hand, Newman said he was comforted that, 'in this day of religious indifference and unbelief' there was a 'silent and secret process going on in the hearts of many' which, in due time, might bring Christians all over the world together.[77]

As noted already, Newman's memories of the truths he had imbibed from evangelical teaching during his early years proved to be indelible influences throughout his life. In his private journal he recorded on 13th June 1874 that from August to December 1816 he 'fell under the influence of an excellent man, the Reverend Walter Mayers, of Pembroke College, Oxford, one of the classical masters at Ealing, from whom he received deep religious impressions'. At the time, Newman states, these were 'Calvinistic in character... and were the beginning of a new life'.[78] The dramatic effect that the Reverend

Walter Mayers had on Newman's intellectual and spiritual progression was also chronicled in the *Apologia*.[79]

Ullathorne, who had been Newman's bishop for many years, died on 21st March 1889. Over these years, Newman and he had worked closely together in Birmingham, developing a deep understanding and friendship. On his last visit to Newman at the Birmingham on 18th August 1886, Ullathorne found the Cardinal 'much wasted, but very cheerful'. They had 'a long and cheery talk'. As Ullathorne was about to leave, Newman, 'in low and humble accents' asked for the 'great favour' of his blessing, for which he knelt submissively. Ullathorne was profoundly moved: 'I felt annihilated in his presence: there is a Saint in that Man!', he said later.[80]

Newman dictated a letter to Cardinal Manning, on 29th September 1889, congratulating him on settlement of the London dockers' strike. Manning replied very cordially.[81] In November 1889 Newman himself 'went out in the snow to act as a peacemaker' in a strike of Catholic women workers at Cadbury's chocolate works in Birmingham, who were obliged to attend daily Bible instruction. Mr George Cadbury and his brother met Newman and 'were charmed by the loving Christian spirit with which he entered into the question'. The matter was settled amicably.[82]

On Christmas Day 1889, Newman said Mass for what was to be the last time. He 'was attempting to learn more or less by heart from a missal for the partially blind'.[83]

At 1 am on Sunday, 10th August 1890, Newman was taken ill, and died of pneumonia during the evening of the following day.[84] His passing was mourned by the great and the humble alike; most of those who mourned 'were younger by more than half a lifetime... Within the year his intellectual legacy was provoking controversy'.[85] During his long life-time, he had been a vigorous controversialist and a gifted writer. On his death, those issues on which he concentrated his powerful intellect for so many years were still largely unresolved. Newman's pervasive influence had been felt first in the Church of England and, later, in the Church of Rome. His talents and energies were directed by his deep personal spirituality and dedication to what he perceived to be his vocation in life. He undoubtedly affected the ways in which Roman Catholicism developed in the Victorian era, but his influence has extended far beyond that period and is active in Christian thought and behaviour today.

The epitaph chosen by Newman for his memorial tablet in the cloister wall of the Birmingham Oratory has a haunting elegiac beauty which reflects the essence of his spiritual odyssey: *Ex umbris et imaginibus in veritatem* – 'Out of shadows and images into truth'.

NOTES

1   Chadwick, 1990, p.58.
2   Newman, 1956, p.120.
3   Cf Maisie Ward, 1948, p.255.
4   *LD* V.303-5, H.J. Rose, 23 May 1836.
5   *LD* VII.244-46, Mrs John Mozley, 25 February 1840.
6   Cf Trevor, 1996, p.47.
7   Norman, 1985, p.28.
8   Dessain, 1980, p.168.
9   Ward, 1913, p.258.
10   *LD* XIV.165, 12 December 1850.
11   *LD* XIV.172-74, 24 December 1850.
12   *LD* XXXI.189, G.T. Edwards, 24 February 1887.
13   Gilley, 1990, p.421.
14   *LD* XV.381, E.H. Thompson, 12 June 1853.
15   *LD* XX.543, D.R. Brownlow, 25 October 1863.
16   Dessain, 1980, p.135.
17   *LD* XVI.341, 2 January 1855.
18   *LD* XX.471, Lady Chatterton, 16 June 1863.
19   *LD* XVI.436-37, Catherine Bathurst, 6 April 1855.
20   *LD* XII.137, 25 December 1847.
21   *LD* XIV.247, 6 April 1851.
22   Maisie Ward, 1948, p.228.

23 Newman, 1851, p.390.

24 Chadwick, 1990, p.41.

25 Newman, 1956, p.328.

26 *LD* XXVI.394, George Fottrell, 10 December 1873.

27 *LD* XXVI.390, 24 November 1873.

28 *LD* XXVI.60-2, J. Spencer Northcote, 9 April 1872.

29 *LD* XXVI.65-6, J. Spencer Northcote, 17 April 1872.

30 Cf Ward, 1913, II, p.484.

31 Coulson, 1970, p.179.

32 Coulson, 1970, p.181.

33 Sullivan, 1993, p.54.

34 Ward, 1913, II, p.147.

35 cf. Trevor, 1996, p.216.

36 *LD* XXIII.274, 21 July 1867.

37 *LD* XXIII.275, 21 July 1867.

38 *LD* XXIII.216, 9 May 1867.

39 *LD* XXIII.197, 30 April 1867.

40 Gilley, 1997, pp.8-9.

41 Dessain, 1980, p.181.

42 *LD* XXIV.381, Malcolm Mascoll, 29 November 1869.

43 Chadwick, 1990, p.13.

44 Murray, 1980, p.127.

45 Newman, 1956, p.257.

46 Dessain, 1980, p.164.

47 Ward, 1913, p.314.

48 *LD* XXIV.241-42, John Hayes, 13 April 1869.

49 *LD* XXIV.391, Edward Bellasis, 15 December 1869.

50 Dessain, 1980, p.164.

51 *LD* XXIX.340, 23 February 1881.

52 *LD* XXX.191, 27 February 1883.

53 *LD* XXX.216 F.W. Chesson, 8 May 1883.

54 *LD* XXX.220, Michael Frost, 17 May 1883.

55 *LD* XXXI.71, 30 May 1885.

56 *LD* XXVI.187 David Brown, 24 October 1872.

57 *LD* XXVI.364, Miss Rowe, 16 September 1873.

58 *LD* XXVI.200-201.

59 *LD* XXVIII.92-93, 24 July 1876.

60 *LD* XXVIII.221, B.M. Pickering, 9 July 1877.

61 *LD* XXVIII.234, John Hungerford Pollen, 23 August 1877.

62 Ker, 1990, p.715.

63 Dessain, 1980, p.165.

64 Gilley, 1990, p.397.

65 *LD* XXIX.76, W.S. Lilly, 12 March 1879.

66 Newman, 1956, p.275.

67 Harrold, 1945, p.376.

68 *LD* XXIX.72, 11 March 1879.

69 *LD* XXIX.Appendix I, p.426.

70 Chadwick, 1972, p.420.

71 *LD* XXIX.137, 19 May 1979.

72 *LD* XXIX.127, *footnote*.
73 *LD* XXIX.127, 19 May 1879.
74 *LD* XXIX.137, Cardinal Manning, 5 June 1879.
75 *LD* XXIX.173, 29 August 1879.
76 *LD* XXIX.334, 28 January 1881.
77 *LD* XXXI.181, William Knight 7 January 1887.
78 Newman, 1956, p.29.
79 1993, p.89.
80 Butler, 1926, p.284.
81 *LD* XXXI.276.
82 *LD* XXXI.277-8 *footnote*.
83 *LD* XXXI.283 *footnote*.
84 *LD* XXXI.299 *footnote*.
85 Gilley, 1990, p.422.

8

Bibliography

The Letters and Diaries of John Henry Newman are identified as follows: (*LD*. Volume No. Page No. Date of Letter).

Amherst W.J. (1886) The History of Catholic Emancipation and the Progress of the Catholic Church in the British Isles – chiefly in England – from 1771 to 1820, London, Kegan, Paul & Co.

Bacchus J. (ed.) (1917) *Correspondence of John Henry Newman with John Keble and Others*, London, Longmans Green & Co.

Bastable, James (ed.) (1978) *Newman and Gladstone Centennial Essays*, Dublin, Veritas Publications.

Barry, William (1905) *Newman*, London, Hodder and Stoughton.

Beard, Madeleine (1992) *Faith and Fortune*, Leominster, Gracewing Books.

Best, Geoffrey (1985) *Mid-Victorian Britain*, 1851-75, London, Fontana Press.

Bossy, John (1976) *The English Catholic Community: 1570-1850*, London, Darton, Longman and Todd.

Briggs, Asa (1990) *Victorian People: a Reassessment of Persons and Themes*, 1851-67, Harmondsworth, Penguin Books.

Butler, Cuthbert (1926) *The Life and Times of Bishop*

Ullathorne 1806-1889 Volume I, London, Burns, Oats & Washbourne.

Butler, Cuthbert (1926) *The Life and Times of Bishop Ullathorne 1806-1889* Volume 2, London, Burns, Oates & Washbourne.

Chadwick, Owen (1971) *The Victorian Church, Part I, 1829-1859*, London, CM Press.

Chadwick, Owen (1971) *The Victorian Church, Part II, 1829-1859*, London, CM Press.

Chadwick, Owen (1990) *Newman*, Oxford, Oxford University Press.

Chadwick, Owen (1996), 'A Consideration of Newman's Apologia pro Vita Sua' in Paul Vais (ed.) *From Oxford to the People, Reconsidering Newman and the Oxford Movement*, Leominster, Gracewing Books.

Coulson, John (1970) *Newman and the Common Tradition: a Study in the Language of Church and Society*, Oxford, Clarendon Press.

Coulson, John (1978) 'Newman's Idea of an Open University and Its Consequences today' in James D. Bastable (ed.) *Newman and Gladstone Centennial Essays*, Dublin, Veritas Publications.

Culler A. Dwight (1965) *The Imperial Intellect; a Study of Newman's Educational Ideal*, New Haven and London, Yale University Press.

Dessain, Charles Stephen (1973) 'Newman's Philosophy and theology' in David J. De Laura (ed.) *Victorian Prose: a Guide to Research*, New York, Modern Language Association of America.

Dessain, Charles Stephen (1980) *John Henry Newman*, Oxford, Oxford University Press.

Ffinch, Michael (1992) *Newman: Towards the Second Spring*, London, Harper Collins.

Gilley, Sheridan (1990) *Newman and His Age*, London, Darton, Longman & Todd.

Gilley, Sheridan (1996) 'The Ecclesiology of the Oxford Movement: a Reconsideration' in Paul Vais (ed.) *From Oxford to the People, Reconsidering Newman and the Oxford Movement*, Leominster, Gracewing Books.

Gilley, Sheridan (1997) 'Newman and the Convert Mind' in Ian Ker (ed.) *Newman and Conversion*, Edinburgh, T. & T. Clark.

Griffin, John R. (1993) *A Historical Commentary on the Major Catholic Works of Cardinal Newman*, New York, Peter Lang.

Gwynn, Denis (1929) *A Hundred Years of the Catholic Emancipation: 1829-1929*, London, Longmans, Green & Co.

Gwynn, Denis (1946) *Lord Shrewsbury, Pugin and the Catholic Revival*, London, Hollis and Carter.

Harrold, Charles Frederick (1945) *John Henry Newman, An Expository and Critical Study of His Mind, Thought and Art*, New York, Longmans, Green & Co. Inc.

Holmes J. Derek (ed.) (1979) *The Theological Papers of John Henry Newman on Biblical Inspiration and on Infallibility*, Oxford, Clarendon Press.

Houghton, Walter (1945) *The Art of Newman's Apologia*, Yale, Yale University Press.

Jay, Elisabeth (1991) 'Newman's Mid-Victorian Dream' in David Nichols and Fergus Kerr (eds.) *Reason, Rhetoric and Romanticism*, Bristol, Bristol Press.

Jenkins, Roy (1990) 'Newman and the Idea of a University' in David Brown (ed.) Newman: *A Man for Our Time*, London, SPCK.

Kenyon, John (1972) *The Popish Plot*, New York, St Martin's Press.

Ker, Ian (1990) *Newman: a Biography*, Oxford, Oxford University Press.

Ker, Ian (1990b) *Newman the Theologian: A Reader*, London, Collins.

Ker, Ian (1991) *The Achievement of John Henry Newman*, London, Harper Collins.

Ker, Ian (1994) Preface to *Apologia pro Vita Sua*, Harmondsworth, Penguin Books.

Ker, Ian (1996) 'What kind of a book is the Apologia?' in Paul Vais (ed.) *From Oxford to the People, reconsidering Newman and the Oxford Movement*, Leominster, Gracewing Books.

Koenigsberger H.G., Mosse George L. and Bowler G.C. (1989) *Europe in the Sixteenth Century*, London, Longman.

Lash, Nicholas (1990) 'A Seat of Wisdom, a Light of the World: considering the University' in Terrence Merrigan (ed.) *John Henry Newman: 1801-90*, Leuven, Louvain Studies, Vol. 15 No. 2–3.

Leys M.D.R. (1961) *Catholics in England, 1529-1829: a Social History*, London, Longmans, Green & Co.

McGrath, Fergal (1951) *Newman's University: Idea and Reality*, Dublin, Brown and Nolan.

McRedmond, Louis (1990) *Thrown among Strangers: John Henry Newman in Ireland*, Dublin, Veritas Publications.

Mathew, David (1936) *Catholicism in England 1535-1935: Portrait of a Minority: Its Culture and Tradition*, Longmans, Green & Co.

Meenan F.O.C. (1987) *Cecilia Street: the Catholic University School of Medicine 1855-1931*, Dublin, Gill and Macmillan.

Meynell, Wilfrid (1890) *John Henry Newman: the Founder of Modern Anglicanism and a Cardinal of the Roman Church*, London, Kogan Paul, Trench, Truebner & Co.

Mozley, Anne (ed.) (1891) *Letters and Correspondence of John Henry Newman during his life in the English Church*, Vol. II, London, Longmans, Green & Co.

Murray, Placid (1980) *Newman the Oratorian*, Leominster, Fowler Books.

Newman, John Henry (1851) *Lectures on the Present Position of Catholics in England; Addressed to the Brothers of the Oratory*, London, Burns, Oates & Co.

Newman, John Henry (1874) *Sermons preached on Various Occasions*, London, Burns, Oates & Co.

Newman, John Henry (1956) *Autobiographical Writings* (ed.) Henry Tristram, London, Sheed and Ward.

Newman, John Henry (1987) *The Idea of a University Defined and Illustrated* (ed.) Daniel O'Connell, Chicago, Loyola University.

Newman, John Henry (1989) *An Essay on the Development of Christian Doctrine*, (foreword) Ian Ker, Notre Dame, University of Notre Dame Press.

Newman, John Henry (1993) *Apologia pro Vita Sua*, (ed.) William Oddie, London, J.M. Dent.

Newman, John Henry (1995) *Certain Difficulties felt by Anglicans in Catholic Teaching* (intro.) Stanley L. Jaki, Fraser, USA, Real-View Books.

Newman, John Henry (1997) *Fifteen Sermons preached before the University of Oxford* (intro.) Mary Katherine Tillman, Notre Dame, University of Notre Dame Press.

Newsome, David (1993) *The Parting of Friends: the Wilberforces and Henry Manning*, Leominster, Gracewing Books.

Nicholls, David and Kerr Fergus (ed.) (1991) *John Henry Newman; Reason Rhetoric and Romanticism*, Bristol, Bristol Press.

Nockles, Peter (1991) 'Oxford Tract 90 and the Bishops' in David Nicholls and Fergus Kerr (ed.) *Reason, Rhetoric and Romanticism*, Bristol, Bristol Press.

Nockles, Peter B. (1996) 'Newman and Early Tractarian Politics' in V. Alan McClelland (ed.) *By Whose Authority? Newman, Manning and the Magisterium*, Bath, Downside Abbey.

Nockles, Peter Benedict (1997) *The Oxford Movement in Context: Anglican High Churchmanship, 1760-1857*, Cambridge, Cambridge University Press.

Norman, Edward (1985) *The English Catholic Church in the Nineteenth Century*, Oxford, Oxford University Press.

Norman, Edward (1986) *Roman Catholicism in England from the Elizabethan Settlement to the Second Vatican Council*, Oxford, Oxford University Press.

Oddie, William (1993) Preface to *The Apologia pro Vita Sua*, London, Everyman Books.

Pawley, Bernard and Margaret (1974) *Rome and Canterbury through Four Centuries: a study of the relations between the Church of Rome and the Anglican Churches: 1530-1973*, Oxford, Mowbrays.

Reynolds E.E. (1958) *Three Cardinals: Newman, Wiseman and Manning*, London, Burns, Oates & Washbourne Ltd.

Rigney, William J. (August 1995) 'Bartholomew Woodford and the Catholic University of Ireland 1861-79', unpublished PhD Thesis, University College Dublin, National University of Ireland.

Selby, Robin C. (1975) *The Principle of Reserve in the Writings of John Henry Cardinal Newman*, Oxford, Oxford University Press.

Sencourt, Robert (1948) *The Life of Newman*, London, Dacre Press.

Sugg, Joyce (ed.) (1983) *A Packet of Letters: a Selection from the Correspondence of John Henry Newman*, Oxford, Clarendon Press.

Sullivan, Emmanuel (1993) *Things Old and New*, Slough, St Pauls Press.

Trappes-Lomax, Michael (1932) *Pugin: a Medieval Victorian*, London, Sheed and Ward.

Trevelyan G.M. (1948) *British History in the 19th Century and After: 1782-1919*, London, Longmans, Green & Co.

274

Trevor, Meriol (1996) *Newman's Journey*, London, Fount/
Harper Collins.

Vargish, Thomas (1970) *Newman: the Contemplation of Mind*, Oxford, Clarendon Press.

Walgrave J.H. (1960) *Newman the Theologian: The Nature of Belief and Doctrine as exemplified in His Life and Works*, London, Geoffrey Chapman.

Ward, Bernard (1909) *The Dawn of the Catholic Revival in England 1781-1803*, London, Longmans, Green & Co.

Ward, Maisie (1948) *Young Mr Newman*, London, Sheed and Ward.

Ward, Wilfrid (1913) *The Life of John Henry Cardinal Newman*, Vol. I, London, Longmans Green & Co.

Ward, Wilfrid (1913) *The Life of John Henry Cardinal Newman*, Vol. II, London, Longmans Green & Co.

Wilson A.N. (1990) 'Newman the Writer' in David Brown (ed.) *Newman: A Man for Our Time*, London, SPCK.

Index

282